MALADJUSTED SCHOOLING

MALADJUSTED SCHOOLING

Deviance Social Control and Individuality in Secondary Schooling

John F Schostak

The Falmer Press
A member of the Taylor & Francis Group
London and New York

First published 1983

ISBN limp   0 905273 87 7
     cased   0 905273 88 5

Jacket design by Leonard Williams

Typeset in 11/13 Bembo by
Imago/Graphicraft Typesetters Limited, Hong Kong
Printed and bound by Taylor and Francis (Printers) Ltd
Basingstoke
for
The Falmer Press
(*A member of the Taylor & Francis Group*)
Falmer House
Barcombe, Lewes
Sussex BN8 5DL
England

Contents

1   Introduction: Maladjusted Schooling

School can be defined by the grand purposes and designs of politicians, educationists and social theorists. An individual's behaviour and accounts of his or her experience can be torn apart in the search for 'facts' or 'evidence' supporting this or that theory, this or that interpretation of subjective experience and this or that grand social policy. Individuals become problems when under the scrutiny of those who have plans for them and design Utopias for them, for individuals rarely go gracefully but must be pushed, pulled and adjusted until they fit the required categories. The individual who remains obstinate is a problem, has a 'personality problem'.

In this book, school will be defined by the experiences of the individuals whose lives it affects. The problem facing such a task is, how can such research take place without tearing the reports of individuals from their subjective intentions yet keeping those intentions within that juncture of the present and the past and the future within which the individual has his social being? When an individual rebels, he or she rebels against a social form – an expected role, rules, beliefs – which have a history and point toward some form of future for the individual in society. When an instance which calls into question the history and the future of social forms is analyzed, that instance 'goes beyond itself', it reaches out like a poetic symbol, like an archetype; it grows in significance, enriches itself, becomes a focus which is able to clarify issues not only for itself but for other instances in other contexts in other times. There is a folklore in school which exemplifies this. The folklore is based upon incidents such as the following:

> *J.F.S.:*   Do you think it's easy to lie to teachers?
> *Paul:* No.

Danny: No.

Paul: They get the truth out of you.

Dave: It is with some of them. . . . You could lie to Mr Jones our tutor, you can lie to 'im.

Danny: The PE teacher, oof'. You can't even lie.

Dave: I can't lie to 'im.

Danny: I got blamed for sayin' 'just as if'. It was the boy next to me.

Dave: You know, um, 'cos 'alf of 'em forgot their kit 'cos it's the um first week, they've only been 'ere a week an' they forgot their kit for the first time for PE.

Danny: Started shoutin' at them.

Dave: An' 'e started shoutin' at them an' 'e said 'It's a wonder you don't get a crack off your mates . . . when this lesson's over 'cos if you forget it again . . . no one'll do it [the sport]. An' I 'ope you'll get battered by your mates'. An' someone said 'just as if'. An' then 'e [the teacher] thought it was 'im [Danny] then 'e thought it was Bill an' 'e [the teacher] was just sayin' 'Was it you?' An' 'e was goin' 'No' [Bill] An' 'e went 'No What?'. 'No, sir'. Then 'e was goin' 'Was it you, Bill Miles?' An' 'e was goin' 'No', an' 'e carried on goin' 'No, what?' 'No, sir! An' just, you know, tryin'.

Sam: An' 'e forced it out of 'im in the end.

Dave: An' yesterday, you know, yesterday we done games an' 'e said 'Just as if, eh Miles'. An' 'e'll never forget 'im. In the fifth year 'e'll probably say 'Just as if'.

Sam: [laughs]

Danny: 'E'll probably carry on about it.

Perhaps surprisingly these were first-years relating an incident in their first week of experience in the school, a comprehensive school. It shows the relentless pressure the PE teacher was able to exert upon the boys – pressure which made it impossible for them to conceal the truth. The incident, in the boys' opinion has now become ossified. The teacher will never forget the boy who said 'Just as if'. The incident has passed into folklore. The rebellious statement 'Just as if' now stands for a rebellion successfully quashed. It will be used as a reminder, or a trigger for the whole incident and the value system and the relations between individuals which were momentarily questioned and then transformed under the will of the teacher. This is an everyday example which illustrates the ways words or phrases conjure up a whole story. Ted Hughes (1976) writes:

> If the story is learnt well, so that all its parts can be seen at a glance, as if we looked through a window into it, then that story has become like the complicated hinterland of a single word. It has become a word. Any fragment of the story serves as the 'word' by which the whole story's electrical circuit is switched into consciousness, and all its light and power brought to bear.
>
> As a rather extreme example take the story of Christ. No matter what point of the story we touch, the whole story hits us. If we mention the Nativity, or the miracle of the loaves and fishes, or Lazarus, or the Crucifixion the voltage and inner brightness of the whole story is instantly there. A single word of reference is enough – just as you need to touch a powerline with only the tip of your finger.

Such stories act as a way of interpreting everyday life and as a way of justifying these interpretations and justifying behaviour. A story is compelling. Character analysis can be undertaken to provide the motivations which are inferred by the story teller as underlying actions. People become imaginatively transfixed by such stories in the drama of an individual's or a community's life. In any one story there are a thousand endings depending upon the point of view from which it is told and heard; and for any one event stories may be simultaneously begun and ended – what is a beginning from one viewpoint may be an ending from another. The observer who witnesses and records such stories weaves his or her consciousness in and amongst the characters who have stories to tell, and who generate insights through their own observations. We are, to this end, all participants in a community of observers and story tellers.

The observer seeks to make a record which will provide a basis not simply for future understanding, but also for the guidance of future actions. An observation fails if it does not throw some light upon a situation, if it does not broaden awareness as to the conditions affecting that circumstance or the implications of certain conditions. No event is so unique that it stands alone without a prior historical development or without contributing to some future development. The uniqueness of the individual is at the level of perspective and experience, not that the individual is without comparison and outside of the influence of culture.

This book has its origins in fieldwork involving one main site and several subsidiary sites and a concern for the historical context of schooling. From what has been written already it should be clear there are good reasons for supposing that a study of one kind of school in one town in England will have relevance for schooling as a whole. The school is a product of a society-wide historical drama. To understand the school we must have some awareness of the context which gave birth to it and which continues to provide the framework by which the members of the school understand themselves, and find their purposes, their motivations, their satisfactions and their frustrations. Particular instances therefore can make us aware of the general structures by which they are interpreted. Just as a penny has its interpretation and its worth in a whole system of economic exchange, so a teacher's act has its value and meaning within a whole network of educational institutions, values and teacher-pupil relations. As phenomenologists have explained, individuals seek out, create or identify patterns of social and physical phenomena. These pattern aid in recognition, recall and prediction. Individuals thus seek out that which is typical in order to be able to deal with what would otherwise be unmanageable complexity, a chaos of impressions. Thus, the observer, by keying into the ways in which a community or an individual typifies the social and physical world, can identify that which is typical for an entire community. In this sense, one instance is able to direct the observer to community-wide typical structures, or typical ways of seeing, doing and interpreting phenomena. One observation of one instance, of course, gives only a very limited grasp of the structures under which it can be interpreted. Thus a multiplicity of observations over a period of time is required.

Teachers will experience school life in a different way to pupils. A researcher can not only key into the ways teachers experience school and the ways pupils experience school but can also set this within a wider historical/political context. Thus the researcher is able to present a description and an analysis of the ways teachers and pupils experience each other in a manner which can throw light upon the nature and purpose of schooling. Everyday life, however, is not simply a framework of typical structures. Everyday life has dramatic qualities. By dramatic I mean the experience of acting in a world, of being an individual who is 'a centre of experience and an initiator of action'.

Data for the study were collected by observations of school life which were recorded in note form, drawings, photos and tape recordings. Interviews were recorded with over a hundred pupils, all the senior teachers, all the housemasters and those classroom teachers and tutors whose lessons and tutor groups were observed of the main school of the study. A questionnaire was also given to third-year boys (88), and third-year girls (92); and fifth-year boys (85) and fifth-year girls (93). The most useful questionnaire page was one which invited the pupils to write anything they wanted about their experience of school. Extracts from these writings will be given throughout the book. The research period in the main school extended over fourteen months. Subsidiary interviews were carried out in other educational institutions for the purposes of comparison and variation in order to describe these features which key into the historical or traditional concerns of schooling. Similarly, in the community of the different research sites, the people, their qualities and their problems keyed into wider networks of meaning, historically produced. Thus, I have created 'Slumptown' as typical of the social and historical process which have produced other slump towns throughout Great Britain.

In whatever community, in whatever school, the quality of an individual's life must be influenced by the physical or architectural, the social and the economic conditions of the community. Resources allocated to whole communities are allocated within the community not by ordinary families who are best aware of their needs but by the decisions of local and state authorities who claim to know better. When a child enters school, the child understands little of this. The community and the school seen through the eyes of the child take on dramatic qualities. These qualities may well be forgotten and no longer appreciated by adults. Adults convince themselves they see through wiser eyes than those of the child. How do the concerns of the child and the concerns of the adult relate one to another? How are the decisions made by authorities far away experienced by members of the community? What is it like to be 11 years old and enter a new school? What is it like to be 16 years old and leave Slumptown Comprehensive for the dole queue? What is it like to be a teacher who loves the job, loves the kids, and watches them, too many of them, leaving to mill around the streets because there are no jobs? How do pupils and teachers react?

In essence, the book will argue that schooling is maladjusted to the needs of individuals; that the individual is rendered impotent to control his or her destiny, to develop his or her initiative, self-reliance, independence and individuality; that schools, in being primarily agents of social control, tend to define individuality in terms of deviance and further set the conditions for the production of deviance.

Chapter 2 will provide a background in the theories of social control, deviance and individuality which find both sociological and everyday expression in the interpretation of social structures and individual action. It will be argued that there is an intimate relationship between forms of social control and the production of deviance and the confusion of deviance and individuality.

Chapter 3 takes us into the community of Slumptown, setting it within its historical context, identifying the economic and political pressures which created it. Within the history of its creation, it is argued, there has been a violation of community and a violation of individual rights in the production of a pool of labour. Community, it is further argued, has become a community of masks and counterfeit relations which engage in dramas which reproduce the conditions of inequality, and the conditions to safeguard the vulnerable self shrouded in masks and deceits. School acts as the community's incubator of images, identities and dramas drawn from the community.

The black individual in the community is confronted with the question of race and the experience of racism. Chapter 4 again sets the experience of racism within the history of English involvement with the black peoples. It is argued that there has been a violation of ethnicity which leads to an experience of strain and the necessity of asserting a black identity. Racial discrimination is experienced in the community and in the schools, compounding the problems of disadvantage. From the standpoint of black identity, white authority and deviance ascription are reassessed.

Chapter 5 focusses upon the cultural and school contexts of sexism and forms of male and female deviance. A case study of a fifth-year girl and a boy is used to illustrate the process of deviance in a movement toward a sense of individuality.

Chapter 6 looks at the ways schools organize themselves to deal with pupils under pressure, and pupils who respond in a troublesome or worrying manner to that pressure. It is argued that the organization of schooling itself contributes to the pressures faced by pupils. Indeed, pastoral care is reduced to administrative functions on the one hand and the management of deviance on the other.

Chapter 7 discusses several of the main forms of pupil strategies in facing the pressure and growing up to get what one wants. This process of growing up under pressure may result in an experience of being torn rather than formed at school. School, it is argued, too often fails to afford those pupils most likely to experience being torn the structures whereby they can fulfil their desires for success, respect and self-autonomy.

Chapter 8 focusses upon the most dramatic strategy, the violent solution, and sets it within a political context to discuss the extent to which violence may be a rational and even creative solution in the community and in school. The extent to which school perpetuates through its organizational structure the conditions for violent eruptions in school is examined.

Chapter 9 sketches a programme for the reformation of maladjusted schooling in order to respond to the senses of grievance and violation discussed in the previous chapters. It tries to take a practical view of the problem of reformation, looking at a reform as an innovation which has to be managed in order to bring it into being. The chapter speaks to those teachers sympathetic to the need for reform.

The strategy of the book is to describe the kinds of pressure experienced by individuals in school and the kinds of response individuals may make to the experience of this pressure. The book is offered in the hope that those who care will be encouraged in their reforms.

2 Theories of Social Control, Deviance and Individuality

The purpose of this chapter is to introduce the reader to the main theories of social control, deviance and individuality not abstractly alone but also concretely through the conversation, cries, caresses and slaps of people as they act within the confines of school. School is a physical boundary where a few adults regularly meet many children. Schooling, it has been argued frequently, habituates children to the notion of the control of the many by the few. Schools, sociologists and historians inform us continually, are agents of social control and agents for the reproduction of social class divisions, inequalities in wealth, in life opportunities, in health and in life expectancy. Theories, however, may disguise rather than reveal the contours of social reality if they are but projections of the theorists' own needs, fears and fantasies upon the social actors the researcher seeks to understand. Particularly important to remember is that schools are formal mass 'child rearing' institutions and hence child rearing practices and education have become intertwined – perhaps to the disadvantage of each. According to De Mause (1974), 'The history of childhood is a nightmare from which we have only recently begun to awaken.' He continues: The use of the child as a 'toilet' for adult projections is behind the whole notion of original sin, and for eighteen hundred years adults were in general agreement that, as Richard Allestree (1676) puts it, 'the newborn babe is full of the stains and pollution of sin, which it inherits from our first parents through our loins. . . .'

Schooling has been shaped not only by concerns to preserve social class distinctions but also by our dominant forms of child rearing practices. There is, of course, an overlap in principle in the way both children and the lower classes have been treated. Both have been dependent 'classes' of individuals in need of control and –

coinciding with political emancipation – training to fulfil social roles. There is a sense, too, in which the lower classes were a 'toilet' for ruling-class projections. Thus, Kay-Shuttleworth, a noted educationist, could say when faced with the thought of the enfranchisement of the lower classes:

> Should the working class legislate in their own interest, 'our entire system of industry and commerce would undergo a revolution and with it every institution of property'; if the manual labour class 'usurped such a predominance as to give it the practical control of the House of Commons', the resultant evils could 'assume the monstrous proportions of a destructive revolution.' (Simon, 1974:357, writing of Kay-Shuttleworth, 1860).

Similarly, Arnold (1932:204) saw the danger of the working classes who, being 'raw and half-developed' were asserting 'an Englishman's heaven-born privilege of doing what he likes' and thus 'beginning to perplex us by marching where it likes, meeting where it likes, bawling what it likes, breaking what it likes.' With the move toward democratizing the political system it became imperative to transform these 'half-raw' and 'bawling' creatures. Education was seized upon as a tool by which to shape the minds of the lower classes newly enfranchised. Thus Lowe (a previous Minister for Education) at the passing of the Reform Bill in 1867 (he had been an opponent of it) stated, 'I believe it will be absolutely necessary to compel our future masters to learn their letters.' This was a theme echoed by Forster in introducing his Education Bill in 1870 and yet again by Fisher at the time of the 1918 Education Bill and extended franchise (for some women):

> We are extending the franchise. We are making a greater demand than ever before upon the civic spirit of the ordinary man and woman at 'a time where the problems of national life and world policy upon which this house will be asked to decide have become exceedingly complex and difficult, and how can we expect an intelligent response to the demands which the community propose to make upon the instructed judgement of its men and women unless we are prepared to make some further sacrifices in order to form and fashion the minds of the young'.... (quoted in Wardle, 1970:27)

In trying to assess our various theories of social control, deviance and individuality we must discover the extent to which each has become coloured by economic and political desires and child rearing practices.

Social Control

As we have seen, when modern mass schooling was being formulated the political masters were clear as to the function of schools in the maintenance of social order. Lowe in 1867 wrote: 'The lower classes ought to be educated to discharge the duties cast upon them. They should also be educated that they may appreciate and defer to a higher cultivation when they meet it, and the higher classes ought to be educated in a very different manner in order that they may exhibit to the lower classes, that higher education to which if it were shown to them they would bow down and defer' (quoted in Wardle, 1970:25).

Social control, however we wish to define it, involves one or more individuals manipulating the behaviour of one or more others and manipulating social and material opportunities as between individuals. How is such control obtained? The most primitive form of control is through the application of force. However, there are more subtle forms which social theorists have provided to the dictators, the managers and the politicians. Conditioning, for example, is now made 'scientific' and consists of the systematic modification of behaviour with or without the other's knowledge and consent. Behaviour modification is widely practised in schools with varying degrees of expertise. But there are other forms of dabbling, perhaps 'psychotherapeutically' or 'spiritually', with the minds of others. Freud, Mead and others showed how individuals 'internalize' the behaviour patterns and moral injunctions of authorities such as parents and teachers. The task, then, is to get children to internalize the 'right' values and behaviour patterns. Obviously, one could always blame parents or 'bad company' for inculcating the wrong ones! In such a manner, however, one individual may become through a series of social adjustments the 'internalized' mirror image of another, albeit perhaps a distorted mirror image. The task, then, is to present to the young 'ideal images' of what they should become. Models of ideal behaviour – heroes, film stars, sports stars, saints – are set for the young to emulate. Social control through emulation

11

has long been practised in education. Hamilton (1980) has shown that it formed an essential component in the 'class' as opposed to the 'monitorial' systems of education influenced by Adam Smith, Jardine and Robert Owen. Finally, one may use 'appeals to reason'. The utilitarians – Mill, Bentham, Smith, among others – had great faith in reason. So, Mill believed, '. . . I have seldom met with a labouring man (and I have tried the experiment upon many of them) whom I could not make see that the existence of property was not only good for the labouring man, but of infinitely more importance to the labourers as a class, than to any others.'

'Reason', or perhaps we may better call this 'rhetorical abuse', could be used to persuade rather than 'force' or 'condition' the lower classes to accept their station in life. This is not to say that Mill, the Liberal, was not aware of the social evil of oppression. Simon (1974:146–7) makes it clear that:

> Mill argues strongly against those who hold 'that the human race ought to consist of two classes – one that of the oppressors, another that of the oppressed.' On the contrary, the question whether the people 'should have more or less of intelligence, is merely the question whether they should have more or less of misery, when happiness might be given in its stead.' Theoretically, therefore, all classes should have 'an equal degree of intelligence'. But there is a preventing cause 'which is this, that "a large proportion of mankind" is required for labour, and therefore has not the necessary time for the acquisition of "intelligence". There are degrees of command over knowledge to which the whole period of human life is not more than sufficient'; it follows that 'there are degrees . . . of intelligence, which must be reserved for those who are not obliged to labour.'

Social control must therefore be exercised to ensure the 'degrees of intelligence' are realized in their traditional patterns throughout society. The theories of social control are available for individuals to use in the manipulation of other individuals. However, some individuals have a greater access to those techniques than others – the wider social pattern is mirrored in school structure: the few control the many. Here is an example recorded in 1981; analysis shows the way adults may weave their webs of control over children.

A student teacher, during dinner time, asked a boy,

Nicky Wragg, to take the teacher's dinner tray of dirty dishes back to the kitchen hatch for him. The boy refused. The teacher insisted. A confrontation developed and the aggrieved boy decided to take the matter to the headmaster. The question was, did the student teacher have the right to compel Nicky Wragg to do something he did not want to do during what was supposed to be the boy's free time?

The headmaster was not a sympathetic audience. Throughout the incident he spoke with an air of exaggerated outrage and disbelief. The boy when I saw him was sobbing hysterically. The deputy headmaster arrived on the scene and the headmaster proceeded to explain to him the cause of the fuss:

'. . . he'd come to complain to me because our student [teacher] had asked him to take a tray back to the [dinner] hatch. And having this, this *enormous* insult and indignity, injustice thrust upon him, he wanted to complain to, to a headmaster. I'm not yet sorting out exactly why but within half-a-minute of my arriving here he'd been *extremely* rude to me as well. . . . Now he wants to tell his probation officer. . . . What do you want to tell your probation officer about?'

Nicky sobbing heavily gasps out, '. . . 'cos he was tryin' to f' force me.'

'Because what?'

'He was tryin' to f' force me.'

'He was trying to force you?'

'Yeah.'

The head lets out a high-pitched 'Wellll' and proceeds to present his case, voice grating, 'you see you have to have a situation in schools where in the end teachers – and this gentlemen is a visiting teacher – can give reasonable orders to people just as you do in a home. Now your problem is young man is that you really don't believe that teachers ought to have authority, ought to be able to say 'do this' and you do it. And until you do understand that you're just going to get into more and more trouble.'

Theoretically, in a free democratic society, especially in an academic community, it is open to dispute and argumentation as to what constitutes a 'reasonable order' in a given situation. Schools are not democratic communities. The headmaster continues by saying,

'You're trying to fight a war old boy. And rather a silly war to fight. It's a bit like the Isle of Man declaring war on the United States or something like that. . . .' In the opinion of the deputy head, 'You know, the headmaster is quite right, you can't tell a teacher what you're going to do . . . for your own good sometime son you're going to have to learn the lesson that there are people who can force you to do things and you're going to have to do them and you've got no choice.' In the opinion of Nicky, 'I'm in the right.' It's a war.

Nicky has run up a unilateral declaration of independence. There are two basic strategies with which to fight a war such as this: all-out naked force or subversion of the will. The latter is the technique used by the deputy head. Nicky sticks to force. He tries to gather reinforcements:

'I'll come with me mum.'
'Well, I'm sure the headmaster would be delighted to see your mum. When is your dad going to call? Is he home?'
'He's in the house.'
'I think it's one of the reasons why you're upset isn't it? That you know that you made such an awful fool of yourself.'
'I've not.'
'Oh yes you have.'
'I'm right, everyone is. . . .'
'But Nicky, you're not right. This is the thing. You're not right. You're *quite* wrong. And you're going to have to learn that you're quite wrong. One way or another son you're going to have to learn. I'm confident. . . . I know you pretty well by now Nick Wragg don't I?'
'Sir, yeah.'
'Yeah. And I'm confident that I know that one reason why you are so upset at this moment is because you realise you made such an *awful* fool of yourself, haven't you?'
'Sir no.'
'Yes you have Nick.'
'I'm in the right.'
'Well that's just you dreaming and I'm not going to argue with you. I'm not going to argue with you at all . . . sit there until you've calmed down.'

The deputy head is trying to define the situation and the identity or role of the boy in the situation. As Thomas noted in 1928, 'If men define things as real, they are real in their consequences.' Thus, if the situation is defined as one where 'you can't tell a teacher what you're going to do', the child who resists must face up to consequence that 'you've got to accept that you're going to get into more and more trouble.' The consequences are real. The definition of the situation is backed up by power. It is the power to apply punishments as well as the power to control any discussion of rights and wrongs, the power to say 'that's just you dreaming and I'm not going to argue with you.' The child's point of view is relegated to 'dreaming'; it is not a real and valid point of view at all. Indeed, the deputy head is able to penetrate whatever act the boy plays because 'I know you pretty well by now Nick Wragg don't I?' It is almost as if the teacher can enter the consciousness of the boy.

Nicky is entangled in a sticky web of subtle rhetoric concerning 'right' and 'wrong', his mother's feelings, his own feelings, and underlying all this is the reality of the force to which he must ultimately submit. Resistance to control makes Nicky a problem, a deviant, a trouble-maker. However, before we take sides and lay blame in this dispute between Nicky and his teachers let us remember that the teachers are not free agents but are acting to well rehearsed albeit perhaps unconscious 'scripts' in which teachers are expected to close ranks and protect colleagues, in which teachers are not expected to lose face in front of pupils and in which adults *are* superior to children. As Woods (1979:141) writes:

> . . . my analysis of the constraints on teachers portrays them in the ever-tightening grip of a powerful pincer-movement, with 'professional demands' on one side, and 'recalcitrant material' in the form of reluctant or resentful pupils on the other, with shrinking aid or the ability to resist either. In the crush, the kernel of their real job, teaching, is lost, and only the cracked shell of their personal defences remains. Teachers labour to piece it together, and as is the nature of repaired shells, it can appear deceptively full.

Social control creates a complex and sticky web enmeshing those who think they control, those who think they are controlled and those who resist. Deviance arises as tears, warps and breaks in the web.

Deviance

If we think of control as having a hold over somebody, the deviant is one who tries to shake or break free. If we think of the well controlled person as one who obeys the norms or rules of society, the deviant is the one who breaks those norms or rules in some way. To understand deviance we must try to understand the interplay or dialectic between deviance and control: the one acts upon the other; each works to shape and sustain the other. Deviance is not a fact of nature but unfolds in everyday social dramas.

The forms of deviance are various: homosexuality, behaving 'odd', promiscuity, drug taking, criminality, delinquency, vandalizing – there are too many to name. For every rule there is a deviant who will break it. Two basic questions can be asked: Why do some people become deviants? Why doesn't everyone become deviant? There is a variety of theories which try to answer these questions and perhaps all contain some partial insight into understanding deviance.

Some forms of deviance, covertly or overtly, confront authority, some withdraw from authority while others are founded upon intentional or unintentional perceived differences from the norm. Some forms of deviance are aggressive or violent while others appear passive or peaceful. The main popular explanations for the occurence of the variety of forms of deviance are as follows:

1 Nobody's perfect. We all have some weakness which makes us 'fall from grace'. Our weaknesses only become a problem when they break some law and cause a nuisance. Then we must seek help to keep our problems under control.
2 We are filled with evil/destructive/violent/aggressive impulses which are genetic or instinctual or 'human nature'. Sometimes these forces 'break loose'. Mostly, these forces are well harnessed by our fear of the law/God/Father. If they are not, then priests and psychoanalysts will help us; if they fail, judges perhaps will imprison us or, in some countries, have us killed.
3 Bad company. John and Jill are good kids really but Billy's 'bad company', he 'leads them on' and they get caught up in the gang. They have to live up to their reputation.
4 'Give a dog a bad name.' People think they're bad so they act bad. But John and Jill aren't really bad. They just can't get rid of their reputation.

5 It's the parents. The mother's a slut and the father's a drunkard – they just don't care about poor Jimmy. So, is it any wonder he's a 'head case'?
6 It's society. There's massive unemployment, poor housing, poverty and mis-education – and you wonder why the kids are running wild!

These popular explanations which gradually shift their focus from the nature of the individual through to the nature of society are mirrored by biological, psychological and sociological theories.

Is man innately 'weak' or even violent? Historians tell us that throughout history violence has been pervasive and endemic (Tutt, 1976). However, Toch (1972), in a psychological study of violence, writes (pp. 33–4)

> ... the concern with violence is directed at a myth. It demands an ocean where there are islands; it constructs a monolith in place of diversity; it calls for formulas to cover complexity; and it presumes cure-alls where we have no diagnosis. Real-life violence has not the glamour, nor the simplicity, nor the unambiguity of the violence of editorials and public speeches. Reality suffers at the hands of our concern.

He continues (p. 36):

> Clinical science assumes that all men are reservoirs of bloody destructiveness. It maintains that civilization equips most people with the means of discharging their hatreds judiciously and selectively – although there are instances in which this effort fails. Some people are presumed to remain unchecked in their aggressiveness, so that they become promiscuously violent upon slight provocation.

He considers that far from being 'promiscuous', 'violence is not blind and random'; furthermore, 'violence is at least a two man game.' He considers that 'if we want to explain why men are driven to acts of destruction, we must examine these acts, and understand the contexts in which they occur' (p. 38). A fuller discussion of violence occurs in chapter 8.

Drawing the discussion back to schools, it is clear they are crowded and frequently noisy places where a few authority figures inhibit the free actions of the many. Waller (1932) argued that the natural relation between teachers and pupils was hostility because teachers must inhibit freedom of action and coerce pupils into doing things they do not naturally or immediately want to do.

In a review of sociologically informed theories of school delinquency, Hargreaves (1981) sees five main analytically distinct positions:

1 control theories;
2 cultural transmission or cultural deviance, or culture conflict theories;
3 subcultural theories;
4 strain theories;
5 labelling theories.

The first two theories of delinquency can be thought of as 'input theories' since they see the causes of school delinquency arising largely outside of school and hence delinquency being imported into school. The remaining three can be thought of as 'process theories' since they stress the role the process of schooling plays in the production of delinquency (or, in wider terms, 'deviance').

Control theory takes as its basic premise that delinquency can be caused by a collapse of social controls. Thus, for example, Thrasher (1927:22) in his study of 1313 Chicago gangs wrote that the gangs formed in the 'twilight zones' or 'interstitial regions':

> Probably the most significant concept of the study is the term *interstitial* – that is, pertaining to spaces that intervene between one thing and another. In nature foreign matter tends to collect and cake in every crack, crevice, and cranny – interstices. There are also fissures and breaks in the structure of social organization. The gang may be regarded as an interstitial element in the framework of society, and gang-land as an interstitial region in the layout of the city. The gang is almost invariably characteristic of regions that are interstitial to the more settled, more stable, and better organized portions of the city.

Control theory allows us to blame parents (and even weak teachers) for weak control and supervision over their children. High staff turnover, shortage of staff, and the difficulty of patrolling the entire school grounds (hence leading to 'interstitial regions') may all contribute to deviancy in schools.

Cultural transmission theory (also called cultural deviance or culture conflict) is exemplified in Miller (1958). It takes the view that lower-class culture generates the conditions for gang delinquency. Lower-class culture is seen to be quite distinct from middle-class culture. Thus Miller:

> takes as a premise that the motivation of behaviour in this situation can be approached most productively by attempting to understand the nature of cultural forces impinging on the acting individual as they are perceived *by the actor himself* – although by no means only that segment of these forces of which the actor is consciously aware – rather than as they are perceived and evaluated from the reference position of another cultural system. In the case of 'gang' delinquency, the cultural system which exerts the most direct influence on behaviour is that of the lower class community itself – a long established, distinctively patterned tradition with an integrity of its own – rather than a so-called 'delinquent subculture' which has arisen through conflict with middle class culture and is oriented to the deliberate violation of middle class norms.

Hargreaves (1981) sees Willis' (1977) *Learning to Labour* as following in Miller's steps. Willis gives us the 'elements of a culture'. However, it is a culture which exhibits 'general and personalized opposition to authority', and which 'involves an apparent inversion of the usual values held up by authority' (pp. 11,12). This counter-culture must 'be placed within a larger pattern of working class culture' (p. 59). And as we know, in Marxist theory, working-class culture is in conflict with the ruling classes. The struggle, however, results only in reproducing class inequalities:

> The state school in advanced capitalism, and the most obvious manifestations of oppositional working class culture within it, provide us with a central case of mediated class conflict and of class reproduction in the capitalist order. It is especially significant in showing us a circle of unintended consequences which act finally to reproduce not only a regional culture but the class culture and also the structure of society itself. (p. 60)

Willis illustrates his thesis amply. However, an alternative explanation of the oppositional nature and the inversion of middle-class values is provided by Cohen (1955) whose theory involves 'subcultural' 'strain' and psychoanalytic elements.

For Cohen, juvenile delinquency is a subculture. He describes a subculture as follows (p. 12):

> Every society is internally differentiated into numerous sub-groups, each with ways of thinking and doing that are in some respects peculiarly its own, that one can acquire only by participating in these sub-groups and that one can scarcely help acquiring if he is a full-fledged participant. These cultures within cultures are 'subcultures'.

He believes that the subcultural elements blend with psychological factors 'in a single causal process, as pollen and a particular bodily constitution work together to produce hay fever' (p. 17). Added to this there are 'strain' elements. Strain theory, according to Hirschi (1969:3), says that 'legitimate desires that conformity cannot satisfy force a person into deviance'. Thus Cohen writes:

> Our view . . . holds that those values which are at the core of 'the American way of life', which help to motivate the behaviour which we most esteem as 'typically American', are among the major determinants of that which we stigma-tize as 'pathological'. More specifically, it holds that the problems of adjustment to which the delinquent subculture is a response are determined, in part, by those very values which respectable society holds most sacred. The same value system, impinging upon children differently equipped to meet it, is instrumental in generating both delinquency and respectability.

The delinquent subculture that develops, according to Cohen, is 'non-utilitarian, malicious and negativistic' (p. 25). This may be compared to the 'corner boy' way of life:

> unlike the delinquent response, it avoids the radical rupture of good relations with even working-class adults and does not represent as irretrievable a renunciation of upward mobility. It does not incur the active hostility of middle-class persons and therefore leaves the way open to the pursuit of some values, such as jobs, which these people control. It represents a preference for the familiar, with its known satisfactions and its known imperfections, over the risks and

the uncertainties as well as the moral costs of the college-boy response, on the one hand, and the delinquent response on the other. (p. 129)

The negativistic delinquent response arises, according to Cohen, through the Freudian process of 'reaction-formation'. In this process the repudiated 'middle-class values' lie 'deep down' in the delinquent's psyche. When the delinquent meets some (possibly minor) external threat he 'overreacts' because he is also attempting to reassure himself against the deep inner threat.

The final perspective on deviance is that of 'labelling theory'. Such theories share in common the notion that deviance is socially produced, shaped and sustained. They tend to focus upon the 'micro' aspects of everyday life rather than the 'macro' or larger social structures the 'economic system', the 'political system', the 'education system'). Hargreaves *et al.* (1975:3) describe the main features of the approach as follows:

> First, deviance is seen as a question of social definition. Deviance does not arise when a person commits certain kinds of act. Rather, deviance arises when some person(s) defines that act as deviant. Second, deviance is seen as a relative phenomenon. If a deviant act is an act that breaks some rule, than since rules vary between different cultures, subcultures and groups, acts which are deviant (i.e. which break rules) in one culture, subculture or group may not be deviant in another culture, subculture or group.

In this approach deviance arises when people meet and one person 'labels' or defines another as deviant. The labelled person's reaction to this label calls out further responses by the labeller. The response of people to the 'deviant' can act to reify and reinforce the 'deviant' behaviour. Lemert (1967:v) writes:

> There is a large turn away from older sociology which tended to rest heavily upon the idea that deviance leads to social control. I have come to believe the reverse idea, i.e., social control leads to deviance, is equally tenable and the potentially richer premise for studying deviance in modern society.

Thus, social control (as Hargreaves *et al.* note, pp. 5–6) exerted to reduce deviance 'creates, under certain conditions, problems for the person who committed the deviant act which can be resolved by the commission of yet further deviant acts and by a self-designation as a deviant person. The paradox is that the social reaction which was intended to control, punish or eliminate the deviant act has come to shape, stabilize and exacerbate the deviance'.

Whatever theory of deviance we embrace they all treat the individual as tossed here or there either by inner uncontrollable forces, or by internalized social norms or social definitions, or compelled by external force. The individual has been invaded by society, perhaps compelled to strive for certain goals or values, and if frustrated in his legitimate strivings he either grows apathetic or finds deviant solutions; or perhaps, when the necessary social controls disintegrate, the individual becomes wild, deviant, delinquent; or the individual is the largely helpless butt of social definition or labelling which arises in interaction with others. Whatever is the case, the individual seems relatively powerless. Wrong (1961:192) has written of the oversocialized conception of man in sociology:

> 'Socialization' may mean two quite distinct things: when they are confused an oversocialized view of man is the result. On the one hand socialization means the 'transmission of the culture', the particular culture of the society an individual enters at birth; on the other hand the term is used to mean the 'process of becoming human', of acquiring uniquely human attributes from interaction with others. All men are socialized in the latter sense, but this does not mean that they have been completely moulded by the particular norms and values of their culture. All cultures, as Freud contended, do violence to man's socialized bodily drives, but this in no sense means that men could possibly exist without culture or independently of society.

Taking this point a step further, Proudhon in 1840 (see Woodcock, 1977:65–6) wrote:

> Man, in order to procure as speedily as possible the most thorough satisfaction of his wants, seeks *rule*. In the beginning, this rule is to him living, visible, and tangible. It is his father, his master, his king. The more ignorant man is, the more obedient he is, and the more absolute is his confidence in his guide. But, it being a law of man's nature to conform to rule, – that is, to discover it by his powers of reflection and

reason, – man reasons upon the commands of his chiefs. Now, such reasoning as that is a protest against authority, – a beginning of disobedience. At the moment that man inquires into the motives which govern the will of his sovereign, – at that moment man revolts. If he obeys no longer because the king commands, but because the king demonstrates the wisdom of his commands, it may be said that henceforth he will recognize no authority, and that he has become his own king. Unhappy he who shall dare to command him, and shall offer, as his authority, only the vote of the majority; for, sooner or later, the minority will become the majority, and this imprudent despot will be overthrown, and all his laws annihilated.

From the anarchist point of view all external laws are a violation of individuality. The subject becomes an independent person when that person exercises his or her critical reflection upon those in command and *acts in response to such critical reflection*. Individuality is born in such independent action, thought and expression. As we shall see, individuality and education arise together. It may well be that to be an individual is to be a deviant (although not necessarily *vice versa*).

Individuality

Neither sociology nor psychology nor educational research has been much concerned with individuality. If recognized at all, the individual is reduced to a part in a whole, a member of a group or a statistical deviation from a population norm or as a 'problem' to be adjusted to the norm. The 'norm' is king! In the following I will consider five relatively distinct theoretical positions regarding the individual:

1   the individual as a member of a species/group;
2   the individual as the nub of a matrix of social relations, at once a production of and an articulation of the whole;
3   the individual as stranger/outsider, trying to become an insider;
4   the individual as moral critic;
5   the individual as the result of systematic self-estrangement.

The list is not necessarily exhaustive but is sufficient to cover the main lines of inquiry concerning individuals.

Psychometricians are pleased to study the individual as a summation of individual differences – a bundle of deviations from population norms. In this way they ignore individuals completely, seeing only IQ scores, personality scores, attitude scores – dividing the individual into shreds. Modern schooling is built upon the norm. We are divided into classes, sorted according to age and frequently according to sex. Our task is to aspire to reach or surpass certain norms attributable to our age-sex class. We may be further divided according to ability and 'interest' or subject-option. Hoskin (1979) has shown how in the history of examinations the invention of the norm allowed individuals to be formed into easily assessable groups. The individual became but a member of a norm-group, a class, a species of individuals. Such an approach dominates modern psychological, sociological and educational research and practice. In a recent paper (Schostak, 1982c) I argued that individuals in educational research were largely seen as materials to be shaped under the hands of skilful or clumsy teachers to reach (or surpass within acceptable limits) production norms. A review of the literature confirms this argument. If the individual is merely a member of a class or group then that individual is available to be assembled, shaped and produced to adult/socially defined standards of 'incompetence' or 'excellence'. Individuality becomes defined in terms of socially acceptable or unacceptable deviations from norms.

More sophisticated but no less production oriented approaches to individuality can be seen in the structuralist, Marxist and symbolic interactionist perspectives. Each takes a socially defined conception of the individual; for each, the individual cannot exist except as a social entity, a relation in the whole, a nub, perhaps, of a network of social relations. The individual has no meaning and no existence apart from society, and is thus defined according to the roles he or she plays in society, the status achieved or ascribed and the power or authority delegated or won. Individuals become reproducers of social structure, their creativity repressed or grudgingly witnessed.

Structural-functionalism focusses upon the needs of society as a whole rather than individual needs. It is argued that a social form persists because it fulfils some socially useful function. Cohen (1968:63) writes:

> Most versions of this doctrine refer *ultimately* to the benefits which certain forms of social organization bestow on the individual members of society; but some refer to the good of

some collective entity in itself – such as the State, the Nation or Civilization – regardless of the benefit accruing to any individuals.

Society is exalted above individuals. Individuals recede in importance, sacrificed to the necessary good of the wider social form: the State, the Nation, Civilization.

Marxism boasts a special understanding of the ways individuals have become alienated; and the ways working-class individuals resist middle- and ruling-class values, norms and power; and the ways working-class individuals, despite their resistance, fall into the trap of reproducing the conditions of their exploitation and oppression. Yet the individual is scarcely seen. Schaff (1970:66) writes: 'Through the prevailing social consciousness, social relations give shape to the individual who is born and educated in a specific society. In this sense, social relations *create* the individual.' Methodologically, the task is:

> ... the real human individual. Thus, when defining the ontological status of the individual, it is necessary to start from the existence of individuals as specimens of a biological species and parts of nature, just as was done by naturalism. When, however, we have the task of further particularization of the concept of the individual, we have to ascend from what is abstract, and therefore simple, to what is concrete, and therefore complicated. According to Marx, it is only by this method that we can obtain a picture of a complex concrete individual not as a hodgepodge of speculation but as a coherent whole. Consequently, observation begins with the real individual whose social analysis should reveal the whole of the relationships that are our frame of reference in intellectual reconstruction of this concrete individual. By his condensed description of human essence as the ensemble of social relations, Marx wanted to explain why a given man, formed as he is by specific social conditions, is characterized by specific attitudes and views. (Schaff:63–4)

When only an 'ensemble of social relations' is analyzed, the individual vanishes. For Sartre, who tried to reform Marxism with an existential concern for the individual, the individual became a central problem (1960, cf.1976 translation:51–3).

Symbolic interactionism boasts that it does not lose sight of the creative impulses of man. For Mead, the self of the individual is an organic whole in two parts: the 'I' and the 'me'. The 'me' is the social aspect formulated out of an internalization of the other. The 'I' is the unsocialized, spontaneous, shadowy and impulsive aspect of the self. From the 'I' there is the creative, child-like aspect of the self; from the 'me' there is the censorial, inhibitive, judgemental social nature of the self. The 'I' is regulated and subordinated to the social. The 'novel' produced by the 'I' is only accepted if it is socially acceptable, or provides an acceptable solution to a problem of social adjustment. In this way, Mead assumes individuality and social control to be compatible:

> social control, so far from tending to crush out the human individual or to obliterate his self-conscious individuality, is, on the contrary, actually constitutive of and inextricably associated with that individuality; for the individual is what he is, as a conscious and individual personality, just in as far as he is a member of society, involved in the social process of experience and activity, and thereby socially controlled in his conduct. (Mead, 1934, 1962 edition:255)

For Mead social control operating as self-criticism 'exerts itself so intimately and extensively over individual behaviour or conduct, serving to integrate the individual and his actions with reference to the organized social process of experience and behaviour in which he is implicated' (p. 255). Mead himself in a note (p. 255) draws attention to the resemblance of this conception of self-criticism to Freud's notion of the Censor. Through interaction, mutual control between self and other is exercised. Each individual internalizes the attitudes of the other (forming the 'generalized other') and criticizes or regulates his or her actions from the standpoint of the internalized other (or generalized other). The self is invaded; autonomy is reduced to a minimum. The individual is a well adjusted member contributing 'novel' social elements only if they pass the process of social self-criticism.

The individual as a product of society, and yet as possibly able to contribute something new, is the ideal 'balanced' individual of social managers. A deputy head says of his function as a teacher:

> I think you are influencing [pupils] in terms of learning how
> to come to terms with life and management, self-

management. I think, you're also trying to influence them in terms of self development and that embraces: Ah, learning times where you've got to submit your individuality to a common good and other times where you've got to follow your individual style wherever it leads. And learning to judge when one or the other is appropriate. Uh, learning good habits almost in the sense of drill, learning to face up to problems, to deal with them rather than put them off. Uh, learning that you have a more peaceful life when something is done than if you're worrying about doing it. Learning to think about the consequences of actions to think beyond the actions to what the consequences of what it may be. Uh, learning to trust people and to be worthy of trust yourself. Uh, learning that other people exist that you have to, as you mature, adopt standpoints other than your own and trying to think what it must be like to be somebody else, another pupil, a parent, a teacher, whatever you like. Uh, because I think until people can adopt the standpoints of others, or in a simulated sense, they are not mature. Uh, I think that is the story of adolescence in a way, that you enter it really, generally, as a sort of egocentric individual and all being well, you'll leave it as somebody who is conscious of other people's needs and vibrations and so on.

Adopting the standpoint of the other towards oneself is a Meadian concept. Autonomy and initiative are recognized as valuable but there is a balance to maintain:

> that we shouldn't be preparing people to fit into society, we should be preparing people to change society from what it is to what it ought to be . . . is a seductive notion. But I think we also ought to bear in mind that there is a limit to how far any individual can change society. If we give youngsters the impression that they can change the world by an act of will, we're misleading them. But I don't rule that out. I think the danger with preparing people simply to fit into society and no more than that is that you are conditioning people into responding in ways which will give them a safe existence.

The individual capable of social as well as self-criticism is here kept alive – just. The individual who is able to break his or her ties with society is either 'maladjusted', 'deviant', 'delinquent' or insane in any perspective which sees individuality only in terms of a network of social relations. Social change within such a perspective is assessed along a continuum between degeneracy and progress or chaos and constructiveness. The individual takes his or her position in the network of social relations, plays his or her role and is judged according to his or her performance. Our deputy head, however, has hinted at another possibility.

The individual may become or be a stranger or outsider to society. This naive individual asks questions which the insider would not ask. Within the phenomenological tradition from Husserl and Schutz the standpoint of the stranger has been frequently adopted as a research technique. The task is to learn the 'taken for granted' assumptions, ways of behaving and values upon which everyday social life is based; that is, to know how to become an insider. There is no overt sense of social criticism in this method. However, it can become, almost despite itself, a powerful form of social criticism. By revealing the tacit understandings upon which social life is based, social actors can feel as if they are standing naked in a crowded street. By correlating the perspectives of 'master and slave', 'Boss and worker', 'teacher and pupil', certain structural similarities can be shown to operate throughout social life. Furthermore, within every society there are structures of knowledge and ignorance: by revealing what is hidden, knowledge is made available which can prove uncomfortable to those who have a vested interest in concealment and in keeping sectors of the community in ignorance. The task of phenomenology is to uncover the hidden and to identify the meaning phenomena have for individuals, groups and societies and 'Man' (cf. Wild, 1963). It is rare for social phenomenologists to reach beyond certain limited phenomenological techniques. Unfortunately the full resources of phenomenology have scarcely been used. For our purposes the important point is that in Husserlian and Schutzian phenomenology the individual is conceived of as being able to 'suspend', 'bracket' or mentally stand apart from society. This is a position radically different from the preceding positions. It is a controversial position – even amongst those who have been strongly influenced by Husserl. They ask: how can one suspend or step outside of the world? They answer: you can't. Or they argue: if you suspend the world you subtly transform that world. For example, try suspending the act of making love. Making love to an 'essence' is not quite the same as making love to a flesh and blood lover. Thus, the disengagement from the world may well distort it and render its results invalid. When we come to look at the work of Schutz (1976), we find 'puppets', not flesh and blood creatures. When we look at Hargreaves *et al.* (1975) we find human categories and a subtle analysis of the social process of labelling but not a living, sulking, loving, hating human being anywhere. Yet when we turn to Schutz's masterpiece (1964) – an analysis of Don Quixote – we find in the analysis of this fiction all the dimensions of being human and being tragic. There are riches in social phenomenology not yet sufficiently explored. Phenomenology has the capability of entering the soul, of seeing behind the masks and roles and of touching the heart beat:

> I've always tried to be myself in the situation. And what I find in my, what fifteen years now in schools, is that uh, it can be very hard being yourself. I've had some real sort of thudding blows because of that. Um, and you do, you get cowardly about it and occasionally adopt the pose and the role and hide behind that just, just to recover at a human level and recharge your batteries.

This housemaster one day 'exploded', saying 'when I get home at night I don't talk about what has happened during the day with my wife. I just hold it all here' (he placed his hands over his guts). I had asked him to keep a research diary. The reason he did not want to think was:

> ... Sometimes y' see John, what they're telling you is so flaming true and real that you don't want to hear it, because it's absolutely loaded, loaded with problems. What, what some kids are telling me in not so many words is that they loathe and detest this system we're forcing them through.... Once you start lifting up stones like that ... y' know you're into really serious sort of problems aren't you, and the ramifications of it for all of us are very serious ... you know, if if you were to reflect on the messages that uh ... these kids ... uh I think, more and more beginning to tell then they're very serious. Very serious indeed. They throw into doubt the whole purpose of what these schools are here for and what we're sending most of our pupils here for in our present society anyway.

The task of phenomenology is to peer under the stones and reveal the hidden social and personal content that resides there. The hidden can throw into doubt the overt. Phenomenology, like psychoanalysis, gives voice to the repressed.

An alternative yet allied position to the phenomenology of Husserl is the existentialism of Kierkegaard. Kierkegaard described three kinds of individual. Burridge (1979:67) gives these as: (1) the 'individual'; (2) the 'special individual'; and (3) the 'man of movement'. The 'individual' 'reproduces in his life the established order of things, is normal, regular, displaying in his existence the life of the universal.' This roughly accords with the structuralist, Marxist and symbolic interactionist perspectives. The 'special individual' is 'one who reflects on the fundamental presuppositions of the established order' and refuses to follow 'traditionally fixed forms of the social order, and no longer reproductively renews in himself the life of that order. Instead, he stands apart, and out of the bosom of his reflections and relationship to God he introduces new points of departure. Occupied with his relationship to God (the source of Truth), classifying himself as immediately under God, he refashions the moral order' (p. 68). Of course, it could be argued that God could be replaced by Marx or 'The Revolution', but I think Kierkegaard is talking of something more radical, more personal and more transcendental than either of these. Finally, 'the man of movement' is a charlatan, one who seems like but is not a 'special individual'. Such individuals:

> may be found in almost any European or Western community. Ranging from, say, renaissance-man and the leaders of political or social movements to small-town political hucksters, noisy clergy busy with social works, the firm's squeaky wheel, and even the habitual moaner, he or she is the 'special individual' manqué, ambitious, embittered, and frustrated perhaps, greedy for power....

Burridge himself describes an individual clearly influenced by Kierkegaard's 'special individual' but not so grand. For Burridge the individual need not attain to be an Old Testament Prophet as in the case of the 'special individual'. For Burridge individuality begins in moral criticism of the social order. Thus, this position turns upside down that of Mead's social control through mutual self-criticism. For Kierkegaard and Burridge there is nothing compatible about individuality and social control, yet Burridge (p. 5) sees an oscillation between being an individual and being a person:

... the moral critic who envisages another kind of social or moral order, the creative spark poised and ready to change tradition. Or, one might say, the individual is one who manifests relations potentially capable of changing the given or traditional moral order. Yet if some people are wholly individuals and others are persons, it is a matter of common observation that most people are in some respects and most frequently persons while in other respects and at other times they can appear as individuals. And this apparent oscillation or movement between person and individual – whether in a particular instance the movement is one way or a return is made – may be identified as individuality.

The process toward individuality, insanity or criminality appears remarkably similar:

> Assertions to autonomy, working against the processes of socialization which create the person, are opposed to and negate a given moral order. They incubate the individual, but they also give rise to mere nonconformities, arrogance, the criminal, or the insane. What distinguishes the individual from his likenesses manqué is a stand on a truth revealed or perceived in the event; positive moral concern springing from a grasp of the truth of things; the transformation of gross negation into moral relevance – something on behalf of others, possible only through participating in their beings. (p.33)

We may dub this individual the 'moral individual' who, like Kierkegaard, jumps across the Abyss to land safely in the moral embrace of God. Yet we have here a theory of the relation between social control and deviance radically distinct from anything previously considered. Within the 'person' or the 'individual' we see echoes of 'control theory'. However, there are few further similarities with other theories.

There is one further distinct position concerning the individual that we may take. I call this the self-estrangement theory of individuality (Schostak, 1982c). Within this position no God awaits the one who leaps over the Abyss:

> As in the archetypal Freudian drama, the rebellion of the brothers against the father, the first step toward freedom from the father, is to join the gang in collective revolt against

the personal relations with authoritative adults. But the gang becomes the new father. A break with the gang is a step into the unknown without the support of the gang and perhaps in the face of resistance from the gang. The reward of individuality is the most terrifying freedom of all, the leap toward self-recognition. At that point I become what I intend myself to be; there is no one left to blame, no one left to fall back on. I become a creative individual.

The result of a progressive detachment from ties with others is 'Aloneness'. There are a number of things an individual who approaches this state can do: go mad, commit suicide, resort to crime, maintain an attitude that the world is 'absurd', 'gross', 'nauseous' or 'meaningless'; or one can dance and sing and explore the new world of freedom.

The task becomes to identify the ways in which self seeks to estrange his or herself from the hold of the other; and the ways other seeks to tie and maintain a hold upon self. The method of analysis suitable for this is intentional analysis, a method distinct from but influenced by Husserlian phenomenology, Kierkegaardian existentialism and Freudian and Jungian psychoanalysis. The focus of attention is upon 'intentionality' which I describe as follows:

> My basic analytic tool will be 'intentionality' which means 'directedness towards'. Thus, as phenomenologists tell us, consciousness is intentional in structure for it is always 'consciousness of . . .', that is, it is forever directed towards objects, as are feelings such a love, hate, fear, and as are actions which are projected toward future goals; and so on (cf. Mohanty, 1972). If this sounds too abstract, intentionality can be made concrete by considering what I conceive to be the primal experience of intentionality: reaching out and touching. Its concrete inverse is the prevention of touch by others, the escape from the reach or the hold of the other. A further concrete aspect of intentionality is a more subtle kind of reach and hold upon the other: it is attraction, a drawing towards, and capture through seductive enchantment or manipulative designs. (pp. 175–6)

Those who escape or resist the social control or manipulative designs of others become 'problems', 'mad', 'bad', 'deviant' or suffer 'false consciousness' and need to be 'turned around', 're-educated', or 'treated':

You see the thing is with Debbie, she wants to take her own lessons. She thinks she can go into a school and just do what she wants to do, which is not right. I mean the teachers are there to teach her, not her teach the teachers. And I don't agree with it.

Debbie's mother, who said this, is confused and worn out. Debbie's own struggle is a matter of life and death – she has attempted suicide twice. And the task of pastoral care in schools is to manage such forms of deviance – and to fail:

Joan's the youngest, um and, just looks a mess. Really does look a mess. And most abrasive, the moment you speak to her she's ready, verbally, to lash out, you know. And uh, if she's punished justly, it makes no difference um, she's 'hard done by', you know, you're really gettin' at her'. And it's spending time unravelling all that and saying 'you know, Joan, you've got to change the image that you're giving to people of yourself.' And uh forgetting all the hassle about coming late but get backtracking and saying 'what do you do that's nice?' you know. To my mind, as I say, apart from normal teaching things, that is what the difference in my job ... of of ... uh ... looking at these kids and giving them some way of seeing daylight but, you know, they need a lot of help and you're only there now and again to sort of uh pull their strings. . . .

The image of the child is to be transformed by the housemaster toward the desirable image of the 'balanced kid'. In the extract we have a partial glimpse of the ways in which teachers systematically, or typically, turn their attention to Joan, and the way Joan experiences this as 'getting at her', which leads her to 'lash out'. As the housemaster appears to want to 'pull their strings', so the pupils appear to want to resist. However, 'pulling strings' is a more subtle form of control than by command. Pulling strings depends upon 'building relations', upon 'caring'. Systematically pupils are brought under the eye of the teacher in both academic and pastoral matters. The pupils are drawn into a web of caressing but manipulative intents directed 'caringly' toward the pupils – until they submit, scream or suffocate. But this is not all the story, for teachers too have been brought within a web of manipulations and their care, their love, their energy is perverted by the demands of organizational control.

Our study will be of the individual as he or she (teacher and pupil) strives to break through the webs of manipulative designs and meet each other as individuals responsible to no one but themselves. Ours is a study of the kinds of pressure exerted upon individuals and the kinds of solution they adopt to resist, overcome or submit to these pressures. Social control, deviance and individuality are inextricably entwined. The individual, by his or her assertion of autonomy, threatens the control structures of society and thus must be severely dealt with. Individuals are deviants within systems lauding social control; but not all deviants are individuals – the gang member is subject to the gang norms. Our question then is: how may individuals face the various control pressures which form or tear them?

3 Deviants, Disadvantage, School and Community

They're spendin' a few thousand on the Town Centre plantin' all trees 'n' things. They'll all be torn down when the bizzies get fed up patrollin'. Spendin' thousands on trees when there's all this unemployment round 'ere. If I can't get a job I won't stay in Slumptown – I don't want benefit or a Youth Scheme an' all that crap.

(Darren Bailey, fifth form)

Individuals are born into community structures not of their making; their lives are shaped by historical influences of which they have no knowledge. At times, individuals are moved from place to place by economic forces beyond their control; their choices and courses of action are delimited by reduced opportunities for economic independence. Indeed, according to the dictates of impersonal market forces (or economic Fate) whole communities prosper or die. Each individual within each community has a monetary value – the current market price at which he or she can sell his or her labour. Some individuals are worth a great deal, some very little. Some individuals have advantages heaped upon them (for they are so valuable), while others have disadvantages heaped upon them (for they are so valueless). To understand deviance we must examine the interplay between deviance and market forces in the creation and destruction of community; and the role of schools in the production of inequality or disadvantage.

Throughout the generations the disadvantaged have been moved for the sake of the profit of others. There was a time, however, when they were not mere wage-slaves but had 'rights' to use common land. With the enclosure of this common land from Elizabethan times until the mid-nineteenth century the peasantry were deprived of their rights and forced to sell their labour at market prices. The once settled peasantry became vagabonds – mobiles, a mob. They moved to the towns. Their fortunes rose and fell according to the booms and depressions of trade cycles. Without rights they were tempted to crime:

> And the resistance movement to the laws of the propertied took not only the form of individualistic criminal acts, but also that of piecemeal and sporadic insurrectionary actions where numbers gave some immunity. When Wyvill warned Major Cartwright of the 'wild work' of the 'lawless and furious rabble' he was not raising imaginary objections. The British people were noted throughout Europe for their turbulence, and the people of London astonished foreign visitors by their lack of deference. The eighteenth and early nineteenth century are punctuated by riot, occasioned by bread prices, turnpikes and tolls, excise, 'rescue', strikes, new machinery, enclosures, press-gangs and a score of other grievancies. Direct action on particular grievances merges on one hand into the great political risings of the 'mob' – the Wilkes agitation of the 1760s and 1770s, the Gordon Riots (1780), the mobbing of the King in the London streets (1795 and 1820), the Bristol Riots (1831) and the Birmingham Bull Ring riots (1839). On the other hand it merges with organized forms of sustained illegal action or quasi-insurrection – Luddism (1811–13), the East Anglia Riots (1816), the 'Last Labourers' Revolt' (1830), the Rebecca Riots (1839 and 1842) and the Plug Riots (1842). (Thompson, 1980:66–7)

Being dispossessed, turned into vagabonds, wage-slaves, impoverished and criminalized by the laws of the propertied classes, they turned to illegal acts. One way of life was dying, another out of the pain and despair was born:

> Again and again the 'passing of old England' evades analysis. We may see the lines of change more clearly if we recall that the Industrial Revolution was not a settled social context but a phase of transition between two ways of life. And we must see, not one 'typical' community (Middleton or Pudsey), but many different communities coexisting with each other. In south-east Lancashire alone there were to be found, within a

few miles of each other, the cosmopolitan city of Manchester upon which migrants converged from every point in the kingdom; pit-villages (like the Duke of Bridgewater's collieries) emerging from semi-feudalism; paternal model villages (like Turton); new mill-towns (like Bolton); and older weaving hamlets. In all these communities there were a number of converging influences at work, all making towards discipline and the growth in working-class consciousness.

The working-class community of the early nineteenth century was the product neither of paternalism nor of Methodism, but in a high degree of conscious working-class endeavour. In Manchester or Newcastle the traditions of the trade union and the friendly society, with their emphasis upon self-discipline and community purpose, reach far back into the eighteenth century. (Thompson, 1980:456–7)

The history of the violation and the assertion of community can be brought up to date with the post-war destruction, and reconstruction of old inner-city areas and the construction of 'new towns' such as Peterborough, Stevenage, Kirkby, Milton Keynes. And the dreams of a fair society, of prosperity, of an end to poverty have yet again crumbled as unemployment in the United Kingdom passes three million in the official statistics. Again, the cities of the nation have heard the screams of the 'mob'. In the 'special' case of Northern Ireland, 274 riots between 1968 and 1973 were reported by Deutsch and Magowan (1973). Peroff and Hewitt (1980), from an analysis of different kinds of policies and their effects on the riots, predicted 'that an increase in housing and a decrease in unemployment will reduce violence overall.' Scott (1977:16) writing of violent behaviour in the United States, gives a 'statistical picture' of the violent criminal as 'most commonly a male between the ages of sixteen and twenty-five, unmarried or divorced, and unemployed.' He continues, 'The obvious method of combating violence in this group is to provide universal employment, not just any old job at a poor rate of pay, but reasonably well paid work under pleasant and satisfactory working conditions.' Similarly, Iglitzin (1970:177) writes that 'sociological data support the finding of a high correlation between economic and social status on the one hand, and violence on the other; those who are poor commit more violent acts. Moreover, whether one includes homicides, assault and battery, or the collective violence of riots, it is invariably true that a large number of the participants are not only economically deprived but also racially disadvantaged.' Mays (1964:147) in the UK sees 'the older and poorer parts of big industrial or commercial cities' as 'delinquency producing' and considers that 'they are characterized by a long history of poverty, casual employment and bad housing.' And so the literature continues in a similar vein. Burt (1925) showed that over half of London's juvenile delinquents came from poor or very poor homes which then constituted only 30 per cent of the population. Bagot (1941) found that 85 per cent of delinquents lived below the 'bare essentials'. Wilson (1962:15) points out, however, that in the UK 'there is by no means a close correlation between dilapidated areas and criminality' since high levels of delinquency can be found in new housing estates. But she finds that child neglect goes with poverty and families with large numbers of children. The families are defined as 'inadequate', their resources overstretched.

The literature can leave us in little doubt as to the relation between poverty, unemployment, poor housing, being 'dispossessed' and violence, or deviant behaviour. In this chapter I will describe certain general features of a town possessing all these features, a town to be called Slumptown. I will then move on to describe its school and its relation to the community. Finally, I will present some of the perspectives of some 'deviants'. We will see that deviance arises out of a 'drama' played out each day – a drama having implications for the whole of society at one level, and having personal, apparently trivial, implications at another. It is difficult, impossible to select any one cause, or point in time where one grievance 'causes' a particular act. Rather, there is a climate of grievance, a climate of resentment, hostility, suspicion which makes certain kinds of acts and interpretations of acts more likely than other kinds.

'Slumptown' I have placed in the North of England but it could be deprived parts of London and few of the details would need to be changed. Thus Slumptown does not exist except as a symbol of the many towns it could be.

Slumptown is not to be thought of as a 'mish mash' of convenient statistics and quotations. It has been constructed out of a unity of experience, the experience of the violation of and the assertion of a sense of community. In practice it has been constructed out of observations of and the voices of teachers and pupils in a large northern comprehensive, a small London boys' school and my own experiences as a teacher involving both a secondary school and two further education colleges, one private and one public. Furthermore, no school and no community is so unique that its concerns and practices do not key into the history of society and of education. Hence the following arguments and illustrations key into the concerns, ideals and practices of politicians, industrialists and educationists in general.

The Community

No one individual or set of statistics holds the key to describing any community. A community reveals itself gradually through a multiplicity of voices, the unities and disunities, commonalities and eccentricities of these voices mark out the divisions and the degree of integration within the community, those qualities which are rich and those which stagnate and fester.

The mother of Debbie Graves says of her home:

> When I first came to Slumptown which is 21 years ago, this street was one of the quietest streets in Slumptown. My sister came here and she said 'It's like walking down a grave yard.' Now this house had been standing empty when I came in it, for twelve months. There wasn't a window smashed, no boards up outside. Look at it now. I mean I don't know what's happened to Slumptown.

It is a semi-detached council house. There is a small overgrown garden in the front. It was dark when I walked along the road. Railings had been torn from a wall and left partway over the pavement. An alsatian snarled at me as I walked briskly by. 'I planted a rose bush', said Debbie's mother, nodding toward the front garden, 'Someone had taken it by morning.'

Ann, Debbie's friend, lives in a newer council house about half a mile away. They are concerned that people condemn Slumptown without actually going there. Her mother says, 'Don't judge before you've not actually been and don't believe everything you read 'cos you can read the same stories about every town in England, good and bad.'

Ann's father says:

> There was nothing at all, just woods and empty fields, you know. We had to build our own church, St Laurence's. We

thought it was a barn at first. And we gradually done our own church and things have gone on from there. But they still haven't kept pace with the population even though it is slowing down now. They're even thinking of closing schools down. But they, they never catered – just threw people out and said, 'well, get on with it.'

This, of course, refers to Slumptown's 'new' face, they feel there were not enough facilities to cater for the young population of the town.

Sharon, as many others in the school, complains that there is little for them to do. There is 'only one picture house', the sports centre is expensive, the swimming baths are fine if you like swimming but there is little else. In 1965 pupils at the school carried out a small local survey and found that the need for entertainment facilities was high on people's priorities. Sharon's mother recalls how there was to be a leisure centre but it 'never came off'. Sharon's father blames it all upon the economic climate, 'Everything's against us.' He goes on to say:

They've killed the place. A lot of it was new estates – Well, same as Newtown. Government give them a grant, cut the rent and all the rest and once the period of, you know, free rent period, free taxes . . . they move out. This has happened all round here.

The whole top and bottom is unemployment. Kids have got no money. People have got no money. So they get bored. They see other people who have got money so they're taking it. . . .

Sharon's father has been unemployed for the last three years. His wife has a job and it hurts his pride, although he is grateful for the money. Of Sharon and her future he says: 'Here children like her and others are studying for 'O' and 'A' levels knowing that soon as they leave school they go right on the dole. And surely this is not conducive to kids really studying?'

Of 354 fifth- and sixth-formers who left Sharon's school in the summer of 1981 forty had found real jobs by 18 November, four of them having entered military service. The remainder were either on Youth Opportunity schemes, the dole, or had re-entered education.

Sharon's father has talked both of the building and the killing of a community. In the building was pride, and at its death sadness, bitterness, helplessness. He suffers the sense of the impersonal violation of his need for a community. He remembers the old days before they were moved to the new estates in Slumptown:

Father: I mean I lived in the old city through the war, I was only a youngster but I went through the war there when it was really gettin' hammered. An' listen to Jean who lived in Yorkshire out on a farm – she didn't know there was a war goin' on.

Mother: No.

Father: Here we thought the rest of the country was the same but obviously it wasn't. I mean, the house we lived in.... And there was me mum an' dad at first, myself an' two brothers an' two sisters all slept in one room with the, ... what we called the kitchen an' a bedroom in a flat. That was seven of us all were sleepin' in one room. Me mum an' dad got in first, then the two girls'd get in bed then the three lads. Then we moved up into the house from the flat onto the uh landin' above. There were two bedrooms, a *parlour!* An' a livin' room.... So me mum an' dad used to sleep in the parlour, the lads in one room, an' the girls in the other room. But we only 'ad gas an' nothin' upstairs. We used to take candles to bed, you know. You got washed out in the back 'cos that's where y' tap was, y' know.

Mother: Y' see I never knew anything like that because um um we had a house with gas ... we had no uh ... but ever after that we had electricity, an' a bathroom.

Father: Well we didn't 'ave a bath or electricity 'till we move up here.

Mother: Oh....

Father: if we wanted a bath ... the baths are still there, we used to go there. If you were goin' out anywhere special you went an' got a bath. You could go an' get a bath for a penny or thruppence an' they'd supply yer with the soap an' the towel an' you 'ad y' own bath an' you'd get in an' get ... you got a scrub otherwise, you get a tin bath in the house y' know, it was bad news with a family....

This was the majority of people in the old city, Jean, like this ... you 'ad a block of, a block of tenements an' say six 'ouses an' two toilets outside an' yet if you 'ad to go to the

41

toilet you 'ad to come out an' there'd be, could be three
people waitin' to use that toilet. An' the water used to be in
the middle of the square, people'd have to go down with
buckets to bring water. I mean that's only twenty-five
years ago...

Like I say where we lived all the parents an' the children,
front doors were open, they came out an' the children
played skippin' rope, or somebody 'ad a squeeze box or
old banjo y' know, it was great....

My life now is, six days a week, is gettin' up of a mornin',
goin' to the shops an' comin' back, an' sittin' ere, an' that's
it.

Mother: Waitin' for me.
Father: That's right. Y' know, nothin'. Ridiculous you go
down to job centre, it's a waste of time. I mean I went in
our job centre last week – I don't go in often, now – but
there was a job there for a ski instructor.... [laughter]

A community was created around industry's need for factory labour.
The influx of people – the population increased 1500 per cent in a
decade – gave the town an atmosphere of excitement. It seemed as if
a dream was going to come true. Booklets were written by the
council to welcome its new inhabitants to create a sense of identity,
of community. The dream was elaborated in the pamphlets giving
the numbers of houses and flats to be built per year, the schools, the
shops, the proposed entertainment facilities. Each major firm to set
up in the area was celebrated in the local papers. The successes of
pupils from the purpose built schools were published, acclaiming the
first to reach university, the first to reach Oxford or Cambridge. The
new community meant opportunity.

The demand for labour in the 1950s meant also the necessity of
attracting West Indians and Asians to Britain. They were to enter a
community where:

your greater problem will be getting on with your white
neighbours. One thing you must always keep in mind, is that
their knowledge of your country is much less than your
knowledge of theirs. Whenever you are inclined to get angry
or fly off the handle at some remark – or because a person

stares at you for a long time – remember that English people are ignorant of your ways and habits, and they may be just displaying a natural curiosity. There are some parts of England where the sight of a coloured man is still an uncommon thing, and there are people who may never have seen a person like you before.... (from *Going to Britain*, published by British Broadcasting Corporation for West Indians)

The multiracial community in Brixton, Deptford, Moss Side, Toxteth, Handsworth grew:

> *Liz:* My sister goes out wiv a whiteman, right, and um 'er baby's um er black but 'er godmuvver's white. And that lady know us from since she was a baby and she's got 'alf cast kids, you know? And then, we love that, you know what I mean? It's best if we can unite – I mean, you don't need to actually unite in that way but at least we can just get on. The neighbours round here. I mean, there was a neighbour across the road, right. I mean, there's a whole load of black people come to my house right, there's a few whites but there's a whole load of black, right. And there's a man over the road an' he's always watchin' us. O.K. One day he was passin', I was passin', right, an' he goes 'You fink you're fuckin' nice, didn't ya, didn't ya, didn't ya? I'm gonna get the Northend mob down 'ere.' Not knowin' that we know the Northend mobs right. And there's a black Northend mob and they're stronger than the white Northend mob, to be frank wiv you. Right?
>
> *White girl:* It's true.
>
> *Liz:* An' 'e's sayin', 'Oh, you fuckin' cunt', you know what I mean, 'You fink you know it all. An' look at yer 'ouse, you know what I mean, you fink that's a palace an' 'ow many people, black people comin' out there', you know what I mean. 'Oh you lot make me sick I've been watchin' it for years', you know?

This experience of racial prejudice will be developed in a later chapter. But common to both white and black youth (although the burden is disproportionately upon the shoulders of the black) is the experience of joblessness and a certain routine ''anging around':

J.F.S.: Is there any problem with unemployment?

Ray: Yeah ... there is round 'ere.

J.F.S.: D' you know anyone who's unemployed?

Frankie: Yeah, my bruvver.

Ray: Yeah, I do.

Alex: About three quarters of my mates are unemployed.
They just 'ang around, they just 'ang around the Boys
Club all nigh',

Ray: Yeah,

Alex: An' they complain,

Ray: Amusements an' things.

J.F.S.: And there's nothing for them to do?

Ray and Alex: No.

Ray: But when there's riotin', when there's riotin' they go to
that 'cos that's the only thing they can do. There's nothing
really to do.

Frankie: My bruvver just normally stays in. An' sometimes
he goes to his clubs an' that, leaves about five, comes back
at ten each day.

Ray: The dole money is not much is it?

Ray, Frankie and Alex are black fourth-year boys. For them and
their white friends, the expectancy of being unemployed is just
matter of fact; it is a legacy. Its roots are in the way resources and
products, employment and unemployment have been distributed
socially. Ray, Frankie and Alex are a part of the 'mob', the mass,
available for both blame and manipulation. History has bequeathed
them a legacy of inequality. The dreams of prosperity were the
carrots to draw their parents to the new estates into wage-slavery and
on into welfare-slavery.

Wedge and Essen (1982) estimate that in 1974 some 1.5 million
children lived in such low-income families. These welfare-slaves in
general inherit shorter life-expectancies, poor housing, poorer
health, lower educational attainment and low-income careers. In the
UK, according to Brown and Madge (1982), 'roughly ten million
people are suffering from poverty, over four million of them in
families with children ... three million are currently unemployed.
One million eight hundred thousand households are living in
physically unsatisfactory housing conditions in terms of overcrowd-
ing, shortage of amenities or general unfitness, and a small minority,
about 50,000 are received as officially homeless in any one year. Over

half the adult population can be termed educationally deprived in that they left school early and have no educational qualifications, and over 14 per cent of children are still leaving school without any qualifications at all.' In 1979 one in six people was living in poverty. This then is the climate of disadvantage that persists today and is the context for perhaps two million or more children (depending upon definitions of poverty and disadvantage) who daily go to school.

The School

Lennie stands wide eyed surveying the school – its great gates, its great towering teaching blocks and the crowds of people. 'I feel so small', he shrieks inwardly. He says several times of the school, 'It's big though. You walk out and you look up at the school – the size of it!'

His friend felt 'dead nervous ... all the atmosphere, all the kids.' It was hard at first to find their way around. To orientate themselves they made comparisons and contrasts with their previous school. In the new school 'you feel lost 'cos it's a bigger school than the other one. Knew your way around straight away in the little one but you can't find your way as good here.'

There are so many things that are different, not simply the size of the place, nor the hundreds of kids but the kinds of relationship you have with each other: 'The teachers are more strict ... um, can't take your tie off.' I laugh at this, eyeing his friend's unbuttoned shirt. He says, 'I haven't got a tie an' this teacher grabbed 'old of me an' pulled me by him.' His aggrieved tone is not lost on his friends who immediately catalogue a host of other wrongs:

'Some teachers won't let you take your blazers off on a hot day, will they?'
'No.'
'Ah' when you're in the other school you could go to the toilet when you wanted. Here, they say, 'wait till break".'
'And when you do go at break the toilets are locked.'
'And you look all smart with your uniform on don't you?'

So despite the moans, there is the excitement and the feeling of 'smartness' and as others put it, 'growing up.' The setting has about it a sense of initiation into another level in one's personal growth. School, whether first school, middle school, or secondary school, presents a number of contrived hurdles, or an emotional obstacle course. The obstacles may create excitement, fear, hatred, joy and a multiplicity of other feelings. There may be a sense of opportunities opening up, or of being closed down, or paradoxically, as in the case of Lennie, an anticipation of both: 'I like it because it's a whole new experience but when we go up to the third year I'll get sick of it.' He'll get sick of it because the novelty will have worn off.

These are children's experiences of an architectural and organizational environment not of their making. As a purpose built school of the 1950s, the school would be built according to the 'house' system of organization, that is, divided into a number of smaller organizational units called 'houses', each administered by a housemaster and an assistant. According to Benn and Simon (1970:218), the 'pure' house system which used 'no other forms of organization – was used in only 17 per cent of British comprehensive schools. . . . Even when combined with other forms (upper and lower school division and year organization) the house system was used as the main form of organization in only 37 per cent of comprehensive schools.' These figures applied in the year 1968. However, in the early days of purpose built comprehensives there was great enthusiasm about the virtues of the house system. It was the pastoral organization which would help Lennie and his friends to settle into their new school, built in that era of enthusiasm for the house philosophy. Lennie's headmaster recalls this sense of enthusiasm for the pioneering nature of the school in the early days and considers in the light of experience and pragmatic realities that:

> I think some of our central ideas [in the 1950s and 1960s] were right. I think that comprehensive schools need to pay an enormous amount of attention to motivation and to children's attitudes. I think they need to be realistic about the fact that in a classroom it doesn't much matter what a teacher's saying if there's too much noise for anyone to hear him. I think they're right in believing that idealism has to be tempered with practicalities; that not every member of the staff of a school is likely to be of superlative teacher quality and therefore something that may work for the gifted and committed teacher is not necessarily simply by virtue of that fact a good school policy because a lot of the teachers won't be that gifted and committed. I like to be realistic about examinations too. I do think that – at any rate until recently,

there is perhaps some swing now if you're talking about the lower end of the ability range. But until recently exam successes represented life chances for children. And I've never had any patience with that kind of teacher who says exam results don't matter or that exams are not my main concern, if only because all my experience is that the notion that you can either teach children in a lively and interesting way or get them through examinations is just nonsense. By and large, the people who interest them are the ones who get them through exams as well and *vice versa*.

This criterion of realism, which surrounds Lennie, is one which must also be applauded by the writers of the *Black Papers* (1970), which so scathingly attacked the comprehensive movement in education. It could also be argued that it is just this emphasis upon 'realities' which emasculates the comprehensive vision. Similarly, Sharpe and Green (1975) appear to have shown how the progressive ideals of a primary school were modified and undermined by practical economic and political realities.

These realities are the realities of inequality, the realities of a school and its community organized to reproduce relationships of inequality. Pupils must be assessed to be allocated according to 'ability', or exam passes, to various kinds of occupation. Pupils must learn to submit their individual will to 'those who know better' – the authorities as represented in school by teachers. However, why is it, for example, that pupils of similar social and home backgrounds, of similar abilities attending the same school, taught by the same teachers take opposing attitudes towards the school? Debbie Graves and her friend Sharon provide an illustration. The former has 'copped out', is violently anti-school and anti-authority, the latter has ambitions of going to university. In the one case opportunities for self-enrichment through school have been closed down, whereas for the other, opened up. *Apparently* the same social structure offering the same life chances to each girl has resulted in opposing experiences.

In 1971 Bernstein argued that schools cannot compensate for society. As I see it, schools provide a setting, both a physical environment and a social structure, which makes available opportunities for individuals to find out something about themselves and the world and to participate later as adults in that world. Individuals create their cultural interpretations of that structure in their day-today meetings with each other. Individuals are at liberty to draw upon any experience in their lives which helps them to give meaning to or interpret any event which happens at school. If society is divided, then schools will reflect that division through the variety of ways events are interpreted by individuals. But schools need not be merely passive mirrors of society even if they cannot compensate for society's ills. Perhaps if we extend the metaphor we can say schools are rather like a hall of mirrors, some of which distort while others are faithful, or at least honest attempts at a faithful representation of reality. Individuals, whether teachers or pupils, enter this hall of mirrors each with his own criterion for assessing which reflection is the faithful representation of reality. Individuals meet and learn how each other sees and interprets reality. Argument, confrontation and quarrels are likely to occur as each individual asserts his own interpretation. Action follows and is shaped by the variety of ways any given event can be interpreted. It could be argued that any school which encourages a 'social mix' rather than an homogeneity of life-styles, abilities, opinions and so on is likely to bring about a greater tolerance for the views and awareness of and concern for the social circumstances of others. At heart this is the justification for the comprehensive school. It is not so much that the comprehensive school compensates for society but that it generates the conditions whereby society may regenerate itself, through tolerance and concern for others. In Lennie's words, it creates the possibilities for 'a whole new experience'; but our task is to understand why 'when we go up to the third year I'll get sick of it', and why for others the 'whole new experience' leads on to other enjoyable new experiences of school and work.

There is no strict division between school and society. In school, just as out of school, there are adults and children, there are those in authority and those who must obey authority, there are scarce resources and the need to allocate scarce resources, there are rich people middle-income people and poor people. The structures of school are infused with and infiltrated by the wider social structures. Some of these may be said to be specifically capitalist but others (such as adult-child authority patterns) are common to virtually all societies and their different cultures, and economic organizations. It is under these circumstances that ideals become modified by practice and political, social and economic realities. However, all such structures have one thing in common, they either open up or close off opportunities to get those things or to indulge in those experiences that we want. Individuals vary in the extent to which they will fight for what they want, can skilfully manage their relations with others to get what they want, or manipulate social structures and interpretations of reality to achieve their goals. Misinterpretation, confusion as between competing interpretations, and a disintegrating sense of self and self-worth, social order, and creative energies are the inherent dangers involved in finding one's way around not only school but everyday life as a whole. The particular course one drives through everyday life I call the social-curriculum; it is a course in the original sense of the word where curriculum meant 'racing chariot', thus individuals take the reins of their own destiny and drive their course with as much skill, daring and energy as can be mustered. The realities of the course are the emotional hurdles presented by economic structures, disequalities of power and social expectations as to how boys, girls, men and women are supposed to behave in whatever circumstances they find themselves. Schools hold out the hope of 'better jobs through better qualifications' but now a variety of Youth Opportunity schemes show the extent to which schools fail in their implicit promise. Each individual must assess the chances of getting what he or she wants and choose the means. Such assessments and choices constitute the individual's self-elected curriculum (cf. Schostak, 1983b) – and the best teachers are not necessarily school teachers. Each individual, however, does not have an equal opportunity to choose, the choice is bounded always within one particular social curriculum, that course of emotional hurdles which alone or with a community one must overcome. The question for each individual is: to what extent are we prepared to live the lives others want us to live, and to what extent are we prepared to resist their influence and their power to control our minds and bodies?

When I ask pupils what they would like to do when they leave school they smile and rattle out their ambitions – work in a nursery, catering, a hairdresser, a secretary, a mechanic – and then I ask what they think their chances of a job will be. Few answer other than 'None!' Dennis and his mate Marty have their own ideas of what they'll be doing. I ask what they intend doing when they leave school.

Marty: Trying to get a job and earn some money.
Dennis: Well, first when I leave school, I'm gonna get me fair share of the dole. I'm gonna 'ave a little holiday, you know, away from school. Experience lying in. Experience

a few, about a month off school ... then soon as we get that, get out and try and find a job. I probably won't though 'cos it's not, ... there's hardly none now, so when I leave there'll be hardly none, definitely not. I must say I'm gonna skive....

Marty: When I leave school I wanna just go an' try an' get a job an' earn some money.

Dennis is going to play the system and Marty is going to work within the system and try to play by its rules. According to the school, both are poor average pupils just as Debbie and Ann are above average pupils. In each case the friends having similar abilities and home backgrounds choose opposing roads to travel. In each case, as we will see, those roads are chosen not indiscriminately but according to an astute judgement of 'payoffs' and risks.

The teachers of the school are well aware of the scale of the problem that unemployment presents and the question that it hangs over schooling. One housemaster says:

I could tell you one significant fact I think, that we had 250 children left us last summer (1980), 49 of them by the end of November had got jobs. 201 were either on the dole or on work experience schemes of one sort or another. 49 had real jobs. Now, I think if I were 14 or 15 years old looking towards leaving school, average ability, I'd be thinking to myself 'Well, what's the point of working at school?' These teachers are telling us that you've got to work hard if you want a good job but there's no jobs there anyway. So I think we're coming up against.... And I've noticed it this year more markedly than ever before, a certain resignation to unemployment when they leave school. And I'm almost having to bully kids in the fifth year at present into getting hold of the *Echo* at night and writing off to jobs because they believe they are of no value. And it all comes back to what I was saying earlier about trying to get kids to believe in themselves a little bit. But having said that even if they all believed in themselves we still know that a lot of people wouldn't get a job. Even if they were all trying like mad, a lot of them wouldn't get jobs. And this is what I meant when I said circumstances outside the school over which we have no control, they have no control.... So perhaps we should be thinking more about political education and perhaps we should be thinking more about encouraging them to be non-conformist in the sense that they are prepared to ask questions, to challenge and not accept glib answers that teachers give out willy nilly; and when they leave, politicians give out. . . .

The question hangs over school and what it should be doing for children. It is an uncomfortable question easily ignored in the hurly burly of day-to-day school life. It is uncomfortable because teachers do not see themselves as revolutionaries, who may act upon an environment, but rather more as the agents of social control, that is, responding to pressures to fulfil social norms. This is made clear when I jumped at the chance to get him to elucidate the question and develop it. I asked, 'Suppose the pupils started organizing themselves into writing letters, protest marches – what would happen to the school?' His response was quick.

I think we would oppose it. I think you would get the situation where the teachers would oppose it. I mean, it's happened. It's happened in the past. It's kind of 'quash the rebellion'. Because generally speaking . . . when they get a bee in their bonnet, they tend not to write letters. It tends to be violent revolution in inverted commas. And that is unacceptable to teachers. Maybe if we were teaching them properly they would know how to protest without just resorting to violence or vandalism of some type, without the first step being breaking the rules; but we don't. You know, I'm not being just critical of this school. I think it's very difficult to envisage a school of 1900 and odd kids where kids are encouraged to disapprove. And what happens, they come to me and they say, as Housemaster, they say 'I'm not going to maths because I don't like that maths teacher. He was rude today and I don't want to sit with rude people and I'm not going anymore.' It requires a complete turn round in the way that teachers have been trained to think. It requires society to allow us to turn round.

Choices must be made and teachers are implicated in those choices. A choice that involves deviance does not arise randomly; it is chosen from a set of alternatives determined historically. In everyday life these alternatives are reproduced and enforced by those who choose to obey, enforce and resist each demand for change from those under authority.

Deviants

If one does not attempt to assert some sense of individuality, some sense of outrage against inequality, some sense of distaste of the way one is treated, one is enslaved, possessed. Thus, Debbie's mother says when asked whether she would like Debbie to stay on at school after the fifth year:

> Oh I'd like her to stay on [at school]. The way Debbie is with the school, she thinks her life's her own and she can do what she likes you see. When they get to the age of sixteen I think they think that they're just.... Aye, some children are far different, like Sharon seems to be more for school whereas Debbie, Debbie isn't. And being honest with you, I honestly wish that I could have that chance.

Day by day as teachers, counsellors, innocent bystanders, we are audience and chorus to Greek tragedies, we try not to get involved, we dabble perhaps. The children we teach are both our hopes for the future and the seeds of the past. We as teachers see them as the materials out of which we produce exam passes and 'well balanced' adults. Parents, perhaps, see them as the chances they never had, perhaps as the future which is but an image of their past. Children become caught in a net of desires and concerns, bad if they do not. On the dangers of this one parent says:

> You might set your heights a bit much, you know, thinking 'Oh well, I'd like her to do this and I'd like her to do that and when it comes to the end of the day – will she, you know, do something completely different. Sometimes I think parents can get this ... you know, minds set on things and it just doesn't work out. And I don't think it's any good telling them what they should do. I work with a man in work and his son was at university [and] ... he's got no relationship with his son because he didn't become a policeman. He was obsessed because his eldest son was a sergeant and he's thwarting [the] attempt to become a policeman. Well he's got no intention to become a policeman. It's just something he didn't want. And because of this he hasn't forgiven him.

This does not mean to say this parent has no ambitions for her daughter but that those ambitions are not narrowed to one specific occupation. The child is kept well away from trouble spots in

Slumptown. Indeed, she is rarely allowed out. This parent is in full control, or possession, of her child. The community has its unconscious, its darkness, the repressed contents of which the child is not allowed to see. To go out at night is to repossess or be possessed by these contents. Parental authority shrinks back from the dark corners, avoids the loitering gangs, withdraws to the light and warmth of the home. But the dark corners and the gangs are all part of the community, a community founded upon mutual violations of rights, individual expression, interests, and agreements. In the home all is safe. This mother is the sort who believes and can enforce, that 'discipline begins in the home'. A community of disciplined homes would seem to be the ideal. Another mother, the mother of Debbie Graves, is also a believer in firm discipline: 'Although I've asked the teachers to chastise her but they said they can't give corporal punishment anymore.' She tries to exert pressure by being 'on Debbie's back': 'Oh, she's told me when she leaves [school] she's leaving home. That's because I keep on her back about the school. And that's being honest. I do get on her back a lot. I'm forever telling her the teachers are there to teach her, not her to teach the teachers. And she doesn't believe it.'

In any one school there may be 500 to 1000 sets of parents each involved in their different life stories – a community of life stories; and up to 2000 or more pupils. The numbers of teachers range from perhaps the smallest at, say, twenty to the largest, say, 150 per school. The cast of *dramatis personae* for even the smallest school is large, too large for the staff to handle in anything but the most superficial manner. Instead of individuals we have: teachers, pupils, parents and Them (about whom we can do nothing and upon whom we blame everything) – four basic groups which can be further classified into 'problem' or 'no problem', academic or non-academic, and further subdivided into 'problem academic' and 'non-problem academic' or behaviour problem, and so on. We start to talk the language of production management, social engineering and name-calling. We have long lost the individuality of the person (cf. Schostak, 1982c).

When does a person become a deviant? When is it that we lose sight of individuality? When is it that we seek the solution of the gang or the police force? Day by day the pressure and counter-pressure is reproduced, shaped, transformed in the small drip drip of parental nagging, or a child's sarcasm and shouting back or a teacher's slap. It is a fight for possession, to possess the life and destiny of one self against the hold of another. We choose our mates and teachers to aid in this struggle – or perhaps, they choose us – and those who oppose us may seem like enemies, or ogres.

Taylor, for example, regards school teachers, with few exceptions, as ogres. He says of the deputy head who teaches him:

Taylor: ... terrible. Like all teachers isn't 'e? Like a sir.
J.F.S.: Terrible?
Taylor: Mm just 'ate 'im.
J.F.S.: What does he do then?
Taylor: Bawls at yer....
J.F.S.: Have you ever had to go and talk to him or anything?
Taylor: Yeah.... Haven't we? [to friend]
J.F.S.: What sort of thing does he say?
Taylor: Ju' that 'e's entitled to 'it you with a whip or a cane, or with rulers.

That the deputy head is entitled to use whip, can and rulers to hit the child is fantasy. However, that the deputy head 'bawls' is true. But the deputy head is shown as a caricature. It would be easy to suppose that the caricature is wilfully misleading. I sat in the deputy head's office day after day talking conversationally to him, watching him at his work, listening as he talked conversationally to others. He is well liked, gentle and kind hearted. Above all, in interviews with pupils many spontaneously said that this deputy head was good, kind and pleasant to know. However, there were those like Taylor who knew nothing or little of the other dimensions of his personality; for them, punishment and control became the sole kinds of interaction with adults like the deputy head. Similarly, Taylor, to his teachers, became little more than a caricature, a wayward, wilful boy, incorrectly uniformed, persistently truanting.

School in some sense is a community of caricatures; we don masks to play out the dramas typical of school. Upon any one day, an observer will see aspects of the drama. The drama will have its phases, its quiet reflective periods, its periods of fun, its periods of rising tension, its crises and its denouements. The school, however, is an incubator for the images, the narratives, the plots of the wider community; each story finds its interpretation in a cultural matrix of images, myths, folk-tales unique to the society which spawned them. Becoming a caricature is not pleasant: to resist is not easy: it becomes difficult to tell what is projection and what is real. The results can be explosive.

A boy allowed me to 'shadow' him for the day. I call him Jacko. I had interviewed him a month or two earlier and had seen him in his tutor group and upon the occasions when he was 'in trouble' standing in the corridor outside the deputy head's office.

Jacko is a big lad, only 13 years old but a good twelve stone and about five-eight. He towers over his friends. We went straight to the tutor room, a science room. Jacko huddled with his friends, sniggering and laughing. I began to talk to Katie. The tutor called to Jacko and the rest of us on that table to come and sit at the front. Someone complained that there were gas taps on that table, but no matter, we were to move. Reluctantly, we moved. A pupils' bulletin was scanned to see if there was anything relevant for the group, then the remainder of the period was spent by the tutor preventing three girls from leaving the room.

The lesson for the first half of the morning was English. After about half-an-hour Jacko was ordered out of the class. I went with Jacko to the house block and there we saw Debbie Graves at a desk in the empty house block dining hall copying out some chemistry notes. She had been banned from all chemistry lessons. Jacko and I sat with Debbie.

Jacko: What are you doing?
Debbie: Copying out some chemistry.
Jacko: Have you been thrown out?
Debbie: No. I'm permanently banned. I'm banned from a lot of lessons. It's 'cos I don't get on with teachers. Nobody can tell me what to do.
Jacko: Well, they told you to come 'ere.

For a while they discussed the extent to which Debbie had the power to determine her own life. Jacko thought the power to be severely restricted. Debbie however emphasized her 'madness' and the way she loved teachers to shout at her: 'Nobody tells me what to do.' The discussion lasted until break. After break the battle with teachers was resumed. The lesson was physics. Much of the lesson was spent having to coax, threaten and seemingly implore Jacko and his mates to be quiet:

[The teacher, Mr Grey, is trying to explain how to work out relative densities; he is writing various formulae on the blackboard.]

Mr Grey: Right, if the relative density is greater than one it's something that won't float....
Pupil: [in a deep 'funny' voice] Won't float....
Mr Grey: If it's less than one....
Pupil: Won't float.
Mr Grey: It will. Right, that's a useful ... shh! ... Oi! Will you stop looking at those bars you're not in a zoo.
Pupil: Where are the bars? [looking around]
Mr Grey: They don't fascinate you....
Pupil: Where are the bars?
Mr Grey: These are ... [pointing to a shelf closed off by bars].
Pupil: (Indicating friend) He's a pig.
Mr Grey: Oi, shhh!
[Several pupils call out.]
Mr Grey: I'm a bit sick and tired of this, if you want to go at ten past twelve you better listen ... ah ... oi....
The chatter continues. There is a rhythmic tapping as somebody plays the 'drums'.]
Pupil: [calling to another pupil] Sheila, lend me that ball.
Jacko: [He is sitting with the boys who were fascinated by the bars. He has been talking to some girls on the other side of the room. He sees one of the girls has a pair of mittens.] I only want one [of the gloves] you lend me one, you're not using it.
Mr Grey: Right, put that down ... oi, you written this down?
Jacko: Yeah.
Mr Grey: You haven't.
Jacko: I have.
Mr Grey: I can see you haven't....

The lesson proceeded much in this manner until we stopped suddenly to see Jacko and a small boy called Billy throwing punches at each other. Some girls began to cry out, 'Jacko leave him.' The fighting moved into the centre of the room. Billy fell to the ground and Jacko began to boot him:

Girl: Jacko leave him.
[Mr Grey strides forward to pull Jacko away. Most of the class is gathered round.]

Mr Grey: Outside now [Billy is helped up] come, you come with me.

Jacko(?): I broke me fist.

Mr Grey: Come with me. The rest of you stay quiet. Don't start the experiment but sit down.

A girl says to some others gathered round, 'Wasn't he tight?' (That is, didn't Jacko act 'mean'?). Many of the class are now talking at once. One boy says to another (probably Lennie), 'Idiot, what did you say?'

Lennie(?): Fat bastard.

Girl: Don't lie, Lennie.

Lennie: 'E did.

Another boy: 'E did.

Lennie: See.

Girl: That's not him. [That is, fighting and calling names is not the sort of thing Billy does.]

Lennie: 'E did.

Girl: 'E didn't.

Lennie: 'E did say it.

This event was not the product of simply one 'drama' but many. Jacko likes to be provocative and thus continually provokes his teachers. As we saw in the conversation with Debbie, Jacko is reflective about his situation and the situation of others like him. Recalling the incident of Nicky Wragg and the headmaster, we see that Jacko and Debbie are well aware that to fight the system is like the Isle of Man declaring war on the United States; however, they declare their war. But there is also another war of interest which led to the fight between Billy and Jacko. Aspects of this war came to light in their interviews which took place with the deputy head-master:

Deputy: What was the cause of it?

Jacko: Sir, we were going to do this experiment with water and we cleared up (and I threw my book at him). And he threw it back. (I threw it to him and) he threw it back to me and called me a fat bastard. I never did a thing to be rude to him.

Deputy: He called you that?

Jacko: Yeah.

Deputy: Do you normally ask him to? To look after your book?

Jacko: Sir, no.
Deputy: Did you want to look after your book?
Jacko: No.
Deputy: Why did you want him to look after yours?
Jacko: Dunno.
Deputy: [beginning to speak louder and more forcefully] Well you didn't just ask him once and he refused. He refused two or three times.
Jacko: No, Sir, four.
Deputy: Yeah, good, there, is there some sort of rule Jacko, that other people in the in your class look after your things when you want them to?
Jacko: (very quiet) Sir, no.
Deputy: . . . Is he a friend of yours?
Jacko: Sir, no.
Deputy: Is he a relation:
Jacko: Sir, no.
Deputy: Have you, have you any *right* to *expect* him to look after your things for you?
Jacko: Sir, no.
Deputy: . . . Then you persisted in this and when he refused, whatever name he called you, . . . you knocked him to the ground and kicked him to the face . . . yeah?
Jacko: (very quiet) Yeah.
Deputy: What a big hero. Look at you, you're twice the size. How heavy are you?
Jacko: dunno . . . about twelve stone.
Deputy: Yeah . . . you're twice the size of Billy . . . and does that give you some sort of . . . feeling of satisfaction, Jacko, that that um you know, here you are the big hero, the biggest lad in the class – knock down the small boy and kick him in the face because he called you a name because he won't look after your book. There is nothing on this earth Jacko, that says he's got to look after it . . . is there?
Jacko: Sir, no.
Deputy: . . . You've made a right fool of yourself.

At this point in the interview we have reached an interesting irony. If we again recall the Nicky Wragg incident where Nicky was told by headmaster and deputy that his role in school life – including his freetime during the dinner hour – was to obey the commands of teachers, the irony stands out. The question is, do rules exist to say that pupils have got to do what teachers tell them? If such rules do exist – and they appear to – what are the limits which govern their application? At what point can a pupil legitimately say, 'No, I won't, you can't force me'? Now the objections may arise. The irony is superficial. Clearly, there is no real comparison because Jacko has kicked a smaller boy to the floor and is clearly a bully. Objection accepted. But this merely produces another irony. The same deputy head has told of an incident where a teacher punched a boy who was causing trouble, an act not infrequent for this teacher. The deputy calls that teacher a bully and has no sympathy for him; indeed, he feels a disgust with that kind of behaviour. However, the action brought praise for the teacher from a number of other teachers. Punching, slapping, poking and so on are not isolated but are everyday occurrences in any school. It would be impossible to place a percentage upon the numbers of teachers engaging in these practices. However, we could call it a significant minority. As one well intentioned teacher put it, 'it is difficult to see how you control a class without there being some form of threat to enforce commands. Oh, yes, I've lost my temper and have struck out.' This was an experienced teacher holding a senior position. Clearly Jacko was wrong. Jacko is a bully. I am in no way trying to excuse his behaviour. I am, however, trying to interpret and understand his behaviour in the light of the traditional power contests between teachers and pupils and between young people competing for dominance in a conflict ridden environment. Of his job, the deputy head sadly says, 'I'm a piece of blotting paper soaking up the mess which people throw at me.' His job is to deal with the tensions produced in the school between pupils and teachers and between members of the staff. He admits he cannot solve anything. He is happy if he can disperse and dampen down some of the tensions and problems. He must act upon his judgement instantaneously – sometimes he is right, sometimes he is wrong. He is surrounded by the structures which produce the occasions for the tensions just as are the children and the remainder of the staff. Together they are caught in dramatic ironies.

Teachers and pupils are tied together in relationships of control and of guidance. Many teachers when faced by rebellious children do not know what to do other than give out punishments or send them to their housemasters or other senior teachers for punishment. Furthermore, even in a tutor system set up to help solve the problems of teacher–pupil relationships and other school induced problems, some tutors are incapable or unwilling to pursue this role. Jacko's teacher says of Jacko:

> *Tutor:* A bit like a wilful child. He is certainly on the surface quite bright. Appears to be quite talented musically. Um he is not prepared to put himself out for a minute. He certainly will not put himself out as regards his lessons. . . . Um he likes stirring things up, keeping in the background . . . uh . . . being particularly unpleasant now at times. . . .
>
> *JFS:* Do you think he's doing it out of nastiness or just. . . .
>
> *Tutor:* I think most things he does are calculated. I don't find him a particularly pleasant lad. But then again, I would say most of the lads in my tutor group I don't find particularly pleasant when compared with the girls. Um some of them are downright unpleasant. Uh, but Jacko, I don't know. I don't know what's the matter with him um he's always in trouble. He can be very insolent.
>
> *JFS:* Has he been like this, you know, say from first year. . . .
>
> *Tutor:* Ah now then, I didn't have much experience with him in the first year. But um, yes, I think he's got progressively worse. Obviously wasn't as bad in the first year. I think he's got progressively worse. He knows how to play the system. . . . I don't know if it's correct but I get the impression he's a bit spoiled at home compared to his elder brother. I don't really know. I know very little of his home background. I've seen the parents at parents' nights and things like this. Um, I suppose really I know very little about him.

Like Jacko's tutor, not all teachers will be committed to a pastoral system – or, if they are sympathetic to the pastoral system's aims of discipline and control, they are not able to go along with the wider implications of pastoral tutoring. Thus we will find in New Town Comprehensive junior and senior teachers saying, 'We are not social workers.' Consequently, little will be known about even the direst of conditions affecting some pupils (cf. Schostak, 1982a) and the possible reasons for their rebellious behaviour. Such children will be said to 'play the system' and present discipline and control problems, or be said to be 'tragic'. Jacko engages in a drama of provocation, of taunting and pushing the patience of others to the limit. Thus, 'using his brightness he can be very cheeky, he knows just where to draw the line. He can bring you right up to the boiling point, as it were, and then cave in. He knows just how far he can go with you...,' but sometimes Jacko goes too far.

Is there an organizational response to this kind of problem? Because Slumptown Comprehensive is a purpose built, house-centred school it may be thought that if the house system means anything at all it would solve this kind of problem, or such pupils as this – who are a minority – cannot be catered for in any school. School organizational responses are delimited by practicalities. The idealistic but practical headmaster as we have described him in this school must respond to such a problem by saying 'not every member of the staff of a school is likely to be of superlative teacher quality and therefore something that may work for the gifted and committed teacher is not necessarily simply by virtue of that fact a good school policy because a lot of the teachers won't be that gifted and committed.' Hence, given school resources in terms of materials and teacher commitment, the headmaster can only design a school which will be the best that can be made with the resources to hand. In short, the responses of schools can only be made within an environment of social and economic pressures. In practice, the committed and energetic teachers of any school work with the system in so far as they can, and work 'between' the system as far as they can by bending the rules, by sliding between the rules, by 'looking the other way', but eventually they may come up against a Jacko or a Debbie Graves.

With Jacko the deputy head spent a long time trying to arrive at the causes of the boy's problems, but simple causes are rarely found. One part of the problem was traced to Jacko's friends 'winding him up'. The deputy head talked to Lennie:

Deupty: Is Jacko popular? ... Don't the lads like him?
Lennie: Dunno [very quietly].
Deputy: What about the girls?
Lennie: Just the same.
Deputy: You get at him a bit?
Lennie: Some of them do.
Deputy: Why, because of his size? ... They wind him up a bit don't they? You got a teacher where perhaps you know you can get away with something. It's easy enough to wind up Jacko isn't it?
Lennie: Sir, yeah.

Deputy: Get him playing. . . .

Lennie: Probably.

Deputy: Do you know what situation he's in at the moment?

Lennie: Prison.

Deputy: Suspension [untranscribable . . .] thought of that? You thought that that little lad had called a name. You didn't even know what that name was. Did you? But you told him that, um . . . called Jacko a bastard, so Jacko picked on a little lad knocked him to the ground and kicked him in the *head*. What?

Lennie: Sir.

Deputy: So you could be responsible for his suspension. . . . So. . . . I'm not getting at you . . . not blaming you . . . but you ought to think about that and the class ought to think about that. Every . . . he's under sentence of death . . . literally out, boom, boot behind him until he sees the headmaster. . . . The very next time he steps out of line right? That was the sentence last time we saw him. Now you and the class have got to realize that every time you wind him up, every time you tell him the wrong thing, every time he gets involved in stupidity with a teacher, he's right on the edge and he's gonna catch it.

In a similar manner the housemaster argued with Jacko and his mates. The deputy and the housemaster both tried to advise on the other of Jacko's problems – his weight:

Deputy: You are heavy son, you are overweight aren't you?

Jacko: Sir, yeah.

Deputy: And . . . I gather that you have been medically examined about this.

Jacko: Sir, yeah.

Deputy: Yeah? . . . And the doctor has said that you've what?

Jacko: Get the weight down.

Deputy: There's n' there's nothing the matter with you physically.

Jacko: Sir?

Deputy: You've not got any um glandular problems which sometimes cause overweight? . . . Eat too much is that right?

Jacko: Sir, yeah.

Deputy: And don't take enough exercise perhaps, is that
   right?
Jacko: Sir, yeah.

Jacko the clown disliked the reflected image of himself, particularly
an image reflected by one who was not a mate. The deputy head
continued:

Deputy: Well, unless you do something about it Jacko your
   weight's not going to disappear magically. It isn't going to
   happen. Somebody of your shape – or my shape – sunshine
   needs to do something about it. Right? I'm going to do
   something about it. You've got to as well. Otherwise
   people will carry on calling you 'fat' and it's not good
   saying 'It's alright for Barry Knight to call me that, I know
   he's just skitting but it's not alright for White to call me
   that.' Because there are some people who don't understand
   that do they?... Well, do they? I mean, you don't mind,
   you just laugh.... If Barry Knight walked in here now and
   said, 'You're a big fat blob' – you'd just laugh wouldn't
   you?
Jacko: Sir, yeah.
Deputy: Or you'd hit him with your bag or something
   wouldn't you? Yeah, or you'd thump him or kick him or
   something. But you wouldn't knock him to the ground
   and kick him in the face.... What you did to White, Jacko.
   That was absolutely unforgiveable man. He's there [in-
   dicating height] compared to you. And you've got to
   suffer for it. Take your punishment. Look at me Jacko. Do
   you understand that?
Jacko: Sir, yeah.

People can change – but not easily. Jacko can be wound up like a
mechanical doll and set to clown about in the class; sometimes he is
wound too far. He does not want to be a wound-up doll – he fights
back, he lashes out, to save some sense of dignity in the eyes of his
friends, a dignity lost in the brutality of his act. Jacko's act has been
produced out of a multiplicity of wars of interests: between control
and individual act; between Jacko and his mates who wind him up;
and between Jacko and the boy who asserted his right not to be
bullied. And underneath all this is the vulnerable Jacko continually

caricatured in the words of others – he is 'blob', 'fatty', sexually unattractive. Jacko is imprisoned by his mates' image of himself.

In the end will such a talking to and taking his punishment work? To change, it seems to me, he would need some positive indication, some visualizable course of action to allow him to see possible changes in the circumstances of his life. The change would necessitate a transformation of his relations with others. Is such a change realistic?

After the headmaster had seen Jacko, talked to him about his weight problem in a similar fashion to the deputy head and settled upon a suitable punishment, the deputy, the head and the housemaster discussed the future. Indeed, little more than a month later Jacko was again in trouble. If the school cannot cope, then some kind of proof needs to be developed in order to show that the school has done everything possible. Has Jacko seen the educational psychologist? His comments would be needed in any case that would have to be presented against Jacko. Every dramatic incident produces a case history which can be used for praise or blame.

In other situations with other teachers and other Jackos the details will vary. In some schools little or no attempt to reveal the underlying causes of problems will be made, others, like Slumptown, will do as much as they can but will also protect themselves for any eventuality. Schools have a job to do. A school will have anywhere between 400 and 2500 children taught by between twenty and 200 staff. Schools will do what is administratively possible. To this end there must be rules and ways of behaving. Such rules must be enforced With so many children the rules are often enforced in a manner which must seem crude; by shouting 'Oi! You, stop doing that!'; by threatening, 'Right, if you don't shutup now, you'll stay in at break time'; and by force – slapping, punching, poking, pushing, calling names, shaming and so on. The rules and the ways teachers enforce them are the most contentious issue between teachers and pupils. Such rules and the ways teachers enforce them lead some pupils to behave like Jacko or Debbie. Others ruefully tolerate the rules, believing, or perhaps knowing, that nothing can be done about them and they cannot raise them as issues with anybody because the tutor 'usually just goes in the other room' during tutor period and 'speaks to the other teachers' or does his own work. Some tutors, however, you can talk to. They will listen. But they won't always do much. They can't, can they? A fifth-year girl wrote:

School is depressing! The teachers ought to have more feelings and understanding towards the kids. If someone bunks the housemaster/mistress doesn't sit down and talk about why they bunked and help them to solve their problem they just stick them on a school detention. School detention is stupid as well. I can understand using detention as a form of punishment and in some cases it can be effective.

The prospect of leaving school and getting a job is terrible and that makes kids unprepared to learn because they feel there is no point.

Also some of the teachers make the lessons really boring and that makes kids (especially me) mess about to liven the lesson up, then we get into trouble, get told off, etc. but it doesn't stop us doing it again.

My main point is the fact that teachers refuse to forget the bad things and never remember the good. I myself and a few of my friends suffer under these conditions. For the first three or so years we got into trouble and were the talk of the houseblocks. Teachers gave us funny looks and talked about us but in the fourth year we tried to settle down, but the teachers tried to get us into trouble. As soon as the word trouble is mentioned our names get mentioned. I can understand that we have built up our bad reputation but they won't give us the chance to get rid of it.

One teacher even admitted to us that it would be 'impossible' for us to settle down because all the teachers are against us and if that isn't proof of the lack of understanding between pupils and teachers I don't know what is.

This girl is amongst the brightest in the school. Her comments are clearly articulate and considered. Reputation is considered by her to stand between herself and the teachers. Hargreaves, Hestor and Mellor (1975) describe in their study how pupils are labelled and that these labels become relatively stable over time, that indeed teachers resist a change in the labels they have used to describe pupils. This girl pins her reputation to having 'messed around' especially in boring lessons. Boredom is a frequent complaint. She also indicates the poor prospects of finding a job. School for her is 'depressing'.

In similar vein, a girl lower down in the academic league writes:

Being around my age is rather difficult, you think you are too old for school and too young to know anything about the outside world.

This is most probably the hardest year of my school days, with all your exams coming and all that all the teachers seem to be getting on your back.

And now I know that I have only a few months left in school I tend to bunk more of my lessons.

My feelings are if teenagers were not forced to education, more teenagers that bunk or slag school would turn up more often.

Most of the teachers treat you like dog muck and surely you are not going to stand for that so you start to treat them like it. Then they don't like it so they send you down the houseblock. Then you get into lumber.

Most teachers can give pressure but just can't take it. They make me sick.

Most people learn more in the outside world than they do in the school itself.

If the teachers treated the pupils with a bit more respect things would be a lot easier.

If a teacher wanted to talk to you about something you have done they might wait until you are by yourself instead of pulling you out of a crowd, instead of making a show of you. They wouldn't like it if you made a show of them.

It would seem there is not much chance of communication between these girls and their teachers. She reacts to the 'pressure' that the teachers bring to bear upon her by giving 'pressure' back. Her refusal to behave as teachers want and her statement concerning compulsory schooling identifies the underlying power structure of schooling, that the teacher's definition is the only legitimate definition and that this can be enforced using a variety of punishments. By definition, good pupils are the ones who do not challenge either the teacher's authority or the teacher's definition of the situation. A pupil's experience of schooling thus depends upon the extent to which that pupil is willing to accept or to rebel against the teacher's demands; or, perhaps, the extent to which the pupil can present an acceptable facade to teachers which cloaks the pupil's real feelings and actions.

Without trust, individuals will hide behind masks, communication will reduce to the rhetorical manipulation of language to create deceptions in order to manipulate the behaviour of others. Relations between self and other therefore rest upon fraudulent principles. Community becomes a community of masks. The vulnerable self tries to maintain a position of being out of reach, hard, inviolable but able to lash out and make the other submit. In such a situation community does not exist for the celebration of uniqueness but for the reproduction of those existing social conditions which maintain the masks and the illusions which protect the vulnerable self. That uniqueness of the individual circumscribed as it is by birth, death and the limits placed by language-masks upon the communication of experience may shrivel and haunt us in nightmares or may explode as 'irrational' rupturings of community order. Although individuals are born into community structures not of their making they may, through critical reflection, create new order, new community forms. But first they must wrestle with their racial and sexual identities – the topics of the following chapters – in the painful struggle toward individuality.

4   Race, Racism, Deviance and Schooling

We can talk of the race of mankind, or we can talk of the black and white races. Too often when we think of race, we think of skin colour and racial hatred, discrimination or conflict. In the host country the individual of a different colour is from birth ascribed a personality, a stereotypical personality, typically detrimental in some way. Like other social problems racial prejudice has a history. Multiracial schooling cannot be understood except within that historical context.

The last chapter argued that for the lower classes in this country there has been a history of the violation of and assertion of a lower-class sense of community. The specific causes of individual acts of deviance – like the Jacko incident – become difficult to find. Yet, there exists a climate of hostility, resentment, and suspicion. Similarly, the history of racial discrimination in Britain is a history of the violation and assertion of racial identity and community. Individual acts of deviance again cannot unambiguously be pinned down to specific causes but occur within a climate of grievance which is built up over time from many hundreds, perhaps millions, of trivial amongst some major experiences of being 'violated'.

It may be difficult for many to appreciate the extent to which racism is woven into our day-to-day lives, historically, dramatically. Daily we disown this history and forget the drama history compels us to play out. However, racism in Britain is yet another by-product of the lust for profit. Kapo (1981.18) and others like him will not allow us to forget the extent to which Britain has violated the black races in its lust for profit:

> The immoralities and inhumanities which froze the souls of millions of slaves can only begin to assume their proper place

in the British economic memory, if it is recognized that this is a land where the profit motive cuts down everything in its path. Which explains why John Hawkins was knighted by Queen Elizabeth for his success 'to take the inhabitants with burning and spoiling their towns.' You may think this an understandable attitude towards other peoples in the context of the rampant violence of Elizabethan England. But what we shall perceive is that Britain's savage treatment of black slaves was malignant; that there exists an active affinity between the treatment of black people as slaves, their treatment in Britain's colonies under the Pax Britannica, and the treatment black people are receiving in Britain today.

It is a savage indictment.

From the Africans the British took their labour, and 'erased' their history and their culture. Bolt (1971:209) outlined the archetypal Victorian negro – first quoting the *Encyclopedia Britannica* (XVII, 1884:318) as saying:

'No full-blooded Negro has ever been distinguished as a man of science, a poet, or an artist, and the fundamental equality claimed for him by ignorant philanthropists is belied by the whole history of the race throughout the historic period.' Political institutions were rudimentary among Negroes, they had no religion worthy of the name, they had never exploited the rich continent they occupied, so the theory went; they were strong, but lacked brain-power, slaves to their own passions and the natural slaves of other races. Children of Nature, the Negroes apparently had no natural rights. Such rights, it came to be believed, depended entirely upon the nature of the possessor, not of the right. These characteristics were thought to belong as much to the Negroes in America and the West Indies as to the black African; indeed, the former were frequently referred to and condemned as Africans throughout the nineteenth century, in spite of the fact that many had no memory of their place of origin, and most had accommodated themselves to their new homes over fundamental questions like religion, dress and language.

Bolt (p. 209) goes on to compare the Victorian images of the negro and Indian:

A crucial point of difference between all black peoples and the Indian races, according to Victorian opinion, was the greater savagery of the former, as demonstrated, for instance, in the South African Wars and the Jamaica revolt of 1865. The Indian Mutiny and the Afghan campaigns could not, of course, be explained away, and it must be admitted that the more martial tribes of both Africa and India won respect, but the myth of the soft, effete Hindu persisted, and its overtones were not unfriendly.

Added to this there is the way the negro became a 'toilet' for British sexual projections where black skin merged with fantasies of black magic and sinful passion. The various fantasies persist today (cf. Husband, 1982).

However, many black immigrants during the 1950s were drawn to this country by the glittering promises of prosperity diligently advertised by Great Britain. British industry needed cheap labour. Indeed, the 'West Indians originally thought that they had much in common with British people and expected to be able to identify with the British way of life' (PEP, 1976:22). However, many saw the 1962 Commonwealth Immigrants Act as blowing 'the guts out of the "Mother Country" hallucination' (Kapo, 1981:11). A similar reaction followed the publication of the British Nationality Bill in 1981. This Bill redefined British nationality, excluding perhaps millions who previously would have been able to claim citizenship. There is a violation of one's sense of belonging; the 'Mother' has slapped down her children.

It all adds, little by little, to a climate of resentment which at street level may be interpreted as by this black girl (Lucy):

> . . . she call us in to do 'er dirty work for her, build 'er up, she wants us out again 'cos she see that we're gettin' education and we're gettin' brainy, and we're comin' into power so she wants us all out before we reach too high. That's why she wants us out.

In the end it comes down to the individual's sense of being violated and the individual's reassertion of his or her pride.

> *Lucy:* I went for an interview from the um people down at the uh job centre, right? So, there was this girl alright, . . . O.K. I was dressed in my best dress, right, an' I saw a white girl in there right. She 'ad punk sort of style, come in

there with jeans an' she looked really off and – 'cos I would never like to get up in the morning an' see that – I'd run, right? That's 'ow she made me feel. So, it's a thing like, she went, or I went before 'er for interview, right? No, she went before me. So she had, I hear that she had to sit back outside. So, I went for my interview an' he said, 'I'll write you in the future', Right? So, I was finkin', 'Ah, right, so I'll sit back outside like 'ow she's sittin' outside.'

So, I was sittin' back beside her. I said, 'Have you got any qualifications?'

'No.'

And I saw her applic', you know, you got to write your name an' who you are?

J.F.S.: Yeah.

Lucy: She couldn't even write properly, much as gettin' a job 'cos it was for um stock control, alright? So, anyway, least I know that I did my application right, better than her – there's more chance for me to get it even though she's white and the whole, an' the whole shop is white, right?

So, anyway I was sittin' down there, I said, ''ave you got any qualifications?'

She said, 'No.'

I goes, 'Oh I'm in the shit as well but at least I've got a certificate sayin' that I've got experience with this an' that.'

'For I knew it they call 'er back in. She comes back out, 'Ooh, I got the job! I got the job!'

And they were gonna fuckin' write me, make me go 'ome, sit down an' wait an' 'avin' 'igh 'opes an' that! And that's what I found.

I said, 'I'm never going to look for a job again.'

I'll continue goin' on YOP schemes until I know that, that world out there is situated in a better advantage for black people, 'cos I know I'm black. I'm proud of it, right. But I know, it's a strain to be black. It is a strain. You could be proud of it or not proud of it. It's a strain. It's a damn strain.

The strain shows up, though blandly, in statistics on housing, unemployment and education (cf. PEP, 1976; Kettle and Hodges, 1982:141–2; Scarman, 1981). The relation between poor housing, unemployment and relations between the young and the police and the riots of 1981 were not overlooked by Scarman and others. However, it was at the street level where the hurt was felt and the scars remain. The riots become explicable within a matrix of stories, incidents, and the anger which accompanies them. One should never underestimate the intensity of feeling, nor underestimate the extent to which individuals experience oppression in their everyday lives.

The riots will be dealt with more fully in a later chapter. However, it is important not to think of the riots as ephemeral. They act as a persistent symbol by which to interpret everyday incidents. The symbol is complex, at once destructive and creative. The symbol illuminates minor incidents and the collection of minor incidents illuminate, explain and justify the larger symbol which in turn unifies the multiplicity of otherwise unrelated incidents.

Something of the relationship between the riots as symbol and everyday incidents can be seen in Lucy's comments on the Brixton riots:

> it was racism, it was about um, it was um the police arrestin' black boys when they see 'em on the street. I mean, I was, the other day I was walkin' down an' I got nicked for fuck all. I didn't do anythin' an' it really hurt me 'cos I've never been in trouble before but because I'm black I have to stay back. An' I'm tellin' yer I'm standin' firm, right, 'cos whatever they do I know I still got white friends – for they still like me, y' know, I'll call them, you know. It's a thing that, I don't like to be bugged at, bugged at all the time, you know. And they do, and that was what the Brixton riot was all about.

Or in a similar vein, Joan a white girl, says: 'I got done for shop liftin', right? My mate got put away. She's black. I didn't though. I walked out.' Such incidents form the ingredients of resentment. But always, against the felt violation of self-dignity and friendship, there is the reassertion of pride and community. But the reassertion takes an oppositional form – it is 'community-despite ...' or 'unity against ...'. This form sets the context for schooling.

Multiracial Schooling

Lucy: I mean, I remember when I was in school an' I tell ya, it was really prejudiced, it was. I mean I, I, I know white

73

people from since I was a baby an' I grow up – I live cool, you get some cool. In every crowd you get a bad one, there 'as to be a bad chick, be frank wiv me right? But at the same time I mean there was a stage when I was in school right, I, you know I'm an athlete right, I still fink I am. O.K.? And I was doin' athletics an' I just, I didn't want to do it because I see that my marks, my ability, my marks it didn't stand with that. An' all the white girls that doesn't even do anything they're gettin' them top marks. An' that used to make me feel the weight. . . .

Yvonne: Or like, what was it now, she wanted me to. . . . They wanted me to run for the school, right. An' from when I said, 'No I'm not running for the school 'cos I don't like the way that only [untranscribable] get to run for the school'; I was going on a school journey they said 'No, you're not going.' No reason.

They come in the toilet an' saw some girls smokin' an' I was standin' up. But all the girls come out, all the girls what were smokin' said, 'Nah, I wasn't smokin'.' I didn't say nuffin' 'cos I didn't 'ave nuffin' to say. I 'ad no point to prove. So, I wasn't goin' to say nuffin'.

She goes, 'Why didn't you say you wasn't smokin'?'

Right? So, I said, 'I 'aven't got nuffink to prove.'

Right? So, she goes, 'Right, you're not goin' on the school journey. Go 'ome.'

Suspended, six weeks I was at home for nothin'. You know?

Everytime I go, everytime I walk into the school, 'eadmaster's peepin' at the window waitin' for me to come in. 'Miss Woods, come here. Go home. Go home. Come back wiv your father.'

Both girls analyzed their experiences in terms of playground prejudice being backed up by school authority. Both girls were 17 years old, born in Britain of West Indian parents. They had been to different schools but were now classmates on a 'Work Introduction Course' at a local further education college. The majority of this class, as in other classes like it, were black. They had previously been on a Youth Opportunities scheme and knew they had no hope of getting a real job. They were being shunted from one course to another. Like many West Indian girls (cf. Mackie, 1982) Yvonne was an unmarried mother. Proud and happy with her baby she had no intention of getting married. Both girls recalled their school experiences with anger, frustration and resentment.

In the playground it is hard to stand up to provocation:

Lennie: There's some soft kids in our year, right, an' they're um they're National Front an' they, an' they act all hard an' they start doin' the Seig Heil an' we feel like to beat them up. But we don't wanna 'cos we'll get in trouble.

Joe: Like there was a boy today.

Dougie: Who got beat up like.

Joe: Doin' Nazi signs to a black boy an' then 'e got beaten up.

Lennie: An' then 'e went down the office an' complained, right. That other kid, um O'Brian may get suspended for doin' the Seig Heil signs.

Children learn the attitudes and prejudices of the adults. A culture of prejudice, like any culture is passed down from generation to generation. The prejudices are fed by resentments and social pressures:

Dave: You've got a few coloured kids in this school. I used ta 'ang around wiv them I don't 'ang round wiv them much now like 'cos, you know, people started callin' me wog lover an' things like that, an' I don't 'ang around wiv them 'cos they started acting stupid now.

Bill: Yeah, they do 'cos I was walkin' down the stairs right, you know, the recent riots like, an' 'e goes to me, there's a bit of paper on the floor [that is, a black prefect said this to him]. And why should he wait for a white kid to come down? . . . The prefects, big 'eaded. Why should they wait for me to come down because I'm white to pick the paper up?

Len: . . . After the riots an' that they get a big 'ead 'n that, after Brixton.

Jim: There's a few blacks isn't there, an' they call themselves the Black Mafia, an' they stick together.

Dave: They think they're something special like. They got a chip on their shoulder. . . . There's a few black kids, a few of them black kids really hate white people.

The group is a strong influence upon individual behaviour as many experimental studies have shown (cf. Milgram, 1977). Name calling led Dave to stop hanging around with some black friends which he rationalized in terms of them having 'started acting stupid now'. The group identification is then reinforced by tales of 'reversed' prejudice where blacks pick on whites. According to Len, the Black Mafia ''ang around in a bunch an' I goes up to them the other day. I go, 'What's the time?' An' they just goes [he haughtily looks down his nose] like I was a bit of dirt. So I just walked off.' Both groups feel wronged. The sense of being wronged fuels the hatred.

Racism is an emotion laden topic and many researchers have responded to the topic with carefully cool language. Their research findings are carefully qualified, their statistics are bland and their tests of racism are constructed to prove or disprove various hypotheses. However, by circumventing the emotion, the very stuff of racism is itself being circumvented. Racism is in action. It is in the heat of the language used. Such language and action can only be caught and assessed through forms of participant observation. Racism must be caught in the act. It surfaces amidst reasoned arguments. Non-racist attitudes continually have to be on the defensive, as shown by four white fourth-year boys arguing amongst themselves:

> *Len:* If you think, back in Africa, places like that, there's not as many jobs because there ain't houses an' fings like that. But if they was to go back to their own country build their 'ouses then the unemployment would stop in this country.
> *Bill:* No, but we brought them over 'ere right. I 'eard on the television last night, we brought 'em over 'ere for cheap labour, didn't we? An' they, they fink it's their right. They built the country. They build the country that they should stay in it. I'm not National Front nor nothin' like that. I think they should stay 'ere. But not in the same quantity as they are. Because they're comin' round, right. . . .
> *Jim:* But what about the one's comin' over now though?
> *Len:* No, the one's comin' over now should be stopped, not the one's that are born 'ere.
> *Dave:* I fink people who're comin' over to just. . . .
> *Jim:* Scrounge off the system.
> *Dave:* Not, not scrounge or ponce 'cos they do work when they get 'ere, Jim.
> *Jim:* They don't though, they live about an 'undred to an 'ouse. They only pay one rent. An' all of 'em are collectin'

dole so they're makin' such a lot of profit.

Len: Whiteway Road, it's just a whole lot of Asians an' Sikhs an' that.

Dave: Not all of 'em are though, are they? I mean look at all these Pakistani shops who would literally stay open Christmas day. They all do don't they?

Jim: Yeah only 'cos they want the money though. What they do, 'ow they make their money is they buy an' sell off each other, they don't 'ave nothink to do with white men. They buy an' sell off each other. So they all make their profit an' no money of theirs goes in white man's 'ands.

Len: It's got to lead to, I fink, a civil war 'asn't it?

Jim: I should fink you'll lead to a civil war of some kind.

A number of racialist clichés were expressed by Jim. Bill took the strongest position against him but was largely on the defensive. Throughout the discussion there was the impression of being swamped by black immigrants whereas the proportion of immigrants accounted for approximately 2 per cent of the population. The feeling is that whole streets are taken over by blacks, they build their own alien communities, make profits which are not ploughed back into white society while also scrounging off the system. This emotional base to racism is not adequately revealed by statistical studies which in their questionnaires and analyses of achievement tests and public examination results never catch racism in the act. Instead, from their results we must back track toward the acts or causal relations which are hypothesized – or more realistically, speculated – to exist. Consequently, Taylor (1981), in carrying out an extensive review of the literature (which is predominantly statistical in nature), comes to few firm and important conclusions which are of use to policy-makers, practising teachers and the black communities who need such 'evidence' to support or test their claims. There is a clear need for large-scale ethnographic research (carried out over, say, two years whilst living with the community researched) into the processes and everyday realities of racism in education from primary school to YOPs and to university. Only in this way can we have hard social facts rather than soft statistics which provide through questionnaires and test results suitable only for speculation.

The evidence that exists, and seems to be beyond serious dispute, is summed up in the important Rampton Report (1981) as follows: 'we are convinced that West Indian children as a group are indeed underachieving in relation to their peers.' One reason thought by many – particularly West Indians – to contribute to this under-achievement was racism. According to Rampton (p. 12):

> Since a profession of nearly half a million people must to a great extent reflect the attitudes of society at large there must inevitably be some teachers who hold explicitly racist views. Such teachers are very much in the minority. We have, however, found some evidence of what we have described as unintentional racism in the behaviour and attitudes of other teachers whom it would be misleading to describe as racist in the commonly accepted sense. They firmly believe that any prejudices they may have, can do no harm since they are not translated into any openly discriminatory behaviour. Never-theless, if their attitudes are influenced in any way by prejudices against ethnic minority groups, this can and does, we believe, have a detrimental effect on all children whom they encounter.

In what way does one analyze *explicit* racist views? Is it enough simply to ask someone! Or should one extend the notion of explicitness, to views expressed, in passing, in conversation? Setting such views as the target for research there is then the difficulty of determining which kinds of conversation will count as data. It is at least conceivable that teachers who are in publicly accountable positions may try to conceal their explicitly racist views from colleagues and government researchers. However, they are less likely to conceal them from the objects of their racism or those who appear to be open to racist views. Unintentional racism may be no more than an example of a research construct which obscures rather than reveals the processes of everyday life.

A head of department, for example, Mr Stone, enters the staffroom doing his 'Sambo' impression – 'Hey ma-a-an, how de do' – making 'rubber lips', palmed hands flapping. Everyone laughs. The comedy makes his racism ambiguous. Afterall, black comics have caricatured themselves in a similar manner. The humour defuses his racism. Yet, he would count as an 'unintentional racist' saying that his racism is not translated into action. His 'rubber lip' impressions, however, are also carried out in front of black children who can do little else but sheepishly laugh – after all, what harm is there in a little humour? To be forced into the role of being a caricature is not funny. Even where teachers assert that they are 'colour-blind':

> ... to regard all children as equal in this sense need not mean that they should all receive the same educational treatment. In fact, to adopt a 'colour-blind' view of children is in effect to ignore important differences between them which may give rise to particular educational needs. A West Indian child in a predominantly white society needs to see that people like himself are accepted in society generally and that it is recognized that ethnic minority groups have made and are making important contributions in all walks of life. (p. 13)

Moreover:

> there seemed to be a fairly widespread opinion among teachers to whom we spoke that West Indian pupils inevit- ably caused difficulties. These pupils were, therefore, seen either as problems to be put up with or, at best, deserving sympathy. Such negative and patronising attitudes, focusing as they do on West Indian children as problems cannot lead to a constructive or balanced approach to their education. (p. 13)

Surely, whatever racism can mean, it must refer to the fact of holding 'negtive' and 'patronizing' views by members of one race to members of another race. Furthermore, even if 'unintentional rac- ism' is accepted as a real phenomenon of social life, the well attested fact that West Indians are disproportionately represented in Educa- tionally Subnormal (ESN) schools (cf. Coard, 1971) cannot be doubted as discriminatory treatment. However, working backward from statistics to classroom acts of discrimination is still in the realms of mere 'hypothesis':

> ... teachers have negative views of some black children, and teach them in an unstimulating fashion. These children fall behind as a result, and react negatively to their relative failure. But teachers in turn react negatively to the disgrunt- lement of these negatively labelled children, and in some cases refer them for transfer to an E.S.N. school. This chain of events is hypothetical, but it has some plausibility in the light of the studies we have received. (Verma and Bagley, 1979:8)

Others, however, may express their concern in harsher language. Kapo (1981:81) writes:

> Due to the unexpected gut buckets of wrath poured out by black parents against the excessive loading of black children into those schools, the eductional Establishment, by virtue of how many black children they had exiled to them, mugged by their undisguised disinterest in black education, suffered withdrawal symptoms. And 'procrastination being the art of keeping up with yesterday' (Don Marquis), the educational Establishment certainly has done so. Keep on keeping on, with the art of sham. This E.S.N. black-loading sham has re-emerged as the Disruptive Pupils Programme (ILEA, 1979), which in secondary schools has resulted in Sanctuaries and Off-Site Support Centres. In primary schools they are aptly entitled Peripatetic Groups, Nurture Groups and Withdrawal Groups. Very magniloquent titles, but what do they mean? They, successors of E.S.N. schools, revamped in name only, *are* E.S.N. schools. The possibility of any of their black pupils being re-admitted to normal schooling is practically non-existent; and white children are prominent by their absence from these units.

And in Lucy's language of personal experience: 'There's a teacher down there. She's a 'eadmaster. She don't care what 'er teachers do. As long as it's a black pupil, O.K. yeah, 'Get out the school.' She doesn't care. In the 'eart of Oldtown there's a majority of black people O.K. an' they send their kids to school. An' before you know it, them kids can't go in there for a year, a good year, without gettin' suspended. And some of it's for some minor cases I got suspended for.' It is deeply felt and a part of the hard evidence of their everyday lives that the education system is failing to meet the needs of West Indian communities. Bagley (1975:291) found in a study of 2000 West Indian 10-year-olds in London that black families are more interested in their children's education than white families; black mothers read more than white mothers; black parents are more concerned about their children's homework, and are more likely to have taken them to a library. This is the way broken dreams appear in statistics.

In a recent study by Rutter (see *TES*, 8 October 1982) of twelve inner-London schools, performance by West Indians 'on average was well below whites' on measured IQ and reading. However, by the time pupils left school Rutter found a transformation in achievement levels due, he believed, to a greater commitment to education by black pupils than by white pupils. *The Times Educational Supplement* reported that:

> nearer to the time of school leaving, the picture began to change, Professor Rutter said. Although the blacks did less well in the fifth year exams, the differences were marked only in relation to small proportion who got five or more O levels – 7 per cent among whites and 1 per cent among blacks.
>
> Otherwise, the groups were much more alike than they might have expected from the findings at ten and fourteen.
>
> When the final exam results were taken into account, for both fifth and sixth year, the blacks had overtaken the whites. 26 per cent had one to four O levels compared with 24 per cent of whites and a further 19 per cent had five or more O levels compared with 11 per cent of whites.

This glimmer of hope, however, was to be set against the statement that 'more than twice as many blacks were out of work (14 per cent of those in the job market compared with 5 per cent of whites).' In the bland statistics reported in *The TES* the pain is hardly noticeable.

The Rutter finding that blacks are more likely to continue education (in school or further education) than whites was found also by Lee and Wrench (1981) for Birmingham when they tried to find out why there were 'so few black apprentices in industry'. Despite more blacks continuing their education, 'in order to try and meet the state examination requirements of employers looking for apprentices ... only rarely would one of these lads be successful, whereas some boys (mainly white) succeeded in getting an apprenticeship without taking any examinations at all.'

The problem they found was that whites were likely to have informal contacts – through friends or family relations – with firms, whereas blacks did not. However, 'black youths can and do over-come these hurdles and more will do so if they recognize the need to make every effort to get an apprenticeship at sixteen, given the fact that staying on at school into the sixth form is very unlikely to improve their chances.' Therefore, 'they should also explore every possible source of informal information about opportunities, as their white counterparts will not wait for the Careers Service to send them to a firm which is recruiting. At the same time, employers should examine their procedures with sensitivity towards the situation of black applicants and ensure that none of their practices can result in indirect discrimination.'

It is a little like an end of term report that reads 'must try harder'. Knowledge and opportunities, like material resources, are allocated amongst people in unequal ways. How can it be otherwise in a society which preaches the morality of competing for limited favours and the accumulation of profit or wealth in the hands of the few? 'Schools should preach the moral virtue of free enterprise and the pursuit of profit, the Education Secretary, Sir Keith Joseph, said this week. And teachers who cannot put across the message are unfit to teach about industry, he said' (*The Times Educational Supplement*, 26 March 1982). To put this another way, 'liberalism has in our time been enfeebled by sentiment and corrupted by egalitarianism' (Boyson, Junior Education Minister, reported in *The Daily Telegraph*, 11 July 1981).

Growing up and leaving school at present is to face the prospect of unemployment. To be black is to face higher levels of unemployment than white school leavers. The unemployed, both black and white, must grow up to know the moral virtue of serving the profit interests of industry to reduce its workforce by over two million between 1979 and 1983! In particular, what does it feel like to grow up black in Babylon?

Babylon, Adolescene and Deviance

> *Lucy:* You're not safe in Babylon. *This* is what we call Babylon – you know, England. Babylon, y' know. To we blacks, it is Babylon.
>
> *JFS.:* Why?
>
> *Lucy:* Why? Because there's so much tribulation goin' on now. I mean, so much racism by the police against black people.... I've gotta carry a 'dool' around with me, right, that's a knife. Got to carry a knife to protect myself. 'Cos I know I ain't lettin' police 'old me up 'cos they disgrace me. They 'urt my pride. An' I'm aware of them so much now that I'd do any fink in my power to do somefink to them to get self satisfaction.

Growing up black is not just a matter of asserting an individual identity; it is a matter of asserting an identity within the context of needing to establish and assert an ethnic identity. Establishing an ethnic identity itself facilitates the assertion of an individual identity. The ethnic identity allows the individual to stand forward and rise above feeling disgraced. According to Lucy:

> They fink, right, as soon as they're police, they're in *power*, they're in the *law* an' 'cos they're the *law:* you're black an' you stay back. Right, an' that is their policy. Black you stay back. Right, an' any fink they do on top of that. You're walkin' down the road, O.K., and they fink they've got their *power* in their 'ands, they can hit someone an' they're the police, they get away with it.

From the standpoint of a black identity, white authority is critically assessed. From a black identity it becomes possible to assert the image of Babylon. It is not simply that an oppositional black culture develops but that it is an opposition built upon the experience of being violated and a culture created through reflection upon black experience and criticism of white authority. It is a constructive and creative culture. The central image of Babylon at once prescribes possible ranges of behaviour, identities and critical stances, as well as closing off as impossible or censoring certain alternative behaviours, identities and critical stances. At every turn friendship is violated by the divisive image, an image which serves to predict and to explain. When Babylon rules there can be no brotherhood between black and white, any apparent friendship does not deceive:

> *Lucy:* The other day I was talkin' to a white guy of mine, right, my neighbour. He said 'Do you want a drink Lucy?' I said, 'Yeah', y' know. And he was standin' there an' every time – the way we talked, right, is that we're brothers, right, 'cos he calls my mum, mum right. An' we talked like, y' know what I mean, 'cos we know one another for years. We was talkin' about 'ow I got nicked the other day, right. An' then he started interruptin' the conversation, 'Ah, yeah them fuckin' old Bills', you know [to her friend] – an' don't you remember the time in which he said we're black bastards, you know? An' I just find that very typical, you know.

In one context a person is a friend. Yet in another context the 'friend' will shout, 'You black bastard.' Why? According to Lucy: 'It's a fing like, I'd be talkin' to Carol, right, and she's with Ann....' And

Carol and Ann are white and all it needs is for one of them to lead the other, censoring friendship, arousing hostility. Thus the other follows because she does not want to lose face with her white friend. Allegiances are formed according to colour and group censorship demands conformity as ritualized insults fly:

> *Lucy:* [At school] there used to be a group of white girls and a group of black girls, right and y' know, they start ... once they're on their own they're alright but once they're with their people they get a bit lippy so they start callin' me black bastard – 'Look at you you mother fucker' – an' all that fing. An' I tell ya I, it really got to me. It burnt my feelings an' I went over there an' I just hit her. An' I kick her down. She had to go to 'ospital, right. But I also was injured 'cos her friends were hittin' me. But yet I was suspended, right, for a long time and she after she came back all she had is a little scratch there but they took 'er to 'ospital just to make it seem serious and she come back in school the next day. I said, 'Oh that's fuckery', you know, 'Oh, that's nice init?'

In response, a white friend of Lucy's says, 'There's too much 'ate in this world an' not enough love.' In the group the love, if any, is inhibited and violated, and the hatred expressed. Thus the group acts rather like a censor, censoring any expression which would break solidarity within the group. Babylon reigns. Babylon speaks continually to the black individual; it has become a part of the poetics of oppression for the black person bringing about a unity of experience which at once elevates the black person into the awareness of a culturally defined self and provides a rhetorical framework for action as a black person in a white world. Babylon, as a symbol, is founded upon particular incidents and experience, drawing these unrelated incidents into the unity of a powerful symbol. Thus, taking a common standpoint, the image, 'Babylon', stands for the repression of black freedom of expression, which degrades the environment for black people, reducing the possibilities for individual expression and dignity. Violence as 'fighting back' and 'standing up' becomes a way of clawing back some dignity:

> *Lucy:* ... I'm black. I'm proud of it, right? But I know, it's a strain to be black. It is a strain. You could be proud of it or not proud of it. It's a strain. It's a damn strain because I

mean, I could be talkin' to 'er [Lucy's white friend] an'
that, at the end of the day she can say, 'You fuckin' black
bastard.' She can say it but, you know what I mean, it can
'appen.

Friend: Yeah.

Lucy: An' I can take that. I've gotta take that. An' I ain't
gonna take it! I'll kick 'er down! An' I feel a, I won't feel no
way for 'er. I'll feel good inside me 'cos she shouldn't dare
to talk to me like that 'cos I've never said to 'er noffink like
that, you know. But that's 'ow it 'appened. It always
works that way you know.

The strain Lucy experiences is based upon the imagination of what
could happen. Her speculated act – 'I'll kick 'er down' – finds its
foundation and interpretation in an imagination formed by anticipation of the kinds of violation likely to be committed against her.

Unemployment in the area amongst black people is high –
perhaps 60 per cent. Amongst black school leavers, finding a job is
practically impossible. Unemployment becomes a symbol of the
neglect by the authorities of the black people. Lucy's black friend
Yvonne puts it this way: On the whole right, it's the people in
authority what brings that tension around, you know, 'cos the black
people are thinkin' 'ow comes they not gettin' all the jobs, you
know. And the lack of money and lack of things to do may lead
towards thoughts of crime:

Lucy: They have nothin' to do so all they 're thinkin' about is
crime 'cos that's the only way we can live, nowadays, to be
frank wiv you that's the only way you can live. To feel
nice, to have a little nice time. 'Cos you're on the dole, as
soon as your money comes – I mean you're prayin' for
your money to come – as soon as it comes it goes. You
know, an' you're wonderin' what 'ave you done wiv it.

Lucy and Yvonne point to two distinct sources in explaining
deviant behaviour: (1) racism and (2) those pressures, such as
unemployment, also faced by white people. However, to assess the
level of black crime in relation to white crime is difficult and
extremely emotive. Nevertheless, as Kettle and Hodges (1982:90)
put it, 'white society has a tradition of associating blacks with
particular sorts of crime. In the 1950s they were supposed to be

living off immoral earnings. Later, drug pushing became a vogue accusation. In the 1970s, the stereotype of the black mugger was created.' In a Home Office study of the inner-city areas of Liverpool, Manchester and Birmingham, reported by Ramsay in *New Society* (25 March 1982), a number of popular press stereotypes were exploded: 'women were not victims as often as men: only 44 per cent of the 311 victims were female.... Nor did elderly people feature prominently. Most victims were young or middle aged, if not able-bodied.' The descriptions of the offenders given by the victims were considered hazy:

> However, it appeared that, in the Liverpool and Manchester samples, white people were responsible for a greater proportion of the muggings than were blacks. Only in Birmingham, where there was the greatest proportion of the less serious offences, did blacks predominate. Overall, all the assailants were black in less than half the attacks....
>
> Although nearly half the muggers were black, it would be a mistake to see mugging as necessarily being a type of crime committed mainly by blacks. In several of the disadvantaged areas where the attacks took place, blacks came close to representing a majority among the younger people in the local population; and it is younger people who are most prone to commit this type of crime.
>
> In the centre of Southampton – a city with a substantial ethnic minority – Home Office research indicated that only one of 21 muggings there in 1980 involved a black attacker. The rest were the work of whites.

Nevertheless, to many, to be black is to be suspected. During the 1970s black people felt they were discriminated against by police in the operation of the 'sus' law (section 4 of the 1824 Vagrancy Act) whereby the police could arrest a person on suspicion. This act was repealed in 1981. When it was in operation, 'black arrests accounted for 44 per cent of London's sus arrests in 1978 and 40 per cent in 1979. In Lambeth, 77 per cent of those arrested for sus were black' (Kettle and Hodges, 1982:92). In place of 'sus' came 'sas' (stop and search). Brogden (1981) quoted a young black youth in Liverpool: 'It's not 'sus' that leads to hassle with the police, but the number of times that we're searched on the street – round here it's a crime to be young and black.' Apart from such experiences and opinions, there is also the possibility of one's home being searched:

Lucy: ... They come in my 'ouse right. Say they come lookin' for bruvver. My bruvver's standin' right in front of them. They come up, charge straight past 'im – lookin' for my bruvver, you know! They know who my bruvver is. Right, an' lookin' for my bruvver come straight past 'im. Dash m'mum down stairs, tup my sister in the mouth. Right? An' turned the 'ouse upside down, an' then go on about their business. Walk straight past m' bruvver again, right? Couple of months later, they went over m' other sister's 'ouse, dash 'er down the stairs, spread my sister on the floor – four big policemen. My sister's only little. They sit on 'er on the floor out in the street. She's 21 – she's 23 now, but she's 21 then. Right, spread 'er on the floor in 'er nighty. Right, an' most of this is sort of residential area and people would talk y' know. And they drag 'er right in the middle of the road, spread 'er out, sit on 'er, pick 'er up, cuff 'er. Don't know what they're cuffin' 'er for! Throw 'er in the van, right. Took 'em to court. Oh, no, um the police won the case [even though] they never 'ad a search warrant.

Lucy and her friends had several similar anecdotes to tell. It is upon such accounts shared in conversation that the hate develops. Such stories form a local culture of 'folk tales' which can be referred to in the interpretation of future acts.

The 'folk tales', the anecdotes, settle like silt to form the contents of a racist imagination. These racist images organize the psychic contents, setting limits upon behaviour founded upon such interpretations. These racist images are too often reinforced by literature, art, film:

Even now books are still being produced which are tainted by the old colonialist assumptions. *The Cay* is a case in point. Like *Robinson Crusoe*, it is an adventure story whose main interest lies in the struggle for survival on a desert island. Both books reinforce racist attitudes. *Crusoe* with its treatment of cannibalism and the dog-like Friday, *The Cay* with its portrayal of Timothy, the subservient West Indian who saves the hero's life. While we cannot expect *Robinson Crusoe* to show many mid-twentieth century attitudes, there is no such excuse for *The Cay*.

Thus Stinton (1979:1–2) reminds us of the racist attitude underlying some children's literature, in which 'black people are often anonymous figures!'. Furthermore:

> There have been many well-meaning attempts, mainly by white writers, to show that black and white are the same 'under the skin'. But there *are* differences, just as there are differences between the sexes.... These differences should be valued, not ignored or dismissed. People should be accepted for what they are, and have to offer – and not be judged by preconceptions.

Racist images inhibit the emergence of individuality and violate any sense of community developing between races. Schools clearly play a role in reinforcing racist social conditions – of this there can be no reasonable doubt. Schools, however, are not necessarily filled with racists – indeed, there are many who vigilantly combat racism. Nevertheless, there is much to do to rid the official and hidden curricula of racist contents. Those who are willing to try may find practical suggestions on managing such an innovation in chapter 9. The task is to overcome the kind of official indifference such as the *New Statesman* alleges in a report by Wilson (25 February, 1983):

> Last November, the head teacher of Little Ilford School, Saul Ezra, told me: 'There is really no problem of racist violence in our school.' Since then (and the events surrounding the arrest of the Newham 8), racist attacks have continued – with two serious incidents last week. At Langdon School, where National Front leaflets were circulated last year, an Asian girl claimed: 'Teachers are not really interested. Every day we get pushed and spat upon in the corridors by white boys. When there is a fight about, it is usually the Asians who get punished.'

Or again:

> Young Asians at Eastlea school say the violence has continued – but now Asians are fighting back, the police who were never interested in what happened to us are now attacking *us*. They find it very hard to concentrate on their school work in this atmosphere – and believe that, because they have traditionally done well academically, the violence is another way of 'putting them down'.

Too often schools will say, 'There is no problem here'; the public image becomes the mask to conceal the climate of fear, suspicion and racism which haunts the community and hence the school.

5   Sex, Sexism and Deviance in School

In the struggle toward individuality one may even have to battle against one's own sex, that is, the sexual identity thrust upon the individual by others. Growing up is sexual in nature. And sexism is a form of social control by which sexuality and youthful energy are canalized toward traditional and comfortable forms of social expression. School provides many models of how boys and girls, men and women ought to behave, including models of male and female deviance.

The Fairer Sex

Women are condemned and controlled by images of female beauty, sexuality and motherliness which men are condemned to learn to project upon them. It is not that beauty, sexuality and motherliness are evils but that certain traditional images of these serve to starve rather than nourish individual expressions of beauty, sexuality and motherliness. Images of 'the fairer sex' are insidious and inhibit expressions of individuality by making attempts to detach oneself from such an image, expressions of deviance: the man becomes a 'queer', the woman, a whore or 'dyke'. It is strange that women are, on the one hand, 'the fair sex' and yet, on the other, womanliness becomes a term of abuse. To say a man is 'a girl', 'a cunt', 'a tit' is a term of abuse. But to say a woman 'has balls' is a term of grudging praise – she is an honorary man (incidentally, it was a term used by President Reagan in praise of Prime Minister Thatcher).

In the *Encyclopaedia Britannica* (4th ed., 1800–10) is written: 'The woman, delicate and timid, requires protection.... The man as a protector is directed by nature to govern; the woman, conscious of inferiority, is disposed to obey.' Such a view may amuse modern enlightened individuals, however, the smile soon fades; sexism like racism is ubiquitous; sexism is one of the pillars upon which most modern societies are founded. The discriminatory relation between men and women is a powerful force for social control. It is learnt in the home and the playground and reinforced in the classroom:

> Like in this school, right, if you want people to get learnt, right, you want people to learn things, it's like certain sets right, when they get alone there's a couple of messers in them like, they get given, you know, like a woman teacher and she's dead scared an' the class are shoutin', you know, tellin' 'er where to go an' everythin', an' she doesn't do nothin', you know, they're all messin' around an' when it comes to the exams, you know, they've never learnt nothin' so, you know, they just mark down anything. But they need like, someone, you know, dead strict like you know, someone who's dead, you know, dead mean with them an' not scared to 'it them or nothin'. You know to tell them, to make them work like. And so people just sit down and they say, 'I'm not messin' in his lesson like, I mean he's a bit mad like.' So people do the work. You know first couple of weeks like they won't take to 'im but after the first couple of weeks, you know, they take to 'im. But if you get given, you know, like, a woman teacher to teach, you know. You need a woman teacher to teach, you know, all the brainy people who wanna work an' don't mess round. Only, that's the type you should give them.

This was spoken by Darren Bailey, a fifth-form boy, (who will figure prominently in a case study in the latter part of this chapter). Male authority is required to control the 'messers' although female authority is adequate to the 'brainy' pupils. Maleness is identified therefore with the messers and femaleness with the brainy: the messers are aggressive, the brainy more passively receptive. Sexism colours his notions of people's relations with one another; it allows him to project certain qualities upon individuals.

Frazier and Sadker (1973:2) consider sexism to be 'a belief that the human sexes have a distinctive make-up that determines their respective lives, usually involving the idea that (1) one sex is superior and has the right to rule the other (2) a policy of enforcing such asserted right (3) a system of government and society based upon it.' The messers exalt their manliness in a sexist manner for only a truly 'mean' and 'dead hárd' man can control them; a woman (or a male teacher weak like a woman) is too soft, too afraid. Under the conditions of pervasive sexism in society it is difficult for Darren to behave any other way.

Spender (1982a:3) goes so far as to write 'that if sexism were to be removed from the curriculum there would be virtually nothing left to teach, because our society in general knows so little that is not sexist. . . .'

She continues (pp. 4–5):

> It is simply not possible for a fifteen-year-old girl, tired of hearing about men's wars in the nineteenth century, to confront the teacher with three possible alternative histories on the nineteenth century, viewed from the perspective of women, and to request that these books be included on the course. Even if such a fifteen-year-old did suspect that women had made just as much history as men but that men had chosen not to enter it in their records, even if she did suspect that the men's records would look very different if women, and not just men, were to comment on them where could she find a collection of books to make her point?

Spender's point is undeniable. There has been a systematic exclusion of the contribution of women to society throughout history (cf. Spender, 1982b). The image of the fair sex is the image of their domination; it is not easy to break free from such an image and assert one's individuality.

School is where young individuals learn to become boys and girls, men and women. It is where they learn to dress in the images provided by their culture. It is where they learn to play games of dominance and submission. Girls, in their submissiveness, are expected to achieve more than boys (Clarricoates, in Deem, 1980:29, 33), however teachers 'saw the boys as having much more imagination, and having real ability.' Stanworth (1981:47) found that girls tended to be somewhat 'faceless' in the classroom. Moreover, teachers tend to give more attention to boys than to girls (Spender, 1982). Girls, in becoming dominated by boys, in many ways become but an audience to the activities of boys. The roles of 'audience' and 'actor' sustain sexist roles and images. Thus, sexism is a dialectical phenomenon. That is, sexism is circular in nature. It is produced in the interaction of the sexes and shaped, therefore, by the acts and interpretations of both. The images and myths of sexuality shape action as concrete action feeds and creates images and myths of sexuality. An image of sexuality contains not only the ideal but also the deviant. The idea of the 'fair sex' contains the image of Beauty and also of Slut, Witch, Gangster's Moll as the shadows which haunt Beauty – only in fairy tales does Beauty never grow old, ugly and embittered and is never anything other than perfect. And Beauty's consort one may remember, was Beast.

The struggle towards individuality is a struggle through the images and myths which key individuals into the sexual dramas of their culture, those dramas upon which their civilization depends. In every incident we find reflected the wider society wide drama. The task now is to look at the relationship between sex and violence which tie together the mythical images of Beauty and the Beast.

The Beast and His Moll

There is a dimension to the male stereotype that casts a male in the role of a beast. It is the Dionysian, violent, orgiastic side of male aggression and assertiveness. A glance at the figures for violent crime and sexual offences shows a far greater number of men than women found guilty or cautioned for such acts: about 59,000 men as opposed to about 5000 women in 1981 (see CSO, *Social Trends*, 1983). Taking the figures for burglary, robbery and 'theft and handling' stolen goods, there were 325,900 men but 77,800 women found guilty or cautioned in 1981. In Slumptown Comprehensive Beauty and the Beast learn their respective roles; however, Beauty may be transformed into a 'Moll' and Beast may never be transformed into a prince. In the Freudian view (1979:48):

> ... men are not gentle creatures who want to be loved, and who at the most can defend themselves if they are attacked; they are, on the contrary, creatures among whose instinctual endowments is to be reckoned a powerful share of aggressiveness. As a result, their neighbour is for them not only a potential helper or sexual object, but also someone who tempts them to satisfy their aggressiveness on him, to exploit his capacity for work without compensation, to use him

sexually without his consent, to seize his possessions, to humiliate him, to cause him pain, to torture and to kill him. *Homo homini lupus.* [Man is a wolf to man.] Who, in the face of all his experience of life and of history, will have the courage to dispute this assertion?

Who, indeed! Organization for war and defence against attack have historically been major principles in the creation of social order; organization for war is a foundation of political organization (cf. Nisbet, 1976). According to Brown (1966:15):

To know the reality of politics we have to believe the myth, to believe what we were told as children. Roman history is the story of the brothers Romulus and Remus, the sons of the she-wolf; leaders of gangs of juvenile delinquents ...; who achieved the rape of the Sabine women; and whose festival is the Lupercalia; at which youth naked except for girdles made from the skins of victims ran wild through the city, striking those whom they met, expecially women, with strips of goatskin; a season fit for king killing, *Julius Caesar*, Act 1.

Brown sees 'politics made out of delinquency'. From this point of view, delinquency, particularly male delinquency, is a basic structure of civilization. Man as beast – the wolf-child – is the theme of a million cinema films, TV dramas, literary works, news stories, folk tales, religious inspirational tracts and mythology; each baby is born to cultivate a violent imagination. Daily, a subliminal world of orgiastic sex and violence is evoked to sell children's toys, soap powder, nuclear weapons and chocolates:

In the mass media of communication, the preoccupation with love and death symbolism is apparent in every newspaper, magazine, and television programme. Genital symbolism is universally used in the media, though rarely recognized by the audience as such. Commonly used phallic symbolism includes neckties, arrows, flagpoles, automobiles, rockets, pencils, cigars and cigarettes, candles, broomsticks, snakes, trees, cannons, pens – the list is endless .... Death, or the fear of death, underlies virtually all the symbols of state, authority, governments, political parties, and military, commercial, and social institutions. (Key, 1973:58, 59)

All around the growing child are the symbols of the violent imagination. It all seems like a madness as young boys exhibit a lust for orgiastic destruction:

> *Pat:* They're mad here, you've got to keep your animals in on bonfire night.
> *Sal:* I know.
> *Pat:* You've no need to go near a fire. Just get, they tie fires to the tail and ... burn their tails off and everything.
> *Sal:* It wasn't even bonfire night, the poor animal they just lit a fire on its tail. . . .

I arrived in the deputy head's office one day to find him fuming with anger. Some boys had been caught tearing newly hatched chicks to pieces.

Is all this 'instinctual', or have young people been crazed by the images of a mad society? These fourth-year girls continue to talk about the boys who are always fighting:

> *Pat:* Used meet er shopping centre but now no one goes there 'cos there's too much fightin'.
> *Sal:* 'Cos there's too much fightin'. When you come out all the lads were fightin' an' that an' the girls. Just do that to the girl to try and make trouble. Maybe just looked at him like that. Just say somethin' like, 'I'm gonna kill ya, you're gonna die, you've been lookin' at me all evening.'
> *Sal:* They're fightin'.
> *Pat:* What they fightin' for? There's no where to go. . . .

With some other fourth-year girls I ask:

> *J.F.S.:* What's the reason for the fightin'?
> *Ruth:* They're just fightin', it's jus' fightin'
> *Pauline:* that's just it, it's good though isn't it? Sometimes. [laughter]
> *J.F.S.:* No I mean. . . .
> *Yvonne:* There's all police, all the police round our school.
> *Val:* There's all the police 'n' everythin'.
> *Yvonne:* Waitin' when they come.
> *J.F.S.:* Well, is it because you can't stand each other or . . .?
> *Yvonne, Ruth and Val:* No.

Val: No it's not that 'cos, all the girls and them are mates.
Pauline: Mates of the other school.
Val: The other school an' 'alf the lads 'ere are mates. But we
  just fight.
J.F.S.: What, just for fun?
Yvonne, Ruth and Val: Yeah, fun.

They describe an incident:

Ruth: I was walkin' down an' then, the next minute.... Oh,
  there was seventeen of the other school's lads that jumped
  us. One lad, an' 'e's got a bad heart, an' 'e took an 'eart
  attack when they were batterin' 'im. An' the school didn't
  do nothin' about it....
J.F.S.: This school?
Ruth: Yeah.
Pauline: They didn't do nothin'.
Ruth: They said they were gonna, 'cos I was there an' Jean
  was there, they said they was gonna take us into the other
  school to identify them. An' they said, well, then, we're
  gonna need police patrol to watch us, watch the school,
  'cos we could get done over ... we'd get jumped an' that.
  So we, we just lucky we didn't, they didn't go any further
  with it.

Everyone, it seems, has a story to tell. It is not the point to ask
whether these stories are true in detail or even rightly interpreted by
the teller. The point is that each story becomes like an emotional
scar, a seeping wound, a drug, or an ecstatic celebration of violence
to the individual. The stories are dramatic, the stuff that TV serials
are made of:

Val: Oh the SRS.
Ruth, Pauline, Yvonne: The SRS.
Val: It's the Slumptown Riot Squad...
J.F.S.: What's that?
Val: The Slumptown Riot Squad, all lads.
Pauline: There's girls there....
Val: Like, one of the girls that was going with a lad from
  Downtown. An' um, they found out.
Pauline: 'We'll get 'im', like....
Val: 'We'll get 'im', yeah.... When they're by themselves,
  you know, the SRS they ... only time, they'll only fight

in gangs. They can't fight by themselves.

Ruth: When they fight they 'ave penknives.

  [all giggle]

Pauline: They don't fight by themselves.

Yvonne to Ruth: They don't!

Val: They do 'ave penknives an' bottles. I know loads of
  them.

Ruth: So do I, I live by them.

Yvonne: They don't throw them.

Ruth: They do.

Yvonne: They don't.

Val: No? Why everyone carries them then?

Ruth: All Estate an' Downtown went down to Poshtown,
  didn't we?

Val: Mmm.

Ruth: An' we 'ad a big fight down there er all the ones on
  motorbikes an' that. Now, we were joined up with
  Downtown last time.

Val: Last year, yeah.

Ruth: This year were they?

Val: Last year we did.

Ruth: We did join up with Downtown in the end.

Val: In the *end*.

  [all giggle]

Ruth: Been fightin' with Downtown until we joined up.
  Fightin', y' know, along the beach.

Largely, the girls are audience and flag wavers to male acts of
violence, but some are happy to participate. It is the old story of boy
meets girl; or how the Mad Beast gets his Moll.

Darren Bailey – A Mob Leader

Darren Bailey um if you know him, is a great lad, um yeah,
he's fantastic um extrovert. Written work is atrocious. If
there ever is a case for an oral exam it would be him, because
if he had to explain any thing to you he could do it, if he had
to write it down, there's no chance. Uh, he could sell you the
shirt off your own back. No messin' about, and uh definitely
the line he should go into you know, some sort of showman,

salesman type person. Um got, he's got fantastic influence over other people. Thinks a lot of himself um ... but he can influence people and uh, I think the school's been very lucky that we've managed 'im to uh influence people ... relatively in the right direction. If he wanted to he could have caused a lot of trouble with a lot of people, Darren. But he's um, he's matured quite a lot. In fact, um yesterday he came up to see me and said that uh certain people he'd got to know, 'cos he's well in contact with the underworld, anything that's going on. They've noticed a fish tank in my room and uh a few people are after parts of it. So he's put me on guard to that, er and that sort of thing. He knows all of what's going on anywhere about anything um. Unfortunately, sometimes he is involved, you know, but I say, I think he's got through that stage, yet, either he's got through it or he's that darn clever that nobody can catch at him. But um, he's a good lad to know. (Greg Bright, Darren's Tutor)

There is no doubt that Darren is a gang leader, a participant in criminal activities, as his housemaster explains:

He was sent to a Detention Centre (for his suspected role in a riot) and he's out. We heard that the court case has been adjourned, um pending some kind of reports, I don't really know why. Um, during the third year he had a very colourful time. He was involved with uh robbery at a GPO place locally and he um.... Anyway, eventually after an awful er investigation in which he and the other kids involved wouldn't react and wouldn't confess, the, the woman in the Post Office identified them there was no disputing that.

School provides many pupils with their first experiences of interrogation, with housemasters taking the role of the police. Darren has now had two encounters with the law and has learnt the arts of fudging the evidence, giving away as little as possible, not reacting to pressure. However, through persistence and friendliness the housemaster has made some progress with him:

... during last year I think I was very fortunate because he pinched a pen from one of the girls in the classroom and I was able to pin him down on it very quickly and he just had to say, you know, there was no denying the fact that he'd taken it. But I think that for me it was a very good thing because since then he's always been very straightforward with me.

The housemaster's influence with Darren was not enough to prevent his involvement with some local rioting:

> I was talking to Darren and saying, 'Do you not think it would be good for', you know, 'you to keep your nose clean, just a low profile during this time [of the riots].' He said, 'My trouble is I'm so easy to spot', . . . at the time Darren was working nights washing glasses at a local club, it seems, connected to the Town centre. And of course, he was going home and it seems got involved in this [riot] and I had a CY thing to fill in.
> *J.F.S.:* What's CY?
> *Housemaster:* Children and Young Persons Act. You know, it's like um a school report on their standards and attitudes. . . .

I give Darren's version of the riot in a later chapter: The Violent Solution. Darren views his world politically, that is, delinquently. It is a world of power differences, where men are dominant and women are mothers, a good fuck, or slags. He describes his first days at Slumptown Comprehensive thus:

> there was all different people, like there was the cock of one school and the cock of the other school an' the cock of that school and they all do, they [are] all put into this school, you know, from about eight different schools, all put into this one. I say people want to see, you know, who's the best fighter an' everythin' an' then we used to go round 'aving fights. That was, you know, I think that was the best [thing] that happen[ed], havin' their own little mobs, you know, from all the schools and then people started splittin' up. They just started splittin' up from their mobs like, when you first come into the school. And when you 'ad your school uniform on and everything, oh you felt dead 'ard when you were goin' over the (Town centre) for y' dinner you'd have like a suit on an' you're goin' over like this [swaggers].

When he speaks he virtually trips over his words, he speaks so fast. The picture he gives is of reassessment of statuses through fighting. In the first days, the various contests led to a break-up of the old 'mobs'. Through fighting the individual begins to stand out from the mob, that is, exist (*latin existere*, emerge, stand out, be visible, be manifest). The uniform reinforced the new status giving the new hero his sense of ''ardness'. The 'Hero' is a universal myth. Burridge (1979:43–4) writes:

> Positionally, the Hero is he or she or that to which members of the community look. A Hero is a centre of interest, a magnet in whose being others participate or would like to participate, see themselves or would like to see themselves. A standard by which persons measure themselves, the Hero is a means by which an aggregation of persons becomes a community, members one of another.

The 'cock' of the school is the playground hero, turning a mere 'aggregate' into a gang, or a community. Certainly, Darren's exploits are legend in the school – exploits which are out of the sight of the official authorities. According to Thrasher (1927:22), the gang develops in the interstices, the 'spaces that intervene between one thing and another'. Thus, for Darren and his mates, the new school provided a new territory which was up for grabs, the lines had yet to be drawn. The school had the effect of creating interstices between the old gangs and ultimately within the old gangs so that new alignments formed. Moreover, the school itself gave status and corroboration of the claims of the pupils to be important, the uniform enabled them to feel ''ard'. Further oppositions arise between the teachers and the pupils helping to knit together a sense of community and common experience if not gang consciousness. The power of the teachers to observe and to control is stretched to the limit upon the borders between classroom and playground, school gates and street. The gangs, as Thrasher rightly says, thrive upon the borders, the boundaries. In such areas no single power can unambiguously rule. Gangs exist in the ambiguous shadows of society, where meaning shades into meaning, where one person's word is as good as another's, and where the final arbiter is the clenched fist. With one's fist one might be able to shape out some sense of individuality, where one creates one's own definition of the situation and enforces it with the strength of one's own body against others. Darren, however, is not only a fighter but a talker. He impresses his mates with his wit and his patter. There is little doubt of his intelligence – except in school work.

Darren's sense of masculinity at one level is frivolous and, at another, deadly serious. On the one hand, he can use his wit and masculine strength of character to dominate and tease girls. For example, I was talking to Darren in a housemaster's office where he was on isolation. Some girls came through the office. Darren stopped talking to me and said, 'She's got blusher on!' The girl he pointed out was wearing cosmetics. Darren continued as the girls giggled. 'She's only twelve, just out of her nappies an' got blusher on. Don't know what it's coming to.' The girl tries to counter-attack, 'I am not, I'm fifteen.' Darren replies sharply, 'Well, you look like a little school girl to me.' She retorts, 'Well, you look like a little school boy to me.' 'Well, I *am*', Darren grins, 'I *am* a school boy. Got blusher on an' eyeliner too. I don't know what it's coming to.' The girl, now lost for words at the way Darren slides out of reach, sniffs, poking her nose up in the air, and leaves with her friends. They giggle as Darren continues the attack. Darren has frequently talked of his harem, and clearly these girls would not object to being a part of it. Yet Darren said to me when they had gone, 'The girls here are alright in the second and third year but they become vomit later.' On the other hand, this merely turned out to be a symptom of a more general complaint. He said, 'There's nothing in Slumptown for me.' He has begun to assess his life chances and has decided that 'life on the dole is crap and so is a youth scheme.' Darren is beginning to distance himself from the youth of Slumptown and their careers on the dole. As he does this he is beginning to reflect upon the gang as a tool by which to get what he wants from life. The gang is no longer simply little more than a playgroup.

Society has nothing to offer Darren. He related how he had gone for a test for a job with BP in London. It was basically an aptitude test. He thought he had done well. In fact he had 67 per cent in the test but the pass mark was 80 per cent. He said, 'There were tears in my eyes when I found out because I thought I'd be passed. It would've changed my life.' Of course, in 1982 there are twenty-six people on average in the country chasing each job. In Slumptown and its vicinity the chance of an unskilled job (as already stated) is 4000 to one against. Darren knows the trap he is in. But Darren is ambitious and impatient. He begins to dream. 'What I need to do is do a nice little bank. That'd set me up, just like Ronnie Biggs. I could go round the world then.' He is desperate to see and do new things. 'I can't see myself staying on at school, seeing all the same people. I want somewhere new.' Possibilities formulate in Darren's mind. He thinks the riots will happen again. Already there have been a lot of incidents. It hasn't really ended. 'There'll be a few who start it in one place then, then others will join in and the original ones will leave and while the bizzies are busy, they'll do a few shops. There'll be a lot like that. Anyway, Slumptown only had crappy little riots. But in the next riots the lads will have had more practice. We've learnt what to do. But the police won't want to be heroes this time round 'cos they'll have experienced what it's like. The lads'll be laughing saying the bizzies are scared.' The bizzies (the police) form a part of the network of observations trying to maintain law and order in the burnt-out blocks of flats, the acres of asphalt and woodland, and the maze-like streets of every Slumptown in Britain.

The Beast hoped to become a Prince but failed.

Debbie Graves – A Moll Fights Back

'I couldn't live without men.' Debbie grinned at her friend, Sharon. 'Let's see, would you like to go out playing football with the lads? I love it. Your life is so dull. You just go home do your homework, go to bed. Girls are so boring. I like to settle down with some rum in front of the telly. It's great.' Sharon preferred to say that Debbie had problems and dwelt upon those problems rather than answer Debbie. Debbie was more than pleased to agree. 'I'm mad. I know.' I then ask what Debbie thinks about those who like the system or at least, don't go against it. Sharon says, 'That's me!' 'They're soft', says Debbie. 'Thank you!'

Her attitude throughout is provocative. It is a style which is repeated with all those she meets. With me it was a challenge to solve her problems. 'She thinks you're a psychiatrist', said her housemaster to me, 'she wouldn't believe me when I said you weren't.' With her boyfriends the challenging tensions persist. She says, 'I like the intelligent ones. Have you noticed? There's Rusty. He's intelligent. And he pushes against the system. I like boys who push against the system.' Rusty, however, is no longer her steady boyfriend, that is, the one she goes with most. On another occasion she told a friend of hers (whose day I was observing) that she'd given Rusty a birthday present. However, she couldn't bring herself to make it seem important to her so she flung the present – an expensive pen – across the table to him. It slid off the desk and onto the floor. She hoped it wasn't broken. It was more evidence of her 'madness', she said. Of her sexual behaviour, her housemaster said, 'She calls a fuck a fuck, y' know.' He described how in the third year Debbie had suddenly gone wild, proclaiming her sexual exploits to all, whether teachers were present or not. She'd say, 'Oh, I fucked so and so last night', and begin to describe her exploits in great detail.

She exploits the taboos of those in authority over her both to shock and to fascinate them. I met her one day when she was on 'isolation'. I was 'shadowing' a pupil, Jacko, who had been thrown out of his class. Jacko and Debbie began to talk. Jacko pushed question after question at her. Why was she not in lesson? Why didn't she get on with her teachers? How could she say she was in charge and manipulating teachers when after all they had ejected her from class? Jacko took the stance of a relentless social analyst who would not be satisfied until all the hidden dimensions were revealed. He was concerned to know how she could be assured of having acted independently, of being an individual rather than a socially manipul-able role player. Debbie danced away from his probing questions and returned to provocation. She began to talk about having babies. She softly smiled, sounded motherly, 'I'd like to have lots of little trogs round me. I love kids. But I like hitting babies. I love it. I like to hear them screaming. It gives me a thrill. I told you. I'm mental.' At all times she did her best to build up an image of an aggressive, violent self. The first part of the process will be to present something attractive – 'I'd like to have lots of little trogs round me.' This typical 'mother image' is then violently distorted – 'But I like hitting babies.' When she speaks she is full of wit, smiles and laughter. Then there is a sudden turn into the macabre. It is a cultivated image which has the dual function of fascinating and repelling. None of these cultivated images is the unique invention of a crazed mind or a scatty adolescent. The images are as ancient as the mythological imagina-tion – the stories have all been told before; the dramas are universal.

Death is one of the great symbols of her life. Her sexuality perhaps moves from and towards death. Her mum says:

> She seems to have gone worse since her dad died. I mean, when her dad was alive all she had to say to him is 'Dad can I have this?' And his hand'd go in his pocket and he'd get it but I'm not in the position to do it anymore. And I think Debbie feels the pinch of it. It could be that he spoilt her, you know. And she's feeling it ain't she? I think the school is getting a come-back on it.

The explanation here is in terms of the wilful child, the spoilt child and the spoiling father. She proudly says, 'Me mum can't control me. I even hit her.' But if her father were alive, 'He'd murder me. Though he was small, he was strong.' There are psychoanalytic riches here!

Death has torn from her her love-object, the source of childish gratification which now haunts her. Death as a solution to conflict (an Oedipal conflict?) is a realistic possibility to her. She has attempted suicide twice. All our futures include death not as possibility but as inevitability. Our education is to avert our eyes from the fact that the meaning of our lives includes the meaning of our deaths. What my life means to another is what my death will mean to that other – will my death be experienced as a tearing of the fabric of life; as a void in the heart of Being? If it is, then suicide is a possible punishment, or possible vengeance to wreck upon the other.

But there is also another layer of explanation. Death can be used as a form of hardening, as a way of making the self inviolable. There is no severer father than Death; there is no stricter Censor than Death. To defy Death is to defy the ultimate Authority; to play with Death is to break the ultimate Taboo. Death can neither deprive nor ravish her – or so the argument may run. And she says, 'I'm not afraid of Death. It doesn't mean anything to me.'

There is in any case a special relationship between adolescence and suicide, a siren attraction; and the drama is full of fascination:

> ... the suicidal adolescent, because he is an adolescent and because he is suicidal, the bearer of desire and of death, arouses the maximum fear. Unconsciously, he arouses feelings associated with an unnatural phenomenon. For everyone, adolescence is synonymous with energy, enrichment, joy, promised satisfactions, invincible hope – that is, with everything that one associates with life. How, then, can one think of death? But adolescence is also, as a result of pubertal maturation, the resumption and resolution of the Oedipus complex, the renunciation of the Oedipal love object and the castration anxiety. It is also a renunciation of childhood pleasures, for which some people retain a nostalgia throughout their lives, a renunciation of childhood dreams at a time when one has to confront the reality of the adult. It is a time of multiple loss, and sometimes of despair, as well as a revival of the most deeply buried emotions, the transitory

disintegration of impulses, and the emergence of hetero-aggressivity and auto-aggressivity. (Smith, 1974:IX)

Although the passage expresses a strangely male-centred notion of suicide, it has its relevance to Debbie. The CSO collection on 'Social Trends' reveals that it is about three times more prevalent among men than women in the 15–24 age group. Taking an overall view, 'although suicides represent less than 1 per cent of total deaths each year in the United Kingdom, the proportion is as high as 12 per cent amongst those aged 25 to 29.' Rutter (1979:133–6) considers that 'attempted suicide, or parasuicide (as perhaps it is better called) . . ., is very much an adolescent phenomenon. Like completed suicide, attempted suicide rates, especially in girls, have risen very greatly during the late '60s and early '70s.' Furthermore, 'parasuicide is associated with a variety of social problems including criminality, unemployment, marital difficulties, and childhood separations.'

According to Grinder (1973:108–12), on American data, 'the number of completed suicides among girls might surpass the number among boys except for the fact that girls' choice of ingestion ensures them reasonable likelihood of survival.' Boys tend to choose more violent methods such as strangulation or firearms, girls tend towards poisons. Debbie chose pills – 'These houses are full of bloody pills!' commented one housemaster. And 'The suicidal victim's life style is a product of a long history of unsatisfying interpersonal experiences, feelings of social rejection, and loss of significant social relationships.' Jacobs (1971) in a study of fifty adolescent suicide attempters found the following common elements.

1 A long-standing history of problems (from early childhood to the onset of adolescence).
2 The escalation of problems (since the onset of adolescence) above and beyond those usually associated with adolescence.
3 The progressive failure of available adaptive techniques for coping with the old and new increasing problems, which leads to the adolescent's progressive isolation from meaningful social relationships.
4 A chain-reaction dissolution of any remaining meaningful social relationships in the days and weeks preceding the attempt, which leads to the adolescent's feeling that he has reached 'the end of hope'.
5 An internal process by which he justifies suicide to himself

and thus manages to bridge the gap between thought and action.

In contradiction to element 4, Janov (1973:346), the originator of Primal Therapy, writes:

> Suicide is attempted, in my opinion, when all the ways an individual has tried to kill his Pain have come to naught. When the neurosis fails to ease Pain, the person may be forced into more drastic measures. It may sound paradoxical, but suicide is the last refuge of hope for the neurotic determined to be unreal to the end.

There is still one further dimension I want to consider before returning to Debbie. For Laing and Esterson (1970) the individual must be set within a family *nexus*; that is, 'that multiplicity of persons drawn from the kinship group, and from others who, though not linked by kinship ties, are regarded as members of the family' (p. 21). They show the complicated relationships which entrap and drive individuals crazy. For example, Ruth was considered schizophrenic and at times suicidal. Her parents are shown to know who she *really* is, that is, when she is 'well'. 'It is only from time to time that Ruth tries to assert herself over against this parental eternal essence, and when she does she wears clothes to her liking and insists vehemently on going where and with whom she wishes.' It is a drama of self-assertion.

Debbie is frequently told what is in her best interests, what reality is like, and how mistaken she is in virtually everything. Rather than simply a family nexus Debbie is entangled in a community nexus where substitute parents vie with substitute parents. The parents of Debbie's friend, Sharon, told me that Debbie frequently came round to their house and called them 'mum' and 'dad'. They felt she really wanted them as 'substitute' parents. Certainly Sharon's parents are well able to cope. Although they are both divorcees making a combined family of six children, they are proud that all the children got on well together. Their one problem is that the father is unemployed and unemployable – disabled by his last job. If it were not for mum's job they don't know where they'd have been. Perhaps Debbie could tell them.

They saw Debbie's behaviour as a cry for help, a cry for stability. Debbie's mother, they believed, had lost control. Sharon's parents were believers in firm discipline. To them, she is a girl going to waste, a sentiment echoed by several of her teachers:

> Debbie Graves is a girl going to waste basically uh obviously very clever, intelligent girl, um but she 'ardly comes into me lessons and the notes she 'as got are all copied up more than being explained to her. Um . . . she spends a lot of time with Mr Brown in the houseblock for one thing or another. I don't know what the reasons are. Um everytime she comes in, this is the time that she's going to get down to it. And uh time keeps slipping by, leaving her behind. As a girl I taught her first when I was in the first year and uh she was mad keen then. Um and I didn't get her back, didn't see her again until the 4th year and uh, it wasn't there anymore. That's about all I've got to say about her. I don't know her all that well personally.

School, with its teachers *in loco parentis*, is very often a place of broken relationships, a teacher you like in the first year is not seen again until the fourth year; a teacher you dislike kills your interest in a subject; and so on. The teacher points out the dramatic difference between the first-year Debbie he knew and the fifth-year Debbie. He points out, too, the lack of knowledge he has of Debbie's situation. This is not a teacher who makes a strict division between his work as a subject teacher and his work as a pastoral teacher, yet there are so many pupils and the organization of subject teaching permits little scope for the building of friendly and caring relationships. School organization contributes to the waste, the sense of deterioration in personal relations.

Many of her teachers eject her from their lessons. She goes to the houseblock where she chats with anyone else on isolation, or works, copying notes from one book into another book. Debbie's mum is sure she knows what the trouble is: 'The way Debbie is with the school, she thinks her life's her own and she can do what she likes, you see.' Debbie's life is, she thinks, her own and is not a substitute for someone else's life. What's more: 'You see, the thing is with Debbie, she wants to take her own lessons. She thinks she can go into a school and just do what she wants to do, which is not right. I mean the teachers are there to teach her, not her teach the teachers.' However, it is difficult to let another live her own life, especially a young adult. Thus Debbie's mother keeps 'on her back about school'.

However, it appears the rows are more generalized than this, as the housemaster says:

Rather than let Debbie go and choose her own clothes [mum's] gone out and spent the little precious bit of money she's got and gone and bought it herself. When she's got home it's not been the right trousers, or whatever. And there's been rows like that which haven't helped at home. No dad to fall back on.

Nevertheless, far from wanting to leave home, Debbie told me she couldn't bear to leave her mum. And far from being a liability mum says of Debbie: 'She can sit down, she can make a meal and she could take over, she can clean all up and everything else.' This is a great asset because every few weeks mum is sick – so ill she cannot move from her settee for days: 'I can't sit for any length of time without going to pieces which I'm gradually doing now....' It is then that Debbie takes over, running the house. What will become of Debbie, a pretty girl, intelligent, just 16?

Debbie is fond of her housemaster, 'I call him gran'pa.' Gran'pa speculates: 'Oh, she'll be married. She will want to get away from home and she'll see a way of doing that by marriage. She'll possibly get pregnant. She's too intelligent to sort of get pregnant now. I'm not worried on that score.' In the immediate future, however, he expects that after the Christmas holidays she will truant permanently; 'I would suspect that she probably will finish up not even taking exams. And this is a girl with a potential of five or six 'O' levels two years ago.'

After Christmas Debbie truanted permanently from school. No one followed up her truancy because it was felt it would cause more problems than it would solve. Occasionally, she came in to bring back books and would talk to 'gran'pa', her housemaster.

Debbie has her boyfriends, including apparently a 50-year-old neighbour of whom she is genuinely fond. She has teased and taunted her friends and in school, 'Debbie won't play the system. She'll play hell.' Thus, 'she will impress you by provocation as well, you know. I mean, she'll actually provoke you to anger with her.... There are times when she's done that with me and then she'll cry. But I've always thought afterwards that's really what she wanted.' Yet Debbie, has retained the friendship of many of the girls. She is witty, good fun and frequently very thoughtful of others. Her housemaster, however, feels 'a tremendous sadness about her'. She has, he feels, 'depressed notions about herself and her situation in the world'. She told me that the day after her sixteenth birthday she felt very depressed, so depressed she attempted suicide. I asked her housemaster if he knew about that attempt (there had been an earlier one):

> I knew about it, yes, but it's something I – I don't know whether I'm right John – I don't push, I don't uh pursue it, I don't, I don't really want to know about things like that unless the kid wants to tell me, you know. It's that kind of thing. If in my opinion it's not leading to a sort of breakdown where the degeneration's so great that the kid is floundering about. That was a one off. That was the way I judged it. It's likely to happen. It happens frequently with our girls, you know, at that age 'cos these houses are absolutely full of bloody bottles – tablets and pills. And many, many of our girls take overdoses you see, a lot of our girls are under enormous pressure in their houses. You won't find that with Sharon. 'Cos I don't think that's the sort of home ... there's not the pressures there ... there's quite a bit of money. A lot of our girls are left with enormous responsibility around the house, bringing up the younger ones, running the house. Mother can't cope anymore and they're broken down. Uh, and these are gestures, you know – help me gestures. I know it's corny that, but it's true. And I can believe that Debbie will do it in the same way as she went through that sex business. That was the same idea really.

Debbie described to me the experience of having her stomach pumped, the wretching, the pain – how much was fantasy elaboration I do not know. But, eyes gleaming, she relished the description.

Debbie's community has provided her with a range of identities (or masks); some of these she has rejected, others attract her. Whenever possible she asserts her independence from the authority of others and revels in her ability to manipulate others. Debbie's community also provided a range of explanations as to her behaviour. *She* liked to think she was mad but independent. But here, her housemaster finds an irony:

> Isn't it amazing that she wants to cover [up her striving for individuality and freedom] by having an ambition to work in

a shop? I mean you can't have anything more normal than that. I mean to me Debbie is looking for a front. Uh she's looking for a front to hide behind. That wouldn't be Debbie Graves working in a grocer's shop, not to me. But that's what she's settled on here. 'Cos I think that will provide her with a ... a way of looking normal around here, being accepted, you know, and then she can carry on with her fellows or live her own life outside the grocer's shop. As long [laughs] as she's got the grocer's shop everyone'll be happy!

Some teachers just have no control over their class the ones that do do it well but that's because I'm in the top sets. In French our teacher always trys to keep complete control over his boring lesson and doesn't do anything until then which is usually twenty minutes from the end of the lesson then he will give us all the work for homework.

As stated before, detentions are sometimes given out when not necessary, lines and sides are similar. Given out to the whole class when, say, two may be the bad ones. There is too much picking on people and if you're not prepared to get up and splatter them they keep on, when you do you're the one who's caught and put in the black book – so you bunk to get out of that lesson and so on, whereas if the teacher had been there all the time and stopped the trouble makers, this would not happen.

This was written by a fifth-year girl who, despite the criticisms, accepts teacher control as being necessary. Without such control trouble naturally erupts. We have seen, however, that many pupils of Slumptown Comprehensive are under pressure. The pressure can lead to 'explosions' or 'unaccountable' behaviour. The assumed need for classroom control can actually exacerbate the problem by increasing the pressure on the individual who finds suddenly that he or she can take no more. Any incident is a climax or crisis in a number of 'stories'. Both pupils and teachers carry their stories with them into school, the clash of stories makes a multilayered epic. Each instance during the day can be interpreted as a component in the many different stories. The poor behaviour in a class may be interpreted as the kind of thing you can expect from these kinds of pupils; afterall, they're not very bright, their parents are inadequate, and there are no books in the homes, and really they've got no values – well, what can you expect?

One boy was sent to the headmaster for being a nuisance. The headmaster punished him, giving him multiplication tables to do as the punishment. The pupil did not do these. Because it was such a trivial matter the deputy headmaster was given the responsibility of further punishing the boy. Again the boy did not do his work set in punishment. It was such a trivial matter and what with the possibility of a riot occuring in the town, the deputy head was far too busy to bother with this. He asked the housemaster to deal with it. The housemaster scornfully replied, 'If he doesn't do it for me who do I pass him on to, the probationary teacher?' This prompted the deputy head to make enquiries as to why the pupil was being a nuisance and defying both the headmaster and the deputy head. In brief, the boy's life-story had all the elements of a Greek drama: the mother had been living with a man who had just sexually assaulted the boy's 10-year-old sister; the mother's brother overheard this fact being told to a social worker and went to beat up the man; the man was taken to hospital and the brother was on an attempted murder charge; the boy's real father was in a mental hospital. On top of this, the mother had just received an electricity demand she could not pay; the electricity was turned off by the board. The demand was to repair damage to the electricity meter caused through robberies.

The school helped by trying to give expert advice on how to deal with the electricity demand. The boy himself will now be treated with understanding. Nevertheless, the fact remains that school can be little more than an interested and concerned observer, only ever scratching the surface of the problems, offering a little help too late. In another situation which had some elements of the above story, though not nearly so dramatic, I asked the father, what do you think the school can do to help? He answered that they try but they can do little. It seems there are external circumstances about which no one can do anything. Oh yes, they try. But really, there's not much that can be done.

We become characters in each others' stories. In the drama of our lives there are the *dramatis personae* who together variously fulfil or frustrate our desires, intentions, needs, ambitions, hopes, and so on. Under the gaze of the other who incorporates us into his or her life-story we lose our individuality, we become features in their landscape, whether grotesque cartoon characters or princes and princesses. If the other is more powerful than I, one way of getting the fulfilments I desire is to incorporate the story of the other into my own story, to become a character in the other's story, an ally in the fulfilment of the other's desires which are now also my desires.

A teacher may live virtually opposite a school, may have several pupils who use his home as a kind of meeting place, may have a rock group made up of local people. In these ways he may intermingle his life-story with the life-stories of others. Such a person is more than a teacher. Most teachers, however, make no attempt to integrate their own life with the lives of their pupils. Instead, they become audiences to the lives of the pupils, or perhaps 'juries' who judge and present verdicts and punishments. Being an audience, or a juror-judge, one sits at a safe distance from the lives of others. One teacher who, intentionally or not, began to integrate his life with the lives of others began to be drawn into their stories as an actor. Unfortunately, there was one story he could not handle, a story of increasing violence which forced him to leave the area. It concerned a young man who's emotional stresses were leading him towards suicide and violent outbursts against others.

In the face of such pressure, what can a teacher or a school do?

Classroom Control

A formal teacher – that is, one who insists upon silence and teaches through authoritarian control – says of his aims:

> I think the good classroom teacher will and has at this school and will continue to do, pursue things in his own way privately. I'm teaching a set, I *love* my subject, I don't make, I'm not ashamed of the fact that I love the academic study of my subject and even at the level of school children, you know, I enjoy teaching it, I enjoy talking to them. You spot someone, admittedly it's going to be spot someone who's, who's got an interest in your subject but children have got an interest in something – probably something in this school which even the academically dimmest child will find exciting and the good teacher of that will spot it and you'll pursue it you know, there.

Of his modest ambitions for those who like his subject he says, 'And

I like to think that we've helped a lot of them but we've not. A drop in the ocean compared to one of the major problems.' By major problems he means the housing problems of the area, its unemployment and the 'inadequate' mothers and fathers of the children. This teacher, like others, is inclined to turn to some form of out-of-school political action, as a counsellor or ultimately as an MP, believing that change can ony be accomplished through politics rather than through education, that schools have no power to change anything. Such teachers who do not try to mix social work with teaching and look to the political structures outside school in order to change society may say that when they leave Slumptown Comprehensive they will 'have an impression of this school which has done an enormous, a lot, enormous amount to try and ameliorate the conditions in which the children find themselves. But that's not enough. It really isn't. When you go into the homes of some of the kids nearby and you see what, what we're up against.' Such teachers' task in school, as they see it, is to bring the best in 'culture' to the working classes. But, as they also recognize, 'it's a drop in the ocean.' Hence they may strive to leave education for the world of local or national politics.

The same teacher ejected from his classroom all the 'social problems', represented by Debbie Graves, as did many other teachers. Classroom control in this method is by imposing obedience upon the compliant and ejecting the trouble-makers. Partridge (1968:172–3) wrote of the effect of rigid discipline upon boys in a secondary modern school:

> The general mood of apathy, disinterest, indifference, and even contempt, which typifies the attitudes of our boys to their classroom work and in some cases to all school activity, is derived, it is suggested, from a variety of factors. Inevitably, to make the boys go through the motions of learning and to create an outward facade of order and purpose, school discipline must be essentially repressive. By the time most boys have reached their third year, they have lost their initial inquisitiveness and any interest they might once have had. As the time approaches for them to leave, they tend to become increasingly concerned about their prospects for a job and more antagonistic to teachers and every form of authority, so that there may sometimes be what amounts to a running war between particular boys and teachers. With many of the

third- and fourth-year classes teaching is a euphemism for repression. Repression takes the form in Middle School of indiscriminate corporal punishment; but this very form of discipline further exacerbates the naturally strained relations between teachers and many of their charges.

This is a picture echoing Waller (1932:195–6):

> The teacher-pupil relationship is a form of institutionalized dominance and subordination. Teacher and pupil confront each other in the school with an original conflict of desires, and however much that conflict may be reduced in amount, or however much it may be hidden, it still remains. The teacher represents the adult group, ever the enemy of the spontaneous life of groups of children. The teacher represents the formal curriculum, and his interest is in imposing that curriculum upon the children in the form of tasks; pupils are much more interested in life in their own world than in the desiccated bits of adult life which teachers have to offer. The teacher represents the established social order in the school, and his interest is in maintaining that order, whereas pupils have only a negative interest in that feudal superstructure. Teacher and pupil confront each other with attitudes from which the underlying hostility can never be altogether removed. Pupils are the material in which teachers are supposed to produce results. Pupils are human beings striving to realize themselves in their own spontaneous manner, striving to produce their own results in their own way. Each of these hostile parties stands in the way of the other; in so far as the aims of either are realized, it is at the sacrifice of the aims of the other.

None of this sounds like what teachers intend when they confront the class. A vision of things 'being in the best interests of the child' motivates most teachers. 'Care' and 'concern' and with many 'a love of children' seem more appropriate than 'dominance and subordination', 'conflict' and 'hostility' at the level of reflective thought. But in the day-to-day being with the class the recalcitrant structures of control are forced upon the teacher – and the teacher must in some way respond.

Smith (1977) in a book on 'underground' literature on education – primarily from 'libertarians' or 'anarchists' – cites a writer, Andy Cowling, who tried to follow his principles:

> Confronted with a room full of rioting fifteen-year olds, I tried to be non-authoritarian. 'If you don't want to sit down or do anything then that is fine with me. I'll sit here and read.' Immediately I'm compromising because I have to bawl my head off to make myself heard. I'm also wondering what's going to happen when the teacher next door comes in to complain about the noise. 'I don't like it here any more than you do, but if we have to be here then let's work out what we can do together that will be useful to us.' Then comes the response from amidst the paper darts, flying chairs, thumping dominoes and twenty different arguments: 'You're the teacher sir. You should make us sit down. You should tell what to do and make us do it.' I experienced that situation many times.

This is a major problem for any teacher who wants to do things differently in school. Henry (1971:23) calls the teacher 'vulnerable': because he does something challenging to given expectations of what constitutes class control and teaching matter, 'the probabilities of getting a rise or even keeping his job are reduced.' Thus, the problem is:

> 'How shall a person who wishes to assert himself in the school system become invulnerable or at least reduce his vulnerablity?' By self-assertion I do not necessarily mean yelling at the principal, although it is rarely that assertion of one's self does not entail standing up to a superior.
>
> By assertion of the self, I mean doing and saying what is in harmony with a self that is striving for something significant, for something which would be a step in the direction of self-realization – in the direction of something that would enable one to say to one's self, 'I have made myself more significant in my own eyes.' It is this 'ownmost self', as Martin Heidegger has called it, that studies and evaluates remorselessly, that I am talking about.
>
> For a teacher, assertion of the self would involve saying what he thinks most enlightening to the students; refusing to use stupid books, or reinterpreting them to make sense; deviating from the embalmed curriculum, and so on.

This then is the scale of the problem – it is a question of self-worth, worth not in the eyes of others, but in one's own eyes. It is a matter perhaps of systematically breaking one's ties with the social order, an order based upon fear of punishment. It is a matter of striving toward a society where we are not merely distorting mirrors, seeing ourselves dimly in the distorted reflections of others, suffocating slowly in the drab uniformity of impersonal organizational control structures.

Is it possible? There are precedents, usually on a small scale, usually short-lived; but short-lived and/or small-scale because of the pressures against them. We can write of Isaacs (1930) or Neill (1973) or of the various 'free schools', amongst many others. All were and still are at the fringe of modern mass schooling. The real problem is to smuggle these liberating ways of teaching and ways of being with kids into schools, particularly secondary schools.

The problem is immediately confronted even during the time teachers are but student teachers. Lacey (1977:84):

> ... both from the point of view of personal relationships and from the point of view of assessment of academic potential, the students are meeting challenging situations and are both distancing and labelling in self protection. Bob had referred to the pupils he taught as 'really strange, really weird'. Lisa had referred to her 4A as 'dumb'. Lora referred to her third year boys who were trying it on and were 'really nasty'. 'You know, they have it all worked out in advance.' Anna talked about a typical challenge. She said she noticed that one boy was eating a sweet but had decided that if he did so fairly quietly she would ignore it. Presently somebody said, 'Please, Miss, David's eating a sweet. What are you going to do about it?' She made him take it out, wrap it up in paper and throw it in the waste-paper bin. It was this constant challenge and having to react predictably to situations that were set up to test them that really upset the students. They felt that they didn't want to react in a stereotyped way to what seemed to them artificial situations

Unfortunately, new teachers tend to move towards the views of their evaluators (Edgar and Warren, 1969); probationers were found to turn to the head teacher and an experienced colleague 70 per cent of the time by Taylor and Dale (1971). It is necessary, therefore, Kohl (1977) advises us, to look for allies within the school if one wishes to try something radical, since nothing can be accomplished without them. The teacher, being vulnerable and if alone, is as much 'the controlled' in the classroom as 'the controller'.

Finding allies, however, may not be easy and the spectre of classroom control with its dimensions of hostility, conflict and dominance wait to confront us. Somewhere at the back of the class will be a Jacko, a Debbie Graves, a Darren Bailey – and they will not leave us alone. If we wish to share our 'knowledge' and our 'experience' or if we care for them we will not want to eject them from our classes.

Within Slumptown Comprehensive there are a number of teachers who try not to eject their trouble-makers, who try to reduce the control barriers between themselves and the kids and yet who *do not* face classrooms of rioters. One such teacher, Mr Brown, however, feels his powerlessness keenly, and feels the need to talk to the :

> flotsam and jetsom, the people . . . the kids who're failing in the system [and] uh [the] kids who, who're . . . probably successful in system but really just need to talk to somebody occasionally, y' know uh.
>
> *J.F.S.:* D' you, do you see a complete divorce between that kind of counselling and teaching? . . . the academic bit. . . .
>
> *Brown:* Yeah.
>
> *J.F.S.:* A complete divorce. . . .
>
> *Brown:* Uh . . . well yes because I really am talking about one to one stuff and that's why I don't think you can do what I'm talking about in a class. . . . I mean it crops up occasionally, spontaneously, y' know. But it's so chancy that way uh and I don't think either if you gave y' self the role or y' know, the title say of school counsellor or whatever that you . . . it would work. All . . . all that I'm saying is that I would like my job and what I do ideally to be like that. The opportunity and the time to just talk to some kids and sound them out . . . or y' know, listen to what they've got to say – have the time to do that. And we don't. I haven't time to really listen and get good feedback from my kids. . . .

Control, we see, has two further dimensions: the number of individuals a person has to interact with at any one moment and time. Of schooling, he says, 'It isn't for all kids – some kids find it excruciating; boring, meaningless and fruitless as well 'cos they're not going to get anything. They haven't got the ability ... y' know, to succeed in a system that by definition says so many will fail.' Control has the further dimension of being built upon systematic 'failure by definition'. Each classroom is stratified according to degrees of failure – the best at the front, the worst at the back. By shifting the failures around or ejecting them, class control can be maintained; alternatively, one may use the technique of 'work sheets' to cater for the 'slow' and the 'fast' at once. Whatever is the procedure, control becomes organized around failure. To challenge such structures of control is a major job. Furthermore:

> We have some teachers who are as much a problem as pupils to the housemaster because its – they really do need the help and not the kids they send to you. The kids are just a symptom of their, of their own shortcomings or inadequacy or sensitivity or whatever or blindspot even, y' know. [But] we're all professionals. And this is another thing which gets in our way. It's not for me to tell another of my colleagues y' know, that they're not up to, you know, up to my ideas of the the 'I would do it this way.' That's not part of our role unfortunately.

His own method is subtle, difficult and emotionally tiring:

> ... you'd be looking for opportunities first of all to project yourself. That, that's one thing I would say (to a new teacher/tutor). The kid sort of looks at you and asks you something, you know, for God's sake give him something back, y' know. Look for a chance uh to get in there and make a contact, Um ... I would ... I'd also tell them [new teachers] uh to ... realise that they're playing a role that, you know, they will be seen as part of a title to the kids and not a person. And therefore if anything happens that that sort of hurts them, not to take it personally. Not to see it as a criticism of themselves. Um, that's the kind of thing I'd be telling them, 'cos that's, that's what happens all the time – teachers want it both ways y' see. They want to be able to tell the kids 'stand up and sit down' but when a kid says to them 'piss off' ... O.K., they then interpret that as the kid telling *them*, who ever they are, 'to piss off' and, of course, the kid isn't telling *them* to 'piss off' because he doesn't know *'em*. All

121

he knows is that *teacher*. He's actually telling the teacher. And this is what I've tried to tell even very experienced staff who get very hot under the collar about this, y' know, and very hurt some of them.... And I would tell a new member of staff that, that any relationship they're gonna make has got to be done in that role ... you know, 'cos I don't accept the role theory for all of its ... uh ... I would accept the idea that we're playing parts and we do have titles and that these mask [us] as our behaviour is structured in certain situations and therefore, you know, we don't project our *selves* as it were ... you know, we're always sort of ... going along certain lines. I accept that much of it. And that's what I would emphasise with uh a new teacher. And as you go along, John, y' see, you try to get rid of that that role you [try to get], you know, a growing relationship with a kid or with another teacher – like me, the housemaster, to my tutors, that should grow and develop to the point where it doesn't really matter what what my title is any more, but they know me so ... got to know me so well in these situations that there is a definite bonding relationship that they can trust. And trust an' all that y' know, that's how it's built up ... y' know just, just by... revealing yourself to them.

The recipe is that of 'social schizophrenia'. We play parts behind which we can hide or from behind which we can step out and reveal something of our individuality. Structurally, the process is the same as that used by, say, Debbie Graves – where her method was overtly provocative and challenging, Brown's is overtly gentle, unobtrusive. However, the break created between conformity and individuality is just as complete and, by affirming the break, is ultimately just as abrasive or corrosive to the 'controllers'. Brown has frequently been heavily criticized, sometimes bitterly by fellow teachers. Nevertheless, his relationship to the kids and his ability to teach is never questioned.

There are yet other techniques used by such teachers as Brown who refuse to eject their 'trouble-makers'. It seems to depend upon the 'personality' or personal qualities of a teacher as to which are used. Some have a natural gift for comedy or have some 'dramatic talent' through which they are able to arouse inner emotions which in turn systematically break down 'masks'. Any teacher, if he or she is to survive in the classroom at some tolerable degree of friendliness with the pupils, must possess and utilize these gifts to some extent.

One teacher, Mr Jones, possessed both comic and 'dramatic' talents to an outstanding degree. He was also a firm (and aggressive) disciplinarian given to booming shouts of 'ratbag', 'arse'ole' and 'toerag' to anyone – pupils or staff – who crossed him. Total silence was imposed upon his class except when given premission to do otherwise. It might seem he should be an ogre and indeed a number of pupils thought him to be so. However, many 'trouble-makers' loved him, as did a majority of his pupils. He was always open and honest, always ready to speak, joke and help pupils. During all break times his classroom was open to pupils to use as a meeting place. He would be there, joining in the fun. In such a way he missed no opportunity to reveal his own – admittedly frequently abrasive but also frequently gentle – personality and create bonds of friendship which lasted for years after pupils left school. By embracing coercive forms of class control and yet also creating bonds of intense friendship and concern he created within himself a tension which led to health problems. To punish and to shout was intensely painful to him – yet he perceived his job as demanding it.

Many pupils are frightened by teachers who 'bawl and shout' – it is a primitive yet pervasive control technique. The consequence of its use is to diminish the individual who shouts and the individual shouted at, both physically and mentally. Some (earlier published) results of a questionnaire I gave *suggest* the extent of this fear. Of the third year 44 per cent of boys and 63 per cent of girls said they felt afraid of teachers; for the fifth-years the percentages were 22 for boys and 46 for girls. (The figures are the sum of those who said 'yes' or 'sometimes'.) Moreover, of pupils who admitted truanting (15 per cent of third-years and just over 50 per cent of fifth-years) 70 per cent gave as their reasons a dislike or outright hatred of school (*TES*, 25 June 1982):

> I am frightened of one of my teachers, not of what he does but what he says. He makes a show of me . . . I have never given this teacher any cheek and yet he makes me feel very uncomfortable. My friends do better than me in the results and I feel like a divy and this makes me feel worse.

Truanting has led her to miss lessons and this shows in her results making her feel stupid (divy). Besides being shown up, other pupils complain of being called names – about 30 per cent of fifth-years – and others complain of being punched or pushed about by teachers.

Also, rarely being allowed to act upon their own initiative and continually being supervised – they are not allowed to go to the toilet without written permission – they feel they are being treated like children, or worse. About 80 per cent of fifth-years complained of sometimes being treated like children and nearly a third felt they were usually treated like children. One of the most extreme expressions came from a fifth-year girl truant:

> Most of the teachers treat you like dog muck and surely you are not going to stand for that so you start to treat them like it.... Most teachers can give pressure but just can't take it. They make me sick. If the teachers treated the pupils with a bit more respect things would be a lot easier. If a teacher wanted to talk to you about something you have done they might wait till you are by yourself instead of pulling you out of a crowd, instead of making a show of you. They wouldn't like it if you made a show of them.

Classroom control at this level of hostility is no more than policing a 'mob'. There is little scope here to 'negotiate' a reasonable work climate for the classroom.

It is sad to think that a climate of command so rules a classroom that any deviation from this makes a teacher seem 'weak' or 'queer'. The teacher who wishes to present an alternative experience must face the structures of command and authority which trivialize education into a series of hollow victories – for one side or the other – in a process of negotiation:

> Command of the process of negotiation is at the heart of being a successful teacher. Quite often, if the teacher overdoes his concessions, the pupils will demand more and threaten to take over the lesson. It is also to be reviled as offending the norm: 'He's a bit of a queer teacher. He's not like a proper teacher. He doesn't tell you off.' If not enough concessions are made pupils might become resentful, and potential colonizers might be turned into rebels. What the standard lesson consists of then, is a number of checks and balances, prompts and concessions, motivations, punishments, jollyings, breaks and so forth, as the teacher displays his professional expertise in getting the most out of his pupils, while pupils, seeking basically the comfort of their

own perspective and reality, will tend to react according to
how the teacher's techniques mesh with that reality. (Woods,
1978:310)

The dimensions of classroom control, starting from the teacher
as 'manager', 'enforcer', 'commander' or 'judge-jury', trivialize
education, turn lessons into the training of caged animals, demean
the individual and prepare the way for a lifetime of playing 'submission' or 'domination' games, a lifetime of mundane 'negotiations' or
a lifetime of violent rebellion.

Pastoral Care

as a housemaster I'm expected to discipline kids who have
misbehaved for other people ... and whom I might be
getting on very well with ... apart from that. Now I have
got to try and build a relationship which allows that situation
to exist. I've got to try and ... kids have got to understand –
I try and teach kids that it's my, part of my job sometimes to
be nasty to them even though they've not done anything
personally to me. Um, and in that sense they've got to
identify me with the institution. And when they hurt the
institution they hurt me kind of situation. Having said that, I
also personally want them to see me ... as somebody that
they can trust and somebody that they can uh have relationship with as a person, as an individual. I don't want to be
just part of the institution.

The housemaster as an individual has to submit his individuality to
the institution. Individual expression is thus subject to institutional
censorship – in a Freudian sense he has internalized the institution as
censor until he is able to take on the role of expressing the will and
the judgement and the action of the censor.

Pastoral care may not overtly intend to be a system for
surveillance, censorship and repression but it can fall into this trap.
Thus Benn and Simon (1970:221–2) could say of the advantages of
house systems that: 'Children with anti-social attitudes are easier to
handle, it is also claimed, because they are divided up among the
houses. More important than this, a good house system does much
to help these children overcome their problems.' However:

. . . as time went on, it became obvious that the house system was not the answer to all problems. For one thing, in a few schools where it was adopted, it was wrongly assumed that it would take care of all social and educational guidance. It was left to the house tutor or house staff to deal with all problems that arose – academic, social, vocational, and medical – and this most were not equipped or prepared to do. Perhaps the most important factor was that there was not enough time. Generally those who are in charge of houses or tutor groups are supposed to be given a lighter teaching load than other staff. But some schools do not do this. In our own smaller sample of schools, we found that out of the thirty-six schools answering the question as to whether a lighter teaching load was given to staff with pastoral duties, eleven schools did not allow the staff in charge of social unit groups *any* lighter teaching load at all.

Of the pastoral care system in Slumptown Comprehensive – which boasts of its pastoral system – a housemaster says:

There's . . . no clearly defined lines or courses of action that a tutor, an individual tutor, should or must take with the groups to which they're assigned. And [it is] quite possible, for example, that the tutor dislikes the group that they're assigned to . They get no say in it. Um, just like I don't get any say in the kind of kids that I deal with. They, they're designated to me like it or not, or like me or not, or me like them or not. We, we're just thrown together. Um and I find I am used as part of this admin. system as the housemaster, kind of like the hub of the wheel and everything flows through me in terms of information and I, I sort of thrust it out again to my tutors, to my groups and gather in any information that's required back to me and fed into which-ever slot it has got to go to. It might be a deputy head that's collecting it, it might be the head or whoever, it might be an outside agency. It doesn't matter. I, I am like a postman . . . um . . . we do an absolutely essential job as housemasters and tutors to the good running of the school as a bureaucratic machine. If we stopped doing that it'd be like a brainstorm at the school because every everything'd clog up. There'd be no messages going backwards and forwards. Nobody'd know what the hell was happening.

But housemasters hope to be more than 'postmen'. This is made clear by another housemaster describing the function of the 'tutor period' – twenty minutes each morning and ten minutes each afternoon:

> First of all it's a method of registering uh . . . I'm not putting these in a priority order. It's a method of registering kids, checking on who is in school and who is not in school. It's a method of checking on things like uniform . . . checking the kids have got pens and pencils that they need for the day. These things are all important for a smooth day for them, for any individual kid. It's a way of doing the routine admin. that needs doing in terms of sorting out . . . well, it's the tutor that prepares the final report for the kid; it's the tutor who does the initial work in option choices [and] it should be . . . the place where teachers are able to make more involved contact with the kids . . . I mean that kids have got an opportunity of turning to an adult and it's to facilitate . . . the ability of the child to be able to turn to an adult and trust an adult. I don't think it happens that way sadly. It does in some cases, it does in individual pockets . . . I don't think it does happen on a wide basis. But it's what I believe should be happening. I mean, it would never always be that the kid would turn to the tutor. I mean kids are always going to find class teachers that they trust more or a housemaster they're going to trust more or somebody else or perhaps somebody who takes the football team who they're going to trust more. But I think a school this size, it is tragic if kids don't feel they can trust somebody, you know, with one hundred and twenty staff that they don't trust somebody. And I think tutor period gives them the opportunity of finding somebody they can trust. A sort of situation like taking a games team where you can build these relations, where you're going to get a higher percentage of kids have trust in you. . . . I don't think it works that way. I don't think it is working.

Perhaps more pragmatically, another housemaster makes more specific the relation of the tutors with himself, that they are an 'extension' of himself. Because he cannot possibly know all the children in the house, he wants the tutors to act as the first line of observation of the pupils and to 'feed problems back to me'. Many of these problems are felt to be problems created by the school itself: its size, the crowds of pupils, its complexity. He considers 'most of the tutors know their children well, get on with them well and have influence with them which is the all important thing.' By influence, he means 'in some respects almost a parental influence, you know, if the child misbehaves then, you know, the tutor will be able to say, "Oh, I've heard about such and such," and the child will take some notice, you know, modify their behaviour. And if it's serious misbehaviour, I deal with it personally.' He goes on to present an anecdote which acts as a parable setting forth the underlying relations between tutor and pupils. Such relations have a power to change or modify behaviour toward a desired moral or socially approved way of behaving:

> [He points outside to two girls] Alison and Mary, the two on the left. They were causing us tremendous problems last year. They're both bright children but they'd got into the way of uh truancy, you know, playing the system a bit um being very stupid women. Now um, they were punished quite severely for it with their parents in.... Now, they were taking quite a bit of punishment from the House, did one or two school detentions. I think we may have even isolated those for a couple of days. And we had both sets of parents in. Um, they did calm down um but they were sort of uncooperative and relatively uncommunicative but they've changed back to what they were before, you know, they were good kids up until then. Now, uh Derek, he's the tutor, has brought them round, you know, they've both swam for his swimming gala, you know, volunteered, no problems. Uh, quite unusual for girls that age. And he done that with a whole group of the girls. Um . . . and it it's that kind of thing I'm looking for in my tutors.

Thus, success or failure in the system is judged according to the extent to which such relations and dramatic outcomes arise. Here we have the elements of a morality story: girls who caused 'tremendous problems', who were classified into the range of 'bright children' but were 'playing the system'; punishment was given out but perhaps was not really working; they were 'uncooperative' and 'uncommunicative' but have now been transformed by the good tutor into 'what they were before', that is, 'good kids'. Relations have built up in the typical manner, through involvement with such activities as swimming and through having 'talked them round'. Such stories as these form the cultural heritage of the pastoral system. Hence, each character of such a 'morality play' can be compared, contrasted and equated with current dramas. Each story with its dramatic characters (the 'good', the 'bad', the 'ugly') functions to classify and make sense of, or give a dramatic unity to, a multiplicity of everyday events. Thus, any particular incident becomes tied into a complex of associations which give meaning to that incident. The structure or organization of the school compels a number of complexes of associations so that certain events are tied into the pastoral complex, other events are tied into the academic complex, and others into the administrative complex. Together they form a complex of observations, which form a matrix into which to fit children and teachers and their particular acts in the drama. This complex of observations can function in three ways: first, it provides a matrix by which a person can grow or decrease in esteem in the eyes of the school staff; secondly, it provides a matrix against which to rebel in order to grow in esteem in the eyes of those who take an anti-school stance; and thirdly, it provides a cloak which can be used to cover subversive or 'underground' activities. Thus we have three kinds of drama. In the following story, told by a housemaster, two of the functions of the complex of observations intertwine to present the way in which an individual pupil is seen to develop into a problem. In this case it is the reverse of the previous case; we have an example of the transformation from 'good' to 'bad':

> . . . a little boy who was in the first year. . . . He went into the slow set into the X set but he, in relative terms, he was a good worker and neat, careful, tidy, super. But unfortunately, uh just since January he just seems to have flipped, you know. Uh, being rude, performing for the class, you know, doing uh just, I suppose attention seeking but, not in a way that paralleled with anything he'd done in the last term. Being rude, uh, you know, 'You can't speak to me like that', 'You can't do this that and the other to me', and uh . . . um, that kept cropping up time after time. Given a report card, given a self recording um little booklet that you use like a diary uh, 'Where's your report card Peter?'
>   'Oh, I didn't like it.'
>   'Uh, well, you do have a self recording . . .?'
>   'Yeah'.
>   'Where is it Peter?'

'Uh, I didn't do it, I didn't like it.'
Comes to that he doesn't want to take it home for his mother
to see.
'Why not?'
'Because she batters me if I don't have four Excellents.'
Needless to say it's very rarely that he he got his Excellents.
Um, and invited the mother to come in. She did do,
eventually. And, single parent family. Always in tangles um
um it, . . . What it amounts to in the end is that we're going
to have to ask mum to come in again. Peter's going to see the
psychologist um to help them manage school and her to
manage Peter, really. She's trying to do the best thing that
she can but it's counter productive, you know, the whole
thing goes wrong. And, I think that's in a sense the job I'm
paid to do in the end, apart from, apart from uh holding
oversight of . . . the academic progress of so many of our
kids as well as the social work. It's, it's um picking up those
that are dropping like flies, you know trying to fit those back
into the pile somewhere.

The network of observations extends outwards from the school and
penetrates the family home, making use of typical observational
techniques: report cards, self-recording and finally, the educational
psychologist is brought in. The child is described in academic terms
initially, the complex of associations being slow set, good worker,
neat, careful, tidy, super. Then as his behaviour changed he became a
pastoral disciplinary concern. The complex of associations became
rude, performing for the class, attention seeking; these associations
are then associated with a further set used to describe the mother –
single-parent family, always in tangles, trying to do the best thing
but counter-productive, needing help. The moment of transformation from good boy to bad boy is described as 'he just seems to have
flipped.' It is rather like a magical moment, a magical transformation, without rhyme nor reason. In comparison with the previous
story where the tutor was considered to have effected the change, no
character is specifically located as effecting the transformation from
good to bad. However, the character of the mother is used in such a
way that the listener will draw conclusions, almost inevitably a
causitive link will be made between the mother's inability to manage
Peter and Peter's change. Peter is seen to 'perform for the class', he is
seen trying to grow in esteem amongst his classmates. The house-

master's task is then to try and fit Peter back into the 'pile', calling upon the help of the educational psychologist.

Pupils may perform for the class, or mates, may perform for teachers, or may cloak all performances to their advantage. These possible forms for the drama interweave to produce complex multilayered events; when face to face the characters engage to produce their drama. It is a drama of 'social adjustment', 'resistance', 'rebellion', 'failure', 'transformation'. It is organized social adjustment against 'individuals', 'deviants', 'gangs'.

Both Waller (1932) and Partridge (1968) saw the use of pastoral or counselling systems for social adjustment. Waller (p.456) wanted the creation of case studies of every child:

> Bureaus of adjustment should be provided and should be presided over by competent psychologists or psychiatrists. This personnel work should follow the model of social work rather than of personnel work in industry, and should look toward the mental and social adjustment of students. It would do well to avoid over-concern about abnormalities of behaviour, and to look rather toward the solution of normal problems of development.

Waller recognizes also that 'there are numerous teachers whose personal problems affect their teaching' and thus 'personnel work with teachers, by enabling such teachers to struggle more successfully against their own interior demons, might bring about radical changes in the social world of school' (p.457). Partridge (p.177), too, felt that one should deal 'with difficult pupils in terms of the social casework approach. At the present time repression is the solution to every behavioural problem in the school. But there are some boys who need the greatest possible help and understanding to enable them to overcome serious handicaps and emotional and psychological difficulties.'

As we have seen, Slumptown in common with other comprehensives has gone some way to realize the case study approach of dealing with pupils although it has not gone so far as to take up Waller's more radical suggestion of extending the approach to include teachers as the objects of social adjustment in the social work style. Nevertheless, Best, Jarvis and Ribbins (1980) have argued that the pastoral care system has tended to be an agent of discipline and control rather than of social care, thus an organization which prevents change rather than encourages it. Indeed, the pastoral care system, we have seen, is frequently defined by teachers largely in terms of the bureaucratic needs of registration, carrying out the process of getting pupils to choose their subject options for examination courses, and providing information concerning room changes and so on, besides having the function of disciplining, finding out the reasons for absences, and so on.

However, in such criticisms we must not fail to overlook the genuine 'care', 'concern' and emotional turmoil felt by tutors dealing with pressures which explode in their faces. Such an incident occurred at dinner time. I was the 'shadow' of a housemaster for the day. We were in the houseblock office with a number of house staff when suddenly the assistant housemaster came leaping through the office – all we caught was, 'he's thrown a knife.'

What seemed to have happened was that one pupil 'hit' another – they were probably 'messin''. One boy threw a chair, the other retaliated by throwing a knife. The matter was dealt with by one of the deputies so I heard little more about the incident for the rest of the day. Amongst the staff some jokes were made about the incident. At the end of the day another housemaster said to me, 'You should've been with me today.' It had been quite a day for him. Amongst the things that had happened was a boy being thrown off a stair wall. His collar bone was broken.

Later I talked to the deputy who had dealt with the knife throwing incident. He said (reconstructed from notes): 'I've never known anything like it. When I asked him why he did it he burst into tears. He said "I'm a psycho".' The deputy was plainly shocked. 'I asked him why he thought that he was "a psycho". "Me mam says I am. I'm just like me dad. Me dad breaks things, threw a knife at her grazin' 'er shoulder".' The deputy said to him, 'I get angry too, and I'll throw things. Just because you've got a bad temper doesn't mean to say you're psycho.' But the boy insisted he was 'psycho'. To prove this he said he was an 'inventor': 'I've invented a way of magnetizing the metal pillars of a high rise block so that the opposing attractions will repulse each other and make the building fall down.' The deputy said, 'You've just got a lively imagination.' The deputy said to me, 'I wouldn't be surprised if he didn't have a high IQ.'

With understanding, caring for his lads as best he can, the deputy, like others in the school, attempts to patch up the tears left by the pressures. I remember the deputy saying to me one day, 'We may not achieve much but by hell we try.'

As a 'punishment' for the boy the deputy asked him to write about his 'inventions'. The educational psychologist was asked to

assess the boy to see in what way help could be given to him. That
appeared to be the end of the story, for other stories soon claimed
their equally pressing attention upon time and caring. However, the
next day quite fortuitously I interviewed some girls about their
experiences of school life. One of the stories they told referred to the
knife incident:

> *Pat:* We were in the dinner hall ah yesterday it was and there
> was these two lads that were fightin' and one threw a knife
> and it caught me in the face,
> *Sal:* By the arms, isn't it. . . .
> *Jan:* Just by there.
> *Pat:* Cut all the face there. And they knocked these chairs
> off. . . .
> *J.F.S.:* That was yesterday?
> *Sal:* Yeah.
> *Pat:* Knocked all these chairs off, hit me in the side with a
> chair. Got this girl, 'old of 'er arm there and then all 'er side
> there.
> *Sal:* 'An she got a big bruise, didn't she?
> *Pat:* I mean, I told Miss Green, she said, she said 'You're
> alright, yeah.' And she started laughing didn't she?
> *Sal:* Miss Green?
> *Pat:* Miss Green was laughing.
> *Sal:* Mm.
> *Pat:* And she just thought it, she thought it was funny that a
> chair had been thrown and a knife.
> *Sal:* But it wasn't funny.
> *Pat:* And she thought it was funny.
> *Sal:* But it wasn't because it was a knife.

I then asked why they thought the boy did it. They said he was
always doing things like that because of wanting 'the attention I
suppose'.

In every such incident people are bruised, scarred, torn – not just
the pupils, but also the teachers. Such casualties are left in the wake
of the incident. One person may be partially helped, others are
overlooked – not because people do not care but because there are
too many to help, too much to do. And the unresolved tension
between care and control prevents teachers and pupils from meeting
as individuals who might be able to share and grow together. The
greatest problem is to overcome mutual suspicion and hostility.

7 Pupil Strategies and the Process of Growing Up at School

School is one of the major institutions shaping each individual's experience of growing up. It confers privileges and favours, imposes handicaps and censors and endorses the behaviour, thoughts, feelings and beliefs of pupils. School is capable of exerting enormous pressure upon the individual, whether teacher or pupil. A number of strategies are open to pupils for coping with or manipulating this pressure.

Since growing up is sexual in nature – that is, we grow up as biologically male or female – strategies for growing up are sexually framed. Identities and social institutions are organized around taboos, expectations, and experiences concerning sexuality. The period of social and biological 'growing up' is not a settled state. It is a period of transition into the socially defined states of being 'grown' men or women. Adolescence has been typically considered to be a time of 'storm and stress' (Hall, 1904). It is a period when the body itself changes, a period when physical attractiveness becomes a pleasure, a liability, a weapon, a curse; for the infant the body is an instrument of play, but for the adult, an instrument of work which yearns to be an instrument of pleasure (cf. Marcuse, 1972). On the one hand, the adolescent must learn to bend sexual energies towards work, learn to tolerate, even find pleasure in submission to authority. The myths of manliness and femininity channel sexual energy into socially approved ways of living and identify rights, duties and behaviours appropriate and necessary to the experience of being a man or being a woman. However, it is also a period when the young challenge the rights of the old to control them; like Debbie and Darren it is a time when the young must break away systematically from the old in order to gain independence economically, socially, psychologically. They do not always succeed. But adolescence is a battle of wills between the young and the old; a battle which is expressed sexually, dramatically, and its battle lines are drawn in images of masculinity, femininity, race, social class and the exuberance of youth.

It is through the energy of youth that revolutions have been able to ignite and transform societies intellectually and physically (cf. Heer, 1974). The energy of youth is dangerous hence the institutions of 'growing up' are essentially instruments for the control of individuals in order to maintain traditional social behaviours. Typically, schools are successful as instruments of control. However, there are competing controllers. There are the teachers, the parents, mates, the gang, the police. Some may form alliances with each other, but each can potentially tear the emerging sense of adolescent selfhood into shreds – each pulling in different directions. This can be done without the participants intending it to happen; or it can be done intentionally, for pleasure, perhaps to gratify a sense of self-righteousness or a sense of power, or a sense of the tragic or the absurd.

Laing (1965 edition:39) has identified two basic psychological states of being: primal ontological security, and primal ontological insecurity. Primal ontological security means simply that the 'person' or the 'individual' (refer to chapter 3 for the distinction between these) within his or her self or being feels secure. Such a person or individual has a sense of his or her 'integral selfhood and personal identity, of the permanency of things, of the reliability of natural processes, of the substantiality of natural processes' and 'of the substantiality of others'. From such a position the experience of being moulded or formed by others may be interpreted and experienced in three ways: as adding to the self, as diminishing the self, or as being irrelevant to the self.

Some young people in the role of pupils, however, will start from a position of feeling insecure in the sense of a 'primary ontological insecurity' where their 'experiences may be utterly lacking in any unquestionable self-validating certainties' (p. 39). Some pupils, while not experiencing primal ontological insecurity, may be desperately hanging on to a few remaining 'unquestionable self-validating certainties'. For such pupils the experience of being moulded or formed (through the socializing forces of, say, school) may result either in being torn or in being healed. The strategy thus will be to move toward those who appear to offer the most persistent or permanent sense of security in terms of 'unquestionable self-validating certainties'; such 'healers' may be found in school teachers, friends, the gang or whoever attracts the young person.

There is a range of strategies young people may use to cope with pressures, to exert their will on the world and to subvert or frustrate the will of others. The strategy may be carried out with confidence or out of desperation. Some young people may, in confidently asserting their will, choose strategies identical to those who are acting out of despair. There can, therefore, be no complete and definitive typology of strategies. The number of strategies is limited only by the skill and imagination of the strategists. Pupil strategies in relation to the process of growing up, however, all centre on the problem of transition ('becoming', 'transformation', or 'change'). To cope with the transition, or to take advantage of the possibilities inherent in transition, I may, for example:

1   *become like others* who have what I want and will give me what I want if I become like them;
2   *manipulate others* through my powers so that they will give me what I want (which may also involve 3);
3   *deceive others* into believing whatever is necessary to get what I want;
4   *avoid others* in order to avoid their pressures and create my own inner world of pleasure or safety; or
5   *destroy opposition* to my will through various forms of violence.

Each of these strategies involves either attaching myself to others or detaching myself from others in order to get what I want. Any combination of strategies may be used, and may be used skilfully, unskilfully, in confidence or in despair. Through a process of self-criticism and the criticism of others I either draw toward a sense of self dominated by concerns to be like certain others, with those others being the judges of my actions; or, I move toward becoming a self independently critical of others, responsible only to myself. The task for the remainder of the chapter is to present in the voices of pupils the ways they move towards a sense of themselves as they desire themselves to be; or as they run from a sense of themselves as they fear themselves becoming – broken, ugly, empty. I will take each of the first four kinds of strategy in turn. The last will be discussed as the 'Violent Solution' – the theme of the next chapter.

1 Becoming Like Others

The process of becoming like others may begin as a result of a conscious choice leading perhaps to a dramatic change in appearance or behaviour. Thus, for example, Willis (1977) has described the lads 'coming out', that is, adopting the dress and hairstyle of some youth culture; of course, the reverse could happen as a skin head becomes a 'city gent'. Or it may be a gradual, imperceptible process, a process perhaps of subtle conditioning and the internalization of the values of one's family, friends or heroes. Becoming like others involves becoming like *certain others* who will be in distinction to, and may be in opposition to, or in cooperation with yet others (or some other relation). The lads that Willis wrote about took an oppositional stance towards school; the Rasta notion of Babylon involves an oppositional stance to white authority; the authoritarian teacher or manager may take an oppositional stance towards pupils or workers (cf. Coleman, 1961; Lacey, 1970; Hall and Jefferson, 1976).

The choice, or the conditioned acceptance, of becoming like others will be wrought within a framework of necessity, or limits to freedom of choice. Thus:

> This school is a necessity to me, if I wish to hold a steady job when I leave school. The importance of this tells me that I must keep on plugging for my O levels. The tutors, teachers and housemasters have all of a sudden this year started to pay special attention, and started to care, in helping me, which has never happened whilst I have been in this school. (fifth-year boy, written statement)

Suddenly for this fifth-year boy, school has found its *raison d'être*. The attention is valued and *recognized* as being a help to achieve a necessary goal. Becoming like others involves this criterion of recognizability at three levels: the recognition of something being a necessity, or a self-validating certainty; the recognition of oneself being like others; and recognizing that others recognize that you are like them. These levels of recognition are brought about through the participants attending to each other, taking notice of each other, interpreting each other's actions in a similar way and through their interpretations guiding each other's behaviour. In becoming like one set of others, by implication one becomes unlike another set of others. It is necessary to reject incompatible images, interpretations of images and behaviours. When a young person frames his or herself within the image of the pupil as presented by teachers such a young person must take a position against those who would reject or break that image:

> In school now, I find that the teachers respect us more than what they did when we first came to this school, because we now particularly at this stage take more notice of what is going on in our lessons in order to achieve a good examination result.
>
> The teachers now express things more and are as determined as us to get a pleasingly good grade in either CSE or 'O' level examinations.
>
> The things I don't like about school are the odd few people who ignore the whole lesson and laugh with their friends interrupting the class.
>
> The things I do find important in school are the lessons and the homework and tests that we have every so often to see if we have achieved anything. (fifth-form boy, written reply)

However, if school is assessed as unnecessary, one may seek one's formative influences elsewhere:

> I reckon exams'll get me nowhere at all. I've got a brother that's took no exams at all. He's on the lump [claiming unemployment benefit plus working on temporary jobs]. . . . I've got a cousin with all kinds of A levels an' everythin'. Can't even get a job. What they're lookin' for, they're lookin' for all kinds of high paid jobs. Not many of them around. When they leave school I don't really reckon brains come into it. Well, some jobs you do . . . all you get now is factory jobs an' things like that don't yer. Government trainees. . . . (fourth-form boy in interview)

Unsurprisingly, this boy found little use for his lessons and redefined school as a social centre rather than as a work centre. One chooses one's mates among those who define things in a similar manner. Another fifth-form boy writes:

> I'm not really worried about school. Only some things I like about it and really like doing. What stops me bunking all the time is being bored of just hanging around. The only good thing about coming back into school is cause I like talking to

my mates, having a laugh. Most teachers thought they could order me about a lot when I was younger. I am not saying they could but now they don't really say a lot to me. I don't think anything is important about school because when I leave I don't think anyone will give me a job. Anyway on some job scheme or something. I think we should be getting learnt how to enjoy and fill in the time after school.

The 'laugh' becomes the criterion by which one such boy recognizes another such boy as a mate. The school as a meeting place to have a laugh and pursue leisure interests (if possible) is an alternative and partially realized interpretation and use of school. The cry that this boy makes is that teachers recognize this as legitimate and construct some form of leisure curriculum to meet social needs. Such needs are self-validating certainties, necessities in a world of massive unemployment.

In becoming like others, a sense of community is created. However, the desired image is not always attainable. Others may reject or so criticize such attempts that the individual falls into despair, or becomes confused and hurt:

I don't think school is a waste of time because it's a place of learning. Most people hate school and are always playing truant. I used to hate school especially in the fourth year because I had a lot of trouble then. My options [subject choices for exam courses] were upset and I felt at that time it was my [subject] teacher's fault, because I thought he hated me (and I still do). There was never a lesson when he didn't throw me out or shout at me for no reason. One day the whole class was doing an exercise and he told us to mark it. Almost everyone told him we hadn't finished and then he got hold of me and dragged me out. No one else got a word said to them. Also I don't like doing music. I like playing trumpet and doing band but I hate the music lesson.

You probably get the impression now that I hate school but I've got over my disputes against it and I have settled down. (fifth-form girl, written reply)

Clearly, there is still resentment underneath the surface. Her desire to be in community with the school has been violated; the experience of the violation is still a potent memory. From such experiences the images of violation form; a violent imagination is created from such a matrix of images. The images serve as a framework within which any new act or experience finds interpretation. Images direct attitudes and predict behaviour: 'The teachers mostly treat you like dirt. Thinks we are slaves telling us to do about 10 pages of work a lesson. It really bugs me. The good thing about school is when you break up. I can't wait to leave' (fifth-form boy, written reply).

The images sediment, become a cesspool of hate:

> Teachers treat you like shit. They think they're great, in other words, smartasses. And Mr White locked you in the Fire Escape if you skitted him. I always had an idea that I would bring an iron bar, wait for the slob to finish school, put a hood on and twat him all around the show. Some of the teachers wear the clothes we can't wear like trainers, no blaizers. I hate teachers. (third-form boy, written reply)

It is upon such an emotional base that a pupil's strategies of growing up within school become transformed into strategies of resistance and rebellion. Opposition thus comes to mark the boundaries between groups; each group forms a violent imagination out of the sedimented images of being violated by the other group. Individuals become the objects of strategic hate or, at least, dislike. Tactics are formed in order to display people as objects of hate: or to display one self as the subject for admiration. Woods (1979:21) sees 'having a laugh' as a way in which pupils generate 'respect and dignity, meaning and identity'. However, if pupils fall:

> foul of official or tacit norms, the most customary antidote employed by teachers at Lowfield is a tactic deliberately aimed at undermining dignity and producing embarassment, shame and degradation. In the pupil's terms it is 'showing them up', and this was by far the most painful experience, the most feared and detested, the biggest outrage against the human person in their school lives.

Naturally, pupils can take their cues from teachers and employ the tactic of humiliating teachers, and through confrontation enhance their reputation with their mates, or at least win approval from and friendship with mates. The strategy is to identify with a group who distance themselves from or openly oppose school values and norms. It becomes play; and play may become serious. The form of the identity may be expressed as 'style'. Willis (1977:12) writes that style 'is lived out in countless small ways which are special to the school institution, instantly recognised by the teachers, and an almost ritualistic part of the daily fabric of life for the kids.' Or again (p.17):

> Opposition to staff and exclusive distinction from the 'ear 'oles' [the conformist pupils] is continuously expressed amongst 'the lads' in the whole ambience of their behaviour, but it is also made concrete in what we may think of as certain stylistic/symbolic discourses centring on the three great consumer goods supplied by capitalism and seized upon in different ways by the working class for its own purposes: clothes, cigarettes and alcohol. As the most visible, personalized and instantly understood element of resistance to staff and ascendancy over 'ear 'oles' clothes have great importance to 'the lads'. The first signs of a lad 'coming out' is a fairly rapid change in his clothes and hairstyle. The particular form of this alternative dress is determined by outside influences, especially fashions current in the wider symbolic system of youth culture.

Fashion, of course, changes and some of the descriptions given by Willis are not relevant for the fashions of the early 1980s. Nevertheless, the point remains. Fashion, in an active sense, fashions community. Through dress the young fashion the images by which to attract and repel. To censor dress is to violate community; this is as true of punk dress as of Sikh dress; but the latter is legitimized through religion.

Willis' emphasis upon opposition to teachers, however, should not lead us to overlook the fact that even many of the biggest trouble-makers (see my discussion of Darren in chapter 5) could respect some of their teachers. Werthman (1963), for example, showed pupils use criteria employed by any sociologist in assessing the behaviour of others. They employed criteria as to the teacher's fairness in marking assignments, in treating pupils without condescension or authoritarianism and in accepting styles of dress. Similarly, 'hard' pupils in my own study would talk as warmly of teachers who sat down to listen to their problems and hear 'our side of the story' as they talked with hostility against those teachers who 'bawled' and would not listen.

Pupils who reject or accept school may turn their attention to each other in order to reinforce the social distance between each other. This may be done at the level of 'having a laugh' or 'piss taking' or at the level of physical violence. At the first level, those who reject school consider the others to have a boring life, always working. One such pupil said that the 'brainy' pupils thought he and his mates were 'amusin'' in comparison to their boring lives. On the other hand, the 'brainy' pupils complained of the behaviour and stupidness of those who rejected school.

In their games of dominance pupils may use physical violence. Size perhaps more than being brainy or being stupid becomes a focal point for violence. A perceived difference is enough to generate taunts and rough behaviour. Thus one pupil writes, 'I can't stand kids who think they are hard on little kids like me.' Another writes, 'Some kids in school treat me okay; about 1/8 are nasty who bug me and I don't get on with at all.' And: 'I won't get a good report in metal work because I am always getting bullied and I always get found lying on the floor after the bullies have left me there.' Not only has this pupil to put up with the fear of being bullied; he also has to put up with the problem of poor reports brought about through the fear of being bullied. Teachers have little effect upon the bully; the bullied hide and suffer. Few teachers realize the extent of bullying in their schools. The accumulation of pressures can become unbearable as each pressure whittles away at the individual's sense of self-worth and security. I become in the eyes of others – those whom I would like to be like – a diminished, fractured self.

The diminished 'i', the eroded self, being torn from the safety of the background, to be 'torn off a strip' by teachers, parents, mates – all these lead toward experiences of generalized insecurity. The whole world potentially becomes a source of threat rather than, say, nourishment. The growing body requiring nourishment, grows towards the source of nourishment; fearing pain, the body shrinks back, the 'i' becomes a covert shivering creature, defined in terms of what it lacks and cannot have: 'I feel teachers aren't bothered about me because I'm not clever as those in the high set although I am better in certain subjects than them but my English and maths hold me back I have no friends in the high sets because of this problem' (fifth-form boy, written reply). The world no longer facilitates but holds one back from a desired object. One's very body and mind is pinned down by a pressure, locking the self into an undesirable identity and position in the social world. The 'i' becomes an object of derisive attention by powerful others: 'Sometimes teachers go a bit far. It scares me when i hear teachers shout. The girls in the class say,

"Oh look at her getting shouted out." Detentions i don't agree with this is what i dread most of all. People skitting me because i don't get all new clothes when they *do*.' With this fifth-form girl I have retained her use of 'i'; I wish I could present her spidery, faint, so very faint, pencil marks which now are fading from the page. Like others she sees herself as mirrored in the words of others. In the words of others images of the self may be caressed or crushed, reflected accurately or distortedly, consistently or inconsistently. The reflected images shimmer and shift, become confused and confusing: '. . . Most of the teachers treat you alright but some really get on your back when they want to. When you are our age if you ever let yourself slip and start to play around the teachers say if you act like children you will be treated like them this get on my nerves because they treat us like children anyway' (fifth-form boy, written reply). This 16-year-old boy truanted because 'school was getting me down.' At the point of transition between child and adult in the eyes of others nothing seems right: 'Being around my age is rather difficult, you think you are too old for school and too young to know anything about the outside world' (fifth-form boy, written reply).

Self and world are sensuously related. The images of ourselves reflected through the words of others bring pain or pleasure; we know the world through the pain and pleasure it affords us. If the world hurts us so much and so consistently, we fear it, our world of safety crumbles, falls to pieces. Becoming like others, therefore, is not easy, particularly if the others reject us or if counter-cultures develop against us. If becoming like others is not easy or not desired, manipulating others may be a useful alternative strategy.

2 Manipulating Others

To manipulate others one must bring them under one's power. To bring others under our manipulative reach we may use sheer force or attract, enchant or charm them. Both Debbie Graves and Darren Bailey are examples of the manipulative use of attraction. However, one may not always be able to control powers of attraction or live up to the images painted in the minds of others. For example, Ricky is about five foot nine, slim, blond, handsome and 12 years old. His housemaster commented that teachers and pupils expected him to act with a maturity they would not expect of others his age:

... he is middle to low (high band) in terms of ability ... er
... very talented athletically, good kid, very popular with a
lot of the children ... er who physically – I mean more than
obviously, he has sort of outgrown his chronological age and
therefore from what I've seen of him, I think that he is, the
thing that causes him most problems is his immaturity. And I
can't help thinking that many people expect him – many staff
and many kids too – look to him to behave in a much more
mature way than he's ever capable of doing. And whenever
there is trouble around he has the misfortune to be easiest to
spot because of his hair (blond) and his height and therefore
gets clobbered very often even when it's not the case.
Particularly, he does enjoy having a lark, messing around
because I don't think he has yet ever experienced any time
when he's known what it's like to have any satisfaction in
terms of academic achievement, you know. He isn't an
academic child. All his success is in the sporting field and all
his credit is there. And uh one of my biggest battles is kind of
liaising with other teachers....

Attractiveness aids the manipulation of attention to one's self. The
kind of attention that Ricky enjoys from his friends is defined by
teachers as messing about or immaturity. Two contexts are being
created by the manipulative designs of these actors: a context within
which to be attractive; and a context within which attractiveness
must be sublimated to work. A contest results between teacher and
pupil as to who can dominate the attention of the others. When all
else fails teachers may use coercion. The housemaster becomes a
mediator between the actors and the different ways they create
contexts for action and their different purposes.

Generally speaking, attractiveness draws the attention of others
towards oneself. This audience then becomes a context for my own
dramatic importance and defines the roles others are to play in this
drama. The central character knits a collection of people into a
cohesive group of some kind. The degree of cohesion may be fleeting
and unstable, to permanent and stable. Through eye contact, body
posture and gestures a group can be formed and sustained. The
attractive one courts the attention of the audience. The sexual basis to
creating attention and maintaining interest is readily observable
between pupils and teachers and amongst pupils. Those engaged in
courtship move face to face, closing out any third party. Similarly,

groups engaged in a kind of mutual grooming or caressing by eye glances and smiles position their bodies to include or to exclude insiders and outsiders. It is not unusual to observe a silent communication (hidden from the eyes of teachers) through eye contact and gestures. It is not unusual to see girls and boys preening themselves. Nor is it unusual to see continual play or quasi-courtship occurring throughout a lesson. For some children the need to engage in a continual sexual play, or courtship, is very high. After all, learning sex-roles involves learning sexual roles.

For some young people, the learning has a bitter edge. Janet, a second-year pupil I interviewed told me that she had raised the youngest children of the family herself. Her divorced mother left her in charge each evening in order to go out. She had not seen her father for two years. Through the help of the school, a social worker had managed to get the mother to give her two nights off a week to enable her to see him. She believes she will find work in her father's business when she leaves school.

Janet looks very much older than she is. She seeks confrontation by not dressing in uniform and further breaks the rules by wearing and flaunting jewellery and make-up. She is attractive sexually, and aware of it. Throughout the interview (carried out in a group with three of her friends) she continually fiddled with a pen, finally dropped it and made a show of picking it up, pulling the unbuttoned part of her blouse tight over her breasts. This act was repeated twice more. Although she spoke little for the first half of the interview she was clearly the group leader; this fact was communicated by posture and taking more space than the others; she dominated the latter half of the interview.

Previous to the interview I had observed her class for the afternoon. During the lesson, while the teacher was there, she did her work without trouble, chatting like most of her friends. She was, however, plainly bored. When the teacher, a housemaster, left the class to attend to a problem elsewhere, trouble immediately erupted. Janet playfully chased other girls, lifting up their skirts with a large, yard-long ruler. The game continued for about a quarter of an hour. When the teacher returned, the class settled. Janet continued her play covertly, by 'walking' her fingers up another girl's legs beneath the table.

Afterwards in the interview she referred to the way the class behaved, 'We always do that when he leaves.' It was clear, however, that she was the prime instigator of the eruption and largely determined its shape. Situations are managed to bring about a drama in which she can manipulate sexual roles.

Generally speaking, the one who manipulates another transforms that other into an object, dominating the other. The other may either acquiesce, actively encourage, or resist the other and engage in a battle of wills. In such a battle the protagonists become repulsive to each other and each must make the enemy repulsive to others. The effect on the protagonists of such a battle may be to leave them emotionally torn. The life of each becomes enveloped in an atmosphere of threat, suspicion and insecurity.

A feud developed between two third-year girls, Janine and Christine, which illustrates many of the strategies young people may use when they feel under threat; strategies which find their more sophisticated expression in adult cold wars and propaganda aimed at the character assassination of individuals, groups and nations. Janine, after receiving what she believed to be a threat, felt terrified. With a friend, Mary Williams, she came into the housemaster's office, eyes red with crying, saying, 'I'll give you one guess.' The feud had a history. Janine believed Christine was out to get her; Mary had heard Christine say so. Mr Brown, her housemaster, called into his office Christine and her two sisters. He felt that the problem involved the entire family. In describing the sisters he said: '... the mum's a jailbird – I say that but I don't let it influence me. She's always come into the school when I've asked her. The sixth former and the two others have been shop lifting. Of course, they deny it. It's a real nest of worms that lot. It all filters out into the community.'

The problem with feuds is that they seem to have no beginning; there is always an earlier violation which one or the other of the protagonists can point to in trying to establish first causes and blame. This makes it difficult for a neutral third party to find the truth, or to resolve the conflict. Faced with the problem, many would simply give up. Many would feel that school time was too valuable to waste upon such trivia. Mr Brown took the problem seriously and spent an entire morning attempting to resolve it. His strategy was typical of many I observed when housemasters or others were trying to establish the truth of some incident. First the facts of the case would be determined, then inconsistencies were examined, then a confession would be sought. The pupil strategy would typically involve, as will be seen in the next section, giving as little information as possible and protesting innocence. The central fact for this incident became whether Christine had talked to Janine's friend who in turn had told Janine that Christine was out to get her. People become tied by insinuations and unclear messages carried by others. Passions are enflamed upon a whisper. The one who tries to unravel such knots must patiently secure each intricate thread. Mr Brown makes the position clear to Christine, who maintains she had not delivered a threat to Janine via Mary:

> *Brown:* I'll ask Mary, if she's spoken to you this morning or if you've spoken to her. You're *sure* about that fact, that you haven't spoken to her?
> *Christine:* Yeah.
> *Brown:* You are? If you have spoken to her....
> *Christine:* Sir, when I walked in....
> *Brown:* Um, let me explain: if you have spoken to her, then on four or five or six occasions now you have deliberately tried to deceive me.

After clarifying his position twice more Mr Brown says he will send Christine home if she has been lying to him. Finally, Christine admits to having said to Mary, 'Jenny's at the bottom gate.' Jenny is a girl from another school. Thus Christine herself is just a link in a longer chain. After further questioning, Shirly, the sixth-form sister, reveals:

> *Shirly:* Jenny's 'sposed to be gettin' 'er, an' she did get 'er.
> *Brown:* Jenny's supposed to be gettin' her? What for?
> *Shirly:* I dunno.

Finally Christine says: 'Sir, Janine's 'sposed to be gettin' some girls down 'cos Jenny's goin' to get Janine.... An' Janine got these girls an' they've sworn to get me and to get Margarite as well.' Christine begins to cry. Her statements become unintelligible. She is a stocky, plain girl and has a popular personality. Her misery seems genuine: 'She's been spittin', in me face....' Through sobs she describes other incidents, none of which she told Mr Brown:

> *Brown:* Do you think she should have told me Shirly?
> *Shirly:* Yes.
> *Brown:* You see, the difficulty now for you Christine is that you ... put the frighteners out this morning again....
> *Christine:* Sir, I didn't do that....
> *Brown:* Oh yes, oh yes ... whether that's what you wanted

or not I don't know but you did. That's what happened. By mentioning the fact that there was a girl waiting at the gates. . . .

For Christine the statement about the girl at the gates was intended to be a warning and not a threat; or so she told Mr Brown. If this is assumed to be the correct interpretation, there is clearly a disjunction between what Christine intended and what Janine interpreted. In each of the girl's eyes the other has become the evil cause. Laing (1969:110) has commented that 'where there is a disjunction between Peter's self identity . . . and his identity-for-Paul . . . , one is not surprised if Peter reacts with anger, anxiety, guilt, despair, indifference. A disjunction of this kind lends fuel to some relationships. It seems the cement almost, that binds some people together. In this bondage, it is the "issue" they compulsively take up with each other again and again.'

For each of the girls their self identity is in question as the other reflects back an unwanted image. Neither wants to become as the other intends her to be, or interprets her as being. Thus, each has the job of forming a group which will reflect a desired image of herself and will project an undesirable image of the enemy. It is a battle of wills between the two girls.

Confirmation of this was found when Mr Brown called Janine to his office and talked to her. Janine felt alone and shown up by Christine during class time as her mates were won over by Christine. She had to fight back. However, she does want to be friends with Christine, but:

> *Janine:* I've tried to be good to Christine but in um drama . . . I started talkin' to 'er just bein' friendly an' all that 'cos everyone was talkin' to 'er. . . . She said, 'Why what's it to you?' Like that.
> *Brown:* Well, you see what it is don't you. You both don't want to be the first to uh give way, do you? 'Cos you're dead worried about what you're friends will be thinking, she's dead worried about what her friends'll be. . . . Probably the same friends, yeah?
> *Janine:* . . . Sally tells me to go in an' say somethin' to 'er. . . .

Both Janine and Christine have manipulated the situation to try and get what they want from it. However, they have also been the objects of the manipulations of others. The result of these many levels of manipulation is to create an object, or phenomenon, which does not actually exist, but exists in a counterfeited manner. Brown tries to put this proposition to Janine: 'Almost all of what has gone on has been nothing but mouth, has it? There's not an incident that I can think of where there's been any aggression like fighting except where *you* have uh got aggressive as well with Christine. Yes?'

Janine tried to think of some incidents but found none. She recalled being shouted at by Christine and friends from a passing bus; she recalled shouts from one side of the street to the other when the one approached the other's territory. Janine, in reflecting upon the past incidents, decided she would try to meet Christine, alone, to talk things through. She did this. At least for a while, the trouble between them ceased.

It is not easy to break through such a network of manipulations. Without the help of the housemaster it is unlikely they would have succeeded. Both have learnt something of the power of reflective analysis and the power of talking things through together. It is an important lesson. It is a lesson which can be extended throughout the school; particularly, it could be used when teachers and pupils have disputes. However, the pastoral function of mediation rarely extends to mediating between a teacher and a pupil. School (as is life generally) is an emotional obstacle course; it is a course which requires reflective study if we are to transform it in any meaningful and desirable manner. It is a course of study schools rarely profess to involve themselves in, and rarely are teachers aware of it.

Janine and Christine may stand as archetypes for those who compulsively pick on each other, tearing at each other's sense of security with the result that each feels victimized. Each is a central actor in the drama which in part they themselves construct, and each lost control of it. Without the help of the housemaster, neither got what they most wanted – security, friendship, leadership.

It is useful to indicate the similarity of the above drama to the classroom situation. Us-Them strategies serve as control techniques and preserve self-identities. As Payne and Hustler (1980:53) show, it is a part of a teacher's professional expertise to manipulate or manage a collection of pupils. One such way in which 'the teacher provides for the identification of the pupils as a collectivity is through setting up the interaction as "one against the rest".' For example: 'By telling the pupils that no one is to sit down until they are *all* ready the teacher is indicating to the pupils that no one of them can move until they are all in a similar state of readiness. They have been told that

none of them can act individually' (p.54). Is it any surprise, therefore, if an oppositional pupil culture arises based upon a need for
autonomy and thus involving rebellion? Furthermore, complexities
arise when certain collections of pupils are rewarded by teachers with
high academic marks and are set apart from others to do higher grade
work. Like Christine and Janine, the teachers try to win others over
to their side, in this case, the academic as opposed to the non-
academic (cf. Keddie, 1971). Thus, a teacher may say of one class, 'I
expect you to behave like A pupils not C pupils' (which may be
translated as O-level not CSE pupils, or even fifth-years, not
first-years). To be a low ability pupil is thus an insult in the teacher
language of control techniques. The obvious counter-strategy is to
invert the situation and thus call A-streams (or their equivalents)
poufs, ear 'oles, borin', or soft; and to reject teacher authority
whenever it is an affront to a sense of individuality, autonomy,
dignity. Thus, the pupil who rebels may complain of the teacher
who responds by punishing him or her, that the teacher 'always
picks on me'. To be picked on is to be picked apart by the overall
demands of classroom control techniques. Pupils are controlled by
the labels teachers use, they react perhaps angrily and the labels
multiply – they are maladjusted, troublesome, problem children. To
unravel the knots which tie pupils and teachers is difficult, especially
when teachers do not ackowledge their role in the problem. In the
case of Nicky Wragg (chapter 2) the role of the teachers was not
questioned in producing the problem against which Nicky rebelled.
It was a matter of social control. The authority of the student teacher
had to be supported by the headmaster against Nicky. Hence, Nicky
by definition was in the wrong. However, it is a counterfeit
situation, a created problem where teachers must be seen to be in the
right and throw blame elsewhere – as in the case of Christine and
Janine where each girl sought to throw the blame upon the other – a
case of manipulating reality.

3 Deceiving Others

Deception is a particular form of manipulation. Its most obvious
form is when a pupil denies some accusation that has been made
against him or her. For the teacher attempting to find the truth, it can
be a long and frustrating process. Deception is a pervasive phenomenon and may be carried out within a climate of deception to

which school itself contributes. School generates a climate of distrust simply by encouraging authoritarian surveillance procedures: classes must be supervised, pupils are not able to leave lessons without permission (preferably written), pupils must be continually engaged in the work demanded by teachers; to protect themselves, to create space for day dreaming, chatting and playing, they must lie: 'Oh, yes sir, I am *working!*'

Some pupils, like most adults, become adept at lying. By the time they reach the fourth or fifth year, school has provided them with enough opportunities to become masters of the craft. It requires a steadfast attitude and the ability to remain silent or give little away under pressure:

> *Paul:* Got taken to the houseblock and we got questioned. People had to stand outside the houseblock looking in while the other one got questioned so no one would discuss things to make them up.
> *J.F.S.:* What was that like – what did it feel like?
> *Paul:* It was terrible. I mean it was really frightening 'cos, because Mr Green our housemaster then, he'd been a police fellow or something, and he had this, regrettably, reputation for shouting. And he did shout a lot. He was big. And it just frightened yer. . . . You get questioned and eventually we gave in. . . . I know we were lying, obviously we were lying and then eventually all our stories were wrong because we couldn't plan one 'cos we were just looking in the window. It was obvious to him right from the beginning probably. But we just wouldn't give in and he couldn't prove it and eventually . . . we did, we gave in.

Paul, at the time of the interview, was a sixth-former with every chance of going to university. He was recalling an incident, with detached amusement, which occurred in his first year at the school. Despite the time lapse, Paul has mentioned most of the features common to the incidents I observed where lying was alleged to occur. A bright boy, well liked, kept off the night time streets by his parents and finding many school activities and lessons enjoyable, for him the incident of lying receded in importance, became trivial, became an amusing anecdote. His self-respect was easily reconstructed along lines which did not violate but indeed revelled in the school norms. In the following incident Dave reveals what happens when a pupil does not give in. (A girl has been threatened, had some sweets and some money stolen. The culprits have been brought by the housemaster, Mr Downy, to be interrogated by one of the deputy heads. The deputy sums up the allegations

Deputy: ... it's causing actual bodily harm, mm it's also theft, one of a variety of theft charges. Right, now, all I've got to do, pick up the phone, pass over to the police the evidence that we've got from the various witnesses that Mr Downy has named. It's not merely you but Benny an' all, get run in for robbery with violence, right? Now, um it seems to me Dave that.... Even *Thommo* says you were there!... What's the point? And what Mr Downy has said to you [is], 'Look, I'm prepared to deal with this as a housemaster, sort it out quietly between us. The girl gets her things back, you get a punishment for thumpin' her, you great daft twerp. And stay away from the gate, you're a fifth year, you're here to work, make that your last mistake.' Or words to that effect. And I'd be very happy if Mr Downy wants to deal with you in that way. But when it's to be dealt with in that way it requires everybody involved to cooperate. Now Mr Downy's cooperating, Benny's cooperating – you're not.

Downy: If I was to bring these two girls along – you quite happy about that?

Dave: Sir, no.

Downy: What would you say if they pointed to you?

Dave: Sir, I was there but I had nowt to do with them.

Downy: Oh but, you know, that 'as changed 'asn't it?

Deputy: Ah, it's that game now.

Downy: You *were* down by the gate. Two minutes ago you were prepared to sort of stake everything on the line that you weren't by the gate.

Dave: [Untranscribable] are gettin' at me.

Downy: ... I ... I haven't *blamed* you for anything.

Dave: Sir, we 'ave been blamed.

Downy and Deputy: [Speaking together – untranscribable – tone suggests amazement.]

Downy: ... two girls have blamed *you* and *him*. I've presented that to you. One girl has got a swellin' below her eye. She claims to have lost 50 pence. She was in a distressed state, went to her housemistress. She's got

> sweets missing. And two fifth year boys who she knows –
> admittedly the girl's about-four-sheets-to-the-wind, I
> know it. But she's not mistaken about being jostled and
> pulled about by two fairly big fifth year boys.
> *Dave:* Sir, after that she came up to us and said, 'Did you see
> 50 pence?'
> *Downy:* Uhu....
> *Dave:* She just walked up to us, we were sittin' on the
> gate....
> *Downy:* What, what, what *is* the truth?

Dave, defending his alleged lies against the combined onslaught of
Mr Downy and the deputy head, was essentially secure enough in his
self to resist the onslaught. However, he has chosen different values
to those of Paul, values which had continually led him to violate
official school norms. Dave had held out despite the overwhelming
evidence against him. His teachers wanted him to give in and
reconstruct his identity more in line with official school norms. He
did not. He appeared secure in himself. The battle of wills came to
stalemate.

Other pupils are not so secure. When someone is called a liar the
authenticity of the personal relations between the actors is being
questioned. It is not simply 'This statement is a lie' but '*You* are a
liar.' The self is diminished in the eyes of the other. However, the lies
themselves may be a necessary cover under which one builds and
projects a self-image to others, a self-image one considers to be one's
authentic self. In the following example two boys go through a
persistent cycle of denials and counter-denials, accusations and
counter-accusations where the self is under threat. (Two girls have
accused Harry and Brian of stealing and of threatening.)

> Joe, the housemaster, stares steadily at Harry. 'So, when I ask
> the girls they'll say it wasn't you but Brian. Is that right,
> Harry? Now, before you answer, think! Think! Think!'
> 'It wasn't me. It was 'im.'
> After a 'grilling' Brian denies Harry's charge and accuses
> Harry. Harry is recalled for a second 'grilling'. Joe recalls
> how Harry had lied once before and had even had to wait in a
> prison cell while the truth of the matter was sorted out. He
> recalled how this had upset Harry's mother who was under-
> going the torment of her eldest son being sent to remand
> centre. Joe recalled too, how it seemed to him Harry's

mother treated Harry as her favourite son. Harry's face seems to melt seems to leave nothing underneath as tears fall. Harry accepts he had been involved in the stealing but denies stealing one of the items, a pen. After a similar episode Brian admits to stealing the pen. Harry, however, denies threatening the girls. Brian also denies threatening the girls. Harry suddenly says, 'He stole some headphones last term.'

Brian looks aggrieved, 'I did not.'

Joe acts surprised. 'So, there are headphones now! And what else have you been up to?'

'He stole some exercise books,' says Brian.

At this point the girls are called in and the boys sent out. After the girls' testimony each of the boys begin the cycle over again by denying they had anything to do with any stealing. The performance is repeated three further times in front of the deputy head and then in front of their parents. All the adults involved become thoroughly exasperated by the situation. Whenever a confession is made, even the confession is later denied as having ever occurred. The boys cry and are obviously upset. Neither of the boys was treated by the housemasters as being evil, or cunning, but as being 'pathetic little boys' who did not seem to understand the gravity of the situation. The boys were going to be punished, that had been made clear. They could gain nothing in terms of reduction by persisting in denying. At no time did they simply 'give in', each partial confession had to be clawed from them only to be revoked moments later. Throughout they were under enormous emotional stress. Furthermore, the denials and accusations did not seem to impair their friendship and within a matter of days both boys had again been involved in a similar incident of petty theft.

Harry is a 'happy-go-lucky' fellow who is typically smiling and light-hearted. Brian is perhaps quieter. Both had likeable personalities. These likeable personalities were under threat. This suggests that a valued image of the self was being eroded by the teachers which continually had to be recreated. However, set against this was another valued image of the self, the image of being one of the 'lads', that is, an individual to be reckoned with; such a model was already supplied by the father of one of the boys, Harry, who, in fights, was a man to be 'reckoned with', and by Harry's elder brother.

It would seem the lies told by these pupils become a part of that fabric by which to construct their authentic self, that is, that desired self which is presented to others as the *real* self underneath the poses and the roles. It is perhaps another matter the extent to which the authentic self as presented is the same as the self as experienced. Growing up to become a self respected by all is not easy, particularly when others pull you in different directions.

The situation is yet more complex. There is a sense in which relations between teachers and pupils generally are counterfeited. That is to say, roles, feigned attitudes, emotions and beliefs come between the real self of the teacher and the real self of the pupil. By real self I refer to that experienced difference between the self-image as presented to others and the self-image reflected upon in the silence of the mind. Within such a generalized climate of counterfeit relations, what strategies must young people develop to retain a sense of authenticity? And how may one act in ways which are not counterfeited? The work done at school, produced by rote, produced from textbook recipes, carried out half-heartedly at best – how can this be other than counterfeit work on counterfeit products?

When relationships and work are counterfeit, all that remains is to negotiate the extent to which one engages in such relationships and work. Such negotiation in school becomes a model for negotiation of relationships and work output and quality in adult life in offices, factories and other places of waged work, where the work product is of little or no interest intrinsically to the worker. It is not unusual to find that pupils in class have hardly listened to the teacher and require constant prodding to complete their class work. (For examples, see chapter 3 and the description of Jacko's day leading up to the classroom fight.) Teachers differ in their power to prevent trouble in class. Many will have to put up with a certain amount of noise and unworklike behaviour simply because they cannot command total silence and work effort from the pupils. Even where a teacher can command something like total silence and can command high levels of apparent work effort, there is frequently a strange disparity between the effort and the quality of the product. For example, one young teacher had no trouble in gaining silence and the apparent attention of his pupils. His lessons were always trouble-free and pupils worked to his command, never daring to mess around. After what appeared to be a perfect lesson where pupils 'discussed' a topic in religion, he set them some work to do.

The discussion period had consisted of the teacher asking a series of questions which the pupils answered. These are top-set first-year pupils regarded as being the best the school has ever had. During the discussion part the teacher asked forty-three questions, the pupils asked fourteen and gave forty-eight answers. Typically, the teacher would affirm (twenty-seven times) the correctness of a response, deny (five times) or instruct (twenty-two times) or give answers to questions concerning primarily requests for information (twenty-six times). The discussion was purely functional in trying to see how much the pupils knew; none of the questions placed in doubt the status of the knowledge being transmitted by the teacher. The teacher gave the following instruction for the second part of the lesson:

> First thing, your first subheading is 'Immaculate Conception' [he points to the board where he has written the subheading]. That's your main heading [he points to the other side of the board which is 'Mary the Mother of God']. Write down what you think Immaculate Conception means. We've discussed it. Think of the words [points to the board] before you go ahead and write it. What the word immaculate means in everyday ... terms and what the word conception means in everyday terms. Think of these. That's your first subheading. Can you do that now?

Immediately, the pupils settle to write. One boy says he has already done the task but the teacher disagrees and points to the blackboard to prove the fact. The teacher walks around. And within a few seconds one pupil says: 'What are we going to write about immaculate conception sir?' Within the next few minutes several other pupils ask what they are supposed to be doing, or whether what they are doing is right. Finally, after having devoted something like a quarter of an hour to the task in hand the teacher asks the class to put their pens down and asks pupils in turn to read out what they've written. Two examples are:

1 Immaculate conception means born without sin and spotless. Mary is the only person we know of who was born without sin.
2 Immaculate Conception is Mary and no one else. Today is her feast day. And we should think that she was the only person who was born without original sin. When she was born she was totally unable to sin for her nature did not know how to.

The lesson, of course, was carried out in a Catholic school. However, apart from the unquestioning acceptance that the above is 'fact', neither example (nor any of the others) actually conforms to the teacher's original instruction of writing what the words mean in *everyday* language. The teacher was satisfied with the examples quoted. Furthermore, from a 'discussion' lasting approximately forty minutes the written content and the understanding it produced seem of dubious quality from the best, brightest pupils the school has.

It seems that there is an underlying fabric of falsity to teacher-pupil relations which leads to the pupil strategy of negotiating the degree of his or her involvement in the production of work during class time. The negotiated position involves presenting an impression of hard work. The collusion, if it is successful, will present an illusion of steady achievement by the pupils, with no one seriously questioning the importance and standard of the work being done – at least in class time. Woods (1978) has examined some elements in the process of such negotiation:

> Schoolwork is ... unreal for many pupils, and they duly transform it into something more meaningful – play or sociation. In this form they can live with it, even enjoy it. But work of the old-fashioned order has lost its structural supports and its accomplishment therefore will not be a result of a pure state of application, but a product of negotiation, bartering, adapting, manoeuvring.

What kind of self and what kind of sense of individuality is it that might arise in such a situation?

Both teacher and pupils stand in a false relation one to another, towards the process of education and toward knowledge (where knowledge may be conceived as critical reflection upon experience, the celebration of understanding, and the feeling of wonder in the face of creation). In such a situation, it is not the exploration of reality, nor the creation of products of intrinsic worth that become the everyday work of education but the management of impressions, the weaving of disarming deceits, and the juggling of identities as between groups.

Birksted (1976:21), in a case study of a 15-year-old boy, showed how this boy, Andrew, managed his identity as between a conformist identity for parents and teachers and a 'one of the lads' identity for his mates. It is a recipe for what might be termed social schizophrenia:

> Thus Andrew's life is split between 'becoming sensible' and 'having a laugh'. Accordingly he plays a double game, presenting himself as 'sensible' to the adult world and as enjoying 'having a laugh' to his peers. He appears to be on everybody's side. This means, of course, that he is first of all on his own side. His best interest is to be accepted by all. He thus gets popularity from his peers and better results from the school.

Andrew appears to be fairly secure within himself. Others, as we have seen, are not so secure. For Andrew, the exercise of managing impressions allows him to juggle identities from a position of strength. For others, the juggling may result in the experience of being torn, or of being but a fool in the hands of Fate. In any case, deception becomes a way of life in attempting to deal with counterfeited relations and counterfeited work. Growing up to become a self respected by all is not easy: sometimes we will need to be alone to think things through.

4 Avoiding Others

Most people at some time or another need to be alone: to think things through; to escape or rest from problems and pressures; to hide from hostile people; or to enjoy the feeling of solitude. Privacy may be thought of as a right by many people. Privacy, however, is not a right enjoyed by pupils. They are compelled to be with others, compelled to be supervised, monitored and assessed. Adults attempt to invade their inner thoughts, attempt to assess the ways they define their own experiences, and to transform those experiences in ways acceptable to adults. Avoiding others therefore must take into account the ways others feel it their right to invade privacy, to destroy solitude and to compel the individual to be a member of an anonymous crowd. Avoiding others, therefore, frequently involves various forms of deceit because it must break a number of social rules, norms and laws in order to be attained.

One pupil, a fifth-year girl, finds truancy a useful strategy:

> I think that school is good but sometimes it's not. People can annoy you and you can say you hate school for this. I don't

mind being 16 but sometimes i can get so fed up that whenever anybody talks to me i get annoyed with them and it's not their fault. When i'm like this i only want to be by myself. That was when i usually bunk to be by myself.

The 'I' diminished – I have retained her change from 'I' to 'i' – and only solitude brings the necessary escape from pressure.

In a questionnaire I gave just over 50 per cent of the fifth-years admitted to truanting more than once (most of these were on a regular basis). Comparison with a figure of 15 per cent for the third-years suggested a progressively developing problem. Reasons for truanting given by just over 70 per cent of the truants involved at best a dislike, at worst a downright hatred, of school, lessons and teachers. The remainder involved such reasons as bullying or simply feeling too lazy to come to school or being lured by spring sunshine (or a warm bed during winter). (These results were first presented in 'The Black Side of School', in *The TES*, 25 June 1982).) Truanters are primarily people under pressure. *The TES* (18 September 1981) reported research by the University of Sheffield's Department of Education:

> Its investigation revealed that poor attenders often came from homes which were financially deprived, where parents were unemployed, suffered from chronic ill-health or depression.
> 'Many of the children were absent because of responsibilities at home or because they were under such stress that school attendance became irrelevant,' adds the Nuffield Foundation.

According to White (1980:1):

> The attendance of some youngsters at their local comprehensive schools is zero. A row of noughts fills the ten spaces in the register each week. At fifteen, after ten years of schooling, some youngsters have gained almost nothing from the experience on offer.
> Three years ago, in a national survey conducted for the DES, it was estimated that in just one week, 800,000 pupils had been 'absent without good cause'. The irony of those inverted commas should not be lost on those of you who work with truanting children, and those who know that very often there is plenty of cause for their absence.

Many have a great deal of cause. One such boy was Billy. His housemaster considered him 'very strange, very interesting'. Billy was just half-way through his first year at the school. During junior school the memorable incident was that he had thrown a knife and had truanted. Sometime during junior school the boy had had psychological assessment but the parents would no longer hear of such help. The reason for the original help was as follows. The boy was being bullied. One incident involved 'being tied up to a tree and having dog shit smeared over him, on his mouth, and just kept there. And he also had broken glass put into his pants and he walked around all day like that. He hadn't dared to tell the teachers.' After a moment's reflection the teacher added, 'Also, I think, he's a bit slow and his dad's a bit over protective. You know, even pointing a finger at the boy is interpreted as "poking". He's also very good at irritating people – pupils and teachers. When told off he's one of those boys who smiles.' (Incidently, my own son told me that his strategy for getting his own back on teachers who tell him off is to 'smile' – he found it extremely effective.) The housemaster, very kindly, very 'motherly', said, 'Once he just poured out everything to me. You know, this is a boy, a first-year who is already hardened to police questioning. I was questioning him about some trouble and so I thought it'd just be water off his back. But in just quietly getting him to talk, without threats, he poured out his tale.'

This is a boy just 11 years old, hardened by emotional scars, damming up the pain. A gentle housemaster encourages him to talk and through the fissures and tears of his emotional defences the story pours out. The housemaster cannot begin to deal with the real problem: those social forces which are systematically tearing him apart, systematically crushing him.

It is strange to think that the boy is defined as needing psychological help when the source of his worst problems did not arise within him. School presented him – in the form of bullies – with an overwhelming problem. It is a wonder such pupils survive at all. In recognizing this fact, one tutor told me of a first-year girl, Hannah. The mother was taking the child of a neighbour and Hannah's younger sister for a walk and as they were crossing the road a car ran them down and killed the neighbour's child. The neighbours began to blame her, saying she should have been more careful. Hannah is just one in a tutor group of twenty-eight, at least ten of whom, the tutor says, have deep problems, with the remainder needing and demanding attention because 'they're a bit immature' – tutor work lasts approximately twenty minutes per day. The tutor commented upon Hannah as follows:

> Um.... Family background is such that she should be.... I don't know where she should be ... if, if I'd gone through what she'd gone through in the first eleven years of her life I think I'd have been in um some form of mental institution. She's just gone through absolute hell. She's gone through a divorce, um ... a very traumatic divorce. She's been in a children's home. She's uh a continual bed wetter. Her family's split now. Her brothes are living with, with her father. She's living with her mother and her sister's still in care. Um two weeks ago there was a road accident [the tutor gives the details as above]. Her mother was in court yesterday listening to her brother being charged with the murder of [one person] and sexually assaulting a girl.... Her mother hasn't tried to protect her at all. She's quite open with it. So is it any wonder the child wets the bed? It has, must have, it doesn't show particularly.... Hannah's not that ... doesn't particularly demand attention as much as some children do....

All this is taken in, remaining unexpressed. And school proceeds as normal with all the daily demands for discipline. Hannah maintains an outer calm, a calm which her tutor believes masks an inner turmoil of which bedwetting is a minor symptom. Her problems, perhaps, are held within the privacy of her nightmares.

Hannah is just 11 years old. Like many other pupils, she faces problems her teachers can barely contemplate and have probably never experienced. The teachers have little chance to help even if they are aware of the problems. Behind masks the players in the daily school drama tantalizingly reveal or conceal their inner intentions, their vulnerable inner selves. The growing individual – like Hannah, like Billy, like Jacko, like Debbie, like Darren – is confronted with a parade of images, reflections of images and distortions of images. Each source of image identifies for the individual the good, the beautiful, the right and the desirable. Day by day the individual learns the extent to which he or she has what the other wants, or *is* what the other wants. Although there may be a knowledge of alternative identities, behaviours and courses of action, choices will be shaped by the powers of the other in relation to the powers of the self. This power is based upon the power to give or to withhold (or to reveal or to conceal). The choice between giving and withholding implies two major forms of growing up (and hence strategies of growing up): growing up to become what others want; growing up to deny what others want. To get what one wants, however, one may *seem* to be growing up to become what the other desires, or *seem* to deny what the other desires. By playing with the desires of the other, the skilful player becomes enchanting, alluring, tempting, teasing; the clumsy player becomes a fool, pathetic, ineffectual, a pawn.

School is a place where people learn to grow up within constraints not of their making. It is a place where they meet adults who act not entirely of their own volition but who embrace the impersonal authority of the role they are hired to play out. For many young people the game is learnt and the social reproduction of inequality and power structures is assured by unreflective consumer-employees moulded by school. Sometimes, however, a rebellion flares; the inner rage is vented; the nightmarish screams are brought to daylight. This is when we must turn to the violent solution and examine its implications and its social functions.

8   The Violent Solution

In 1981 the nationwide street disturbances came as a 'surprise' (cf. Schostak, 1983a) to many, but such violence has a long history. Many, including senior government ministers, saw the root causes of the violence as a breakdown of traditional morality, and particularly of traditional forms of school discipline (for example, 'Teaching in a Vacuum', in *The Daily Telegraph*, 11 July 1981.) Almost incredibly, in the spring of 1982 a so-called 'riot' occurred in a primary school – St Saviours in Toxteth – where the teachers reportedly lost control of the pupils (see *New Society*, 4 March 1982). However, such eruptions by their infrequency may disguise rather than reveal the endemic and pervasive nature of violence in our society (cf. Tutt, 1976). Unlike deviance, violence has official, legalized and, indeed, heavily government funded forms (organized violence in the form of military aims and actions). Similarly, from a research point of view at least, violence in schools cannot be defined exclusively in terms of 'pupil violence'. Thus in February 1982 the European Court of Human Rights ruled that Britain was wrong to allow corporal punishment in schools if it is against the parent's wishes. On the other hand, there are pupil assaults against teachers which teacher unions are now monitoring. For example, the Leeds branch of the 'National Association of Schoolmasters/Union of Women Teachers, reports seventy-three recorded assaults on staff by pupils during the school year 1981/82, and 178 recorded incidents of abusive behaviour towards staff by pupils' (*TES*, 26 November 1982). Schools are under pressure.

Why Does Violence Occur?

Violence is frequently thought of as an extreme form of aggression and aggression is thought of as an instinct; hence, violence is thought of as having an instinctual basis. Thus, the argument often runs, man is essentially (because instinctually) destructive. Such notions key into many religious views of the inherent corruption of the flesh. It also keys into the Darwinian notion of the 'survival of the fittest' and the 'struggle for existence'. However, this notion has been demonstrated to have been derived from the classical economic view of man and society rather than *vice versa* (see Harris, 1968). At the other pole, we find the biological work of Kropotkin (1904) who established the principle of 'non-aggression' in nature which was based upon extensive observations. Kropotkin postulated an 'instinct of cooperation' or 'mutual aid', viewing aggression as largely between species rather than within species. Indeed, Fromm (1974) has attempted to demonstrate the thesis that man is not naturally destructive but that social conditions pervert man's nature. Fromm, like others, has distinguished between two forms of aggression, the benign or defensive aggression, and malignant (or destructiveness and cruelty). The first is instinctual and has survival value, the second is caused through repressive or inhuman social structures. This is a departure from Freud, whose notion of Thanatos (or a death instinct) is perhaps the most pessimistic expression of the innateness of human destructiveness. It is a thesis which researchers (including most psychoanalysts) have preferred to overlook, or reject (cf. Jacoby, 1975). Since historians (cf. Tutt, 1976) tell us violence has been pervasive and endemic throughout history, and with the modern stockpiling of nuclear devices and the propensity for nations to war amply demonstrated during this century, Freud's thesis is difficult to reject.

Yet, Freud also saw a positive aspect to violence. In *Civilization and its Discontents* (1979 ed.) Freud argued that it was upon the violent act of rebellion by the Brothers against the Father that civilization was founded. It seems to me, however, that in the formulation of Thanatos Freud overlooked a socio-political dimension, the dimension of the individual within a social context and the expression of individual 'rights', or self-assertion within a group. Nisbet (1976) has argued that our modern nations are founded upon a military model of society (rather than kinship or tribal, or religious forms of community) and that the state has successively usurped the traditional 'rights' and 'powers' of the family and church, granting 'rights' to individuals only under state law. Deviance then becomes a violation of state laws (or more broadly, a violation of state approved cultural norms). The inverse of this is that state laws are (or were) a violation of kinship, tribal and religious norms, power, and rights. Thus, for example, CCCS (1981:25) can write of compulsory education that it 'was certainly a breach of the father's right to dispose of the labour of his children' and that this led to resentment against compulsory education amongst many of the lower classes. Resistance or rebellion against such violations of such 'rights' may then be interpreted not as destructive but as a constructive form of aggressive, an assertion of 'rights'. Consequently, Sorel (1915) could advocate violence in the pursuit of political rights. According to Proudhon, of course, all externally imposed laws violate individuality. Thus, we may begin to develop an existential definition of violence as a violation not of norms by the individual but as a violation of the individual by externally imposed norms. Violence, it would seem, is like beauty, in the eye of the beholder – the norm-maker.

Violence occurs when the 'I want' meets the 'You can't' and neither force will submit. The violent individual and the violent gang are quite normal – a part of family and social life. As Gelles and Straus (1979) state:

> With the exception of the police and the military, the family is perhaps the most violent social group, and the home the most violent social setting, in our society. A person is more likely to be hit or killed in his or her home by another family member than anywhere else or by anyone else. Nearly one out of every four murder victims in the United States is a family member. Similarly, in Africa, Great Britain, and Denmark the greatest proportion of murders are intra-familial.

Perhaps we should recall R.D. Laing's (1967:24) statement that 'normal men have killed perhaps 100,000,000 of their fellow normal men in the last fifty years.' We should also recall that 'normal' people – among them world leaders – will argue forcefully that peace in the Western world depends upon the strategy of nuclear deterence based on 'Mutually Assured Destruction' or MAD.

If we focus only upon criminal violence, a claim can be made that there are subcultures of violence. Wolfgang and Ferracuti (1967:263) write:

> ... our thesis contains principally the notion that the man from a culture system that denounces the use of interpersonal violence will be restrained from using violence because of his

positive perspective that conforms to his value system, not because of a negation of it. The absence of that kind of value system is hardly likely to be a vacuous neutrality regarding violence. Instead, it is replaced by a value system that views violence as tolerable, expected, or required. As we approach that part of the cultural continuum where violence is a requisite response, we also enter a subculture where physically aggressive action can quickly and readily bleed into aggressive crime.

Since our culture does not 'denounce the use of interpersonal violence' universally, it is clear the authors are writing about certain kinds of violence under certain circumstances – primarily working-class criminal violence. The writers make a case that homicides and assaultive crimes are overwhelmingly attributable to the lowest social classes (p. 261) and negroes (p. 264) as well as relatives, close friends, same ethnic group and so on.

Toch (1972:38) takes the view that one should place violent men in their social context where 'violence is at least a two man game.' He takes as his basic psychological unit of study the 'violent incident' which is 'an interaction which begins when one person approaches another with some purpose in mind and ends in an act of aggression' (p. 69). However, for our purposes 'act of aggression' is still too narrow. What constitutes an 'act of aggression'? And do all acts of aggression result in an experience of participating in violence or being violated or violating someone? For an act to be considered as violent it must be interpreted and/or experienced as such by *at least one* of the participators. At an existential level – in the gut, the bones, the heart – one feels torn, raped, violated. There is a pain which perhaps cannot be articulated. However, the images of those involved in the felt sense of violation, their acts, their words, their postures remain. Such images may stay personal, never finding expression in communication to others. Perhaps the imagination plays with the images at night, in dreams. If communication becomes possible, images become shared. They may be shared in conversation as anecdotes or may come to serve an almost mythic purpose. This matrix of violent images, anecdotes, folk tales, myths forms a context within which any future act is interpreted as being violent and becomes communicable to others. As Cohen (1955:53) writes: '"The facts" never simply stare us in the face. We see them always through a glass, and the glass consists of the interests, preconceptions, stereotypes and values we bring to the situation. This glass is our frame of reference.' The frame of reference permeated by the personal images of violent incidents and the anecdotes, the folk tales, the myths shared in conversation or identified with in literature in turn foment a violent imagination. The violent imagination in turn limits the kinds of interpretation which can be made concerning a particular incident or situation. Interpretations in turn influence action. One may then be caught within a cycle involving violent images and actions. It is hard to break out. Cohen (p. 51) writes:

> If we want to explain what people do, then we want to be clear about the nature of human problems and what produces them. As a first step, it is important to recognize that all the multifarious factors and circumstances that conspire to produce a problem come from one or the other of two sources, the actor's 'frame of reference' and the 'situation' he confronts. All problems arise and all problems are solved through changes in one or both of these classes of determinants.

The two classes of determinants however are not entirely distinct. For our purposes the 'situation' involves an initial violent act experienced as such. The image of this act then becomes a part of the 'frame of reference'. The 'frame of reference' then acts to filter interpretations of, and experiences of, other 'situations'. In the previous chapter we saw a few of the strategies young people use in the often precarious process of growing up. Some retain a deep sense of security during this process while others experience being torn. Both the secure and the insecure may use violent means but are likely to interpret acts of violence differently and will certainly experience them differently. Our question, framing the remainder of this chapter is: is violence a reasonable solution? Our answer must take into account the reasons for insecurity and the different interpretations upon the different states of being.

Is Violence a Reasonable Solution?

From the point of view of creating and maintaining social order and deterring aggression from other nations, violence or the threat of violence against those who are perceived as threats to the social order may be considered to be a rational, reasonable and practical solution. Such rational violence as an organizing principle for society is entrenched in both political theory and practice. It permeates all our institutions, including school, and frames the historically dominant forms of child rearing practices. From the point of view of social order arising naturally from some instinct or human propensity for cooperation and mutual aid, rational violence, however, becomes at best superfluous and at worst may become a violation of one's need for community and communal resources. Capitalist social order enforced by rational violence presupposes a community ruled by the impersonal forces of supply and demand with the accumulation of personal wealth in the hands of the few. The community under capitalist social order has no rights to the produce of the community except to the extent to which members are owners. Capitalists have a respect for property rather than people. Cohen (1955:91–2) puts it well when he writes that the capitalist middle-class respect for property:

> includes an emphasis on the *right* of the owner to do as he wishes with his belongings *versus* an emphasis on the *claims* of others who may stand in primary-group relationships to the owner. It includes an emphasis on the explicit consent of the owner prior to the use or conversion of his articles of property *versus* 'helping yourself' with the understanding that the willingness and the obligation to share is implicit in your relationship to the owner. It includes a quasi-sacred attitude toward things, whether others' or one's own or collective property. Things are to be husbanded, treated carefully, not wantonly wasted, carelessly abused or destroyed.

We have a situation of consumption based upon rights of ownership rather than rights of claimants based on needs.

The distribution of goods through market forces in classical economic theory finds its ideal expression in the theory of perfect competition. If all the assumptions of the theory were to be put into practice, it would revolutionize society. For instance, it assumes that both producers and consumers are so numerous that any one decision taken by an individual to buy or sell in the market place will have no effect upon price. In short, no individual was to have monopoly power through wealth or capital. With these assumptions in practice demand and supply would allocate resources, goods and services in ways which best met the wants of people. Any monopoly power would seriously distort the allocation of resources, goods and services.

Even the most cursory glance around the market place will show gross inequalities in the distribution of wealth. Honderich (1976) has classified inequalities in terms of time alive; economic and social life; and political freedoms. For example, of 'time alive' he writes (p. 5): 'About *half the world's population*, . . . have average lifetimes about twenty-nine years shorter than another quarter of the world's population.' More specifically, the lowest social class in England and Wales at age 25 has a life expectancy of 3.5 years less than the top social class. Similarly, in the USA non-whites live about 6.5 years less than whites.

Taking a global view, what attempts have there been to change such inequalities?

> . . . not much more than nothing has been attempted. In 1964 a number of the economically-developed countries pledged to 'contribute' a percentage of their future gross national products to the less-developed countries. This 'contribution' was to include loans and private investment. The figure agreed upon was 1%. Since that time, a number of the countries in question have failed to reach this percentage. None has exceeded it by much. The pledged total of 1% of the gross national products of the developed countries in question has not been met in any year. This is not the *kind* of thing to be kept in mind in considering the question of capability. A better thing is the 'war efforts' of the past.
>
> All of these generalizations about lifetimes have *all* of their importance in the fact they have to do with *individual human experience*. It is a banal truth that typically we escape this proposition, or give it the attention of a moment. It is necessary to come closer to the reality of experience. (pp.: 7–8)

Inequalities violate the quality of a person's life. In Britain, perhaps the most intractable problem is that of the distribution of power and wealth. The Diamond commission in 1976 estimated that the top 1 per cent of the population owned 25 per cent of the personal wealth of the country, with the top 10 per cent owning 60 per cent. If we develop the study of wealth and power we find that although, for example, only about 5 per cent of the population go to public schools and Oxbridge, 47 per cent of MPs, 60 per cent of permanent secretaries, 81 per cent of principal judges, 86 per cent of army officers, 85 per cent of Anglican bishops, and 65 per cent of company chairmen went to public schools. According to *New Society* (22 July 82):

> In 1979, 2.1 million people, living in 1.4 million families, were estimated to have incomes below the official (supplementary benefit) poverty line. That is to say in 1979 one person in six, on this definition, was in poverty. Because the government, due to reasons of cost, cannot afford to publish the yearly figures on poverty, the figures relating to 1981 will not be available until sometime in 1983.

Furthermore, in the *New Statesman* (22 February 1982) we find:

> According to the Central Statistical Office, between 1976 and 1980 the spread of incomes *before* taxes widened and the greater inequality was carried through to incomes after taxes had been levied and benefits paid.
>
> In 1976 the bottom fifth of the population's original and final income stood at 0.8 per cent and 7.6 per cent of the national total respectively. In 1980 the equivalent figures were 0.5 per cent and 6.8 per cent. The top fifth's original and final income stood at 44.5 per cent and 37.5 per cent respectively in 1976. By 1980 this had widened to 45.5 and 38.8 per cent.

As the poor have become poorer, the rich have become richer. The figures for the period following 1980 are likely to be much worse. In July 1982 there was unemployment of 3,190,621 which was the highest since records began – unemployment was 13.4 per cent of the working population. According to the Department of Employment's *Gazette* in January 1979 355,000 people were unemployed for more than one year but in January 1982 this figure and risen to 906,000. Against such facts of social and economic life those who are not a part of the power and wealth elites feel powerless to bring change towards a more equitable society; and those who are a part of the power and wealth elites have a vested interest in maintaining the present levels of inequality.

Schools are predominantly organized to perpetuate inequality. The extensive system of examinations separates winners from losers; the state and independent schools separate the upper and lower classes. Research has shown how social class bias, sex bias and racial discrimination are endemic in the school system. Schools are not organized to bring change. In a democratic society they are not even organized to give pupils the experience of democratic control over their lives.

The comprehensive system was an innovation which did not seriously make fundamental changes to education. All the old evils of streaming – covertly or overtly – continued to exist; social mixing was minimal; the success of such schools progressively depended upon the extent to which they could send one or two of their pupils to Oxbridge and others to universities who would not otherwise have had a chance under the tripartite system of secondary modern, grammar school and technical school. But this cannot be a serious criterion of success for the thousands who did not reach such heights.

When headmasters do seriously try to bring about change they become political targets. If such headmasters are also politically inept or brash they are likely to be ousted from their schools, as seems to have been the case with Risinghill (Berg, 1968) and Tyndale. The American experience of innovators also seems to be primarily negative (Kohl, 1974). Teachers who try to bring about less authoritarian styles of teaching, unless they are very skilful, appear to fall foul of the traditional expectations of both pupils and colleagues of what a teacher ought to be (Smith, 1977). Sharpe and Green (1975) have also argued that progressive techniques introduced into primary schools are shaped by the economic power structures outside the school. It would seem that significant change is unlikely, and if it occurs is rare. On this theme Jules Henry (1971:20) has written:

A bureaucracy is a hierarchically organized institution whose purpose is to carry out certain limited functions. Thus a school system, the army, a university, the government, are all bureaucracies. It is common knowledge, however, that bureaucracies have three functions, rather than one. Although the first is ostensibly to carry out the tasks for which they were established, the definition of roles and the routinization of procedures in bureaucracies brings it about that an important function of the organization becomes that of preventing anything within it from changing. Even small change might make it necessary for the entire organization to change because each part is so interlocked with every other, that to alter any procedure in a bureaucracy without changing the rest is often like trying to increase the height of one wall of a house without modifying its entire configuration. A third function of a bureaucracy is to perpetuate itself, to prevent itself from disappearing. Given the functions of preventing internal change and struggling to survive, bureaucracies tend to devote much of their time to activities that will prevent change.

As Henry points out, all are vulnerable within the large bureaucracy which is overlooked and supervised by bureaucrats in other bureaucracies. Those who deviate from the expected are likely to be punished in some way, whether they be headmaster, teachers or pupils. Henry goes on to say that 'the history of American education in the last hundred years, as set forth cogently by my colleague, Professor Callahan, shows that education has not considered the child's interest but that of industry; and I am not yet convinced that what is good for General Motors is good for our children.'

Is it not possible that through the violent assertion of individual will, constructive change may take place? Is it not possible that individuals may cooperate violently to end inequality? Honderich (1976:9) defines political violence us '*a considerable* or destroying use of force against persons or things, a use of force prohibited by law, directed to a change in the policies, personnel or system of government, and hence also directed to changes in the existence of individuals in the society and perhaps other societies.' If change is desired and felt to be necessary, and if change is not willingly brought about by the authorities, then force becomes a compelling and rational solution. It would seem that a strong argument can and in the past has been made to justify political violence. To right injustices, violence may be necessary if the injustices are maintained wantonly and through force entrenched in the institutions of a society. However, much violence does not have such a nature and may be entirely negative in its personal and social effects.

The Interpretation of Violent Acts

Political action forms a context for interpretating individual actions. Individual actions may be interpreted as novel, conformist or deviant and criminally deviant according to whether they further or militate against the prevailing order. In a violent situation the individuals take sides. An action may be interpreted as being for a 'proper reason' or 'for the hell of it'. During the 1981 'riots' some black boys said:

Ray: Some kids just like goin' for the fightin'.
Frankie: Yeah.
Ray: That's all they like.
Alex: They're just usin' it as an excuse to go out an' fight an' loot.
J.F.S.: Mm.
Alex: But some people are fightin' for a proper reason.
Ray: Yeah.

The proper reason, it was felt, included the fight against alleged police harrassment, unemployment, poor living conditions, lack of money and opportunity to acquire the better things of life and a decent quality of life. But whether those who fight are 'fighting for a proper reason' or are fighters and looters, the effect is the same:

Dave: You got to fink there's a great atmosphere there to burn, fight, loot, 'cos they've seen it 'appen before an' all it takes is one person to kick something an' make a sound an' that's it. They all start. [He continues on the same theme later] I mean youngsters nowadays ... nineteen year olds. They're easy to wind up, aren't they, you can really wind someone up so easy. An' all it takes is a lot of little kids to go an' say 'Go on smash that'. Or 'You're frightened' or something, an' they do it. I mean all the little kids jump in there an' get all the stuff don't they? [And finally] I mean it's a natural mutual feeling now, isn't it, if you can nick something, nick it without gettin' caught. It's quite natural.

Dave has begun to analyze his experiences of the 'riots' in which he has participated. He takes a view very different from Alex who considered there were 'proper' and by implication 'improper' reasons for fighting in the streets at that time. Dave is more interested in the thrill, the 'great atmosphere' (Toch's category of catharting).

Dave is a natural leader, a big lad of 15 who has been 'expelled' from three secondary schools, with time spent in a detention centre before coming to Slumptown Comprehensive. He likes his new school because 'you know where you are'. He likes its emphasis upon strong discipline. According to Dave: 'One machine gun up the end of the road would've stopped all riots everywhere.' He is enthusiastic about the violent solution to end violence. He did not like his previous schools because teachers were too soft. According to Dave, if the teachers and the police are hard they will keep him under control and so he will not get into any more trouble – at least, for most of the time.

Dave, in his interpretations of violent acts, does not typically use a political frame of reference. His frame of reference is 'a great atmosphere' which enables one person to 'wind up' another. The whole atmosphere leads to a 'natural mutual feeling' which makes stealing seem natural. The atmosphere is permeated with feelings of excitement. To lead an exciting life adds to one's reputation and fuels the imagination. Eddy, for exmple, now a sixth-former told me of the time when he was against his school and was 'soccer hooligan'. He loved the excitement that football gave. Wherever the team went, Eddy would go, and he went to 'hit out at the opposite number'. He describes meeting 'a lad from Chelsea who 'ad half of his left hand missin'. And his bald head – he was a black wasn't he, a coloured fellow – and he's got lines running all over across the back of this and he said it was bricks and bottles broke 'is head open.' He described the awe which he felt for this lad at the time, he 'looked up to him'. To have such scars was 'a very great honour.' Why? 'To me then it seemed like scars of experience. He had more experience . . . had more experience. I mean . . . meet after the pub, it'd all be pretty excitin'. Everyone was after a bit of excitement then. And I thought I'd like to 'ave the excitement and the scars to prove I 'ad, I'd led an excitin' life.'

Eddy has 'calmed down a bit now.' It was his uncle – now in his 20s – who introduced Eddy to all the football but he too has calmed down. He has married. As Thrasher (1927) has noted, the gang is largely an adolescent phenomenon and marriage its greatest threat. But Eddy does not appear to be merely emulating his uncle. He is also reflecting: 'I think I can feel what he feels. Feel a lot better. I feel wiser. Calmed down in school. And like you were saying about the system either beat it or use it and there's no way you're gonna beat it. It's not us who made the system but we need it to get through things together. And that's why I feel a lot better for that. And that's why I'm back in the sixth form now, to get on a bit better.' He's hoping to 'squeeze into an apprenticeship'. He is not academically successful but now wants to try to get what he can out of the system. Eddy is, at least for the time being, trying on the attitude of the 'clever' pupils, the 'ones who wanna work'. He realizes that the 'system' can be used to get what he wants. However, he realizes also that the chances of getting an apprenticeship are slim. What if he fails? His answer is that he'd 'like to be one of the bosses'. He has the possibility of joining a family business. It would seem, like the prodigal son, he is returning to the fold. Eddy has taken on a different frame of reference which he now uses to reinterpret his previous experiences as a soccer hooligan. This alternative frame of reference provides him with feelings of 'calmness' since there is less conflict with the dominant 'system' as he now aspires to be a 'boss' within that system. From the point of view of this alternative frame which embraces the school approved social roles, system of production and career structures, his previous violent self at best seems immature, at worst appears like madness. From the point of view of the school approved frame of reference, one sixth-form girl described her daily experience: 'It's got worse since we've been here. I live in a really rough part now. . . . It's terrible, the gangs there every night. We can't sleep. They, they're always tryin' to let our dogs out. . . . They, they set fire to rabbits an' everythin'. They've stolen my brother's rabbit, I don't know how many times but he finds it. . . . There's nothing you can do about them.' There was a sense of hopelessness in her voice. She had no comprehension of the acts of those around her.

It is not easy for one person using one frame of reference to communicate with another person using an alternative frame of reference. Moreover, it is difficult for each to see that they frequently draw upon a common fund of cultural images. We will see this to be so if we move now to the dramatic context which allows different people to interpret and enact cultural images in different ways.

The Dramatic Context for the Interpretation and Enactment of Violent Episodes

If we start from Toch's view of violence being at least a two-man game, 'the fight' may be analyzed as an example of a violent social drama. The fight can be seen to have the function of creating a dramatic unity out of previously unrelated individuals. It may produce in its wake a new social order or reinforce existing social orders.

Taylor is a principal character in many fights. He has a hatred of school, truants frequently, walking in and out of school when he feels like it:

> *Taylor:* [Teachers] make me feel terrible like, make me feel stupid 'cos they're callin' me all names.
> *J.F.S.:* Yeah.
> *Taylor:* An' all the class start callin' out then.
> *J.F.S.:* So the other kids do it too? As soon as the teacher does it. . . .
> *Taylor:* Soon as the teacher says it.
> *J.F.S.:* Yeah.
> *Taylor:* It's them that start it.
> *J.F.S.:* Yeah. . . . Why do you think the teacher does it?
> *Taylor:* I don't know . . . it's just that they don't like me and I don't like them.

Taylor, after the interview, asked to hear the tape recording I had made. He repeated frequently, 'I sound just like a little girl.' He was small, slender and had a high-pitched squeaky voice. In many interviews I heard explanations as to why a particular pupil was violent attributed to 'he thinks he's big'. It seems to me there is a need or a desire to grow big, or seem big in the eyes of the other, that is, to grow in stature. Willis (1977:35) has written on the role of masculine violence in the social world of 'the lads' that:

> It should be noted that despite its destructiveness, anti-social nature and apparent irrationality violence is not completely random, or in any sense the absolute overthrow of social order. Even when directed at outside groups (and thereby, of course, helping to define an 'in-group') one of the most important aspects of violence is precisely its social meaning within 'the lads' own culture. It marks the last move in, and final validation of, the informal status system. It regulates a kind of 'honour' – displaced, distorted or whatever. The fight is the moment when you are fully tested in the alternative culture.

The images of violence, however, that Taylor revels in are not alternative to 'straight' culture but are embedded in and nurtured by whatever may be meant by British, European, Western or world culture. These are the images of the hero, the righteous war (as in the case of the recent Falklands 'war'), the right of the state to enforce its laws and the images of the relatively powerful taking from the relatively powerless. In his day-to-day life Taylor reproduces the forms of violence upon which a violent society thrives.

One of the deputy heads talked of Taylor's fighting prowess and the role fighting plays in his social relationships:

> He had five fights in the week we're away (at the school's outward bounds centre). Not always because he was ... uh ... arguing with somebody but he would interfere when two other people were arguing and decide which side he was on and then resolve the argument between the two others by fighting the one whose side he wasn't on. An' ... he got really vicious actually ... and we had to drag him off on one occasion and sit him in the bus for ten minutes and calm him down.... For example, he arrived a day late ... he didn't come the day we went. Uh, somebody drove him up the second day ... and within an hour of arriving he had fought every boy in the group ... except one who refused to fight and ran off home. You know, I mean, it was absolutely incredible. He just had to demonstrate he was cock of the group. And havin' arrived late it was the only way he could do it 'cos they'd already set up their pecking order.

Through his fighting Taylor appears to find stature within a group. Walking home with some pupils I noticed Taylor's name written in large letters sprawling across the entire side of a house. The pupils with me assured me it was the Taylor I know. Taylor, they said, is famous. To be famous in a community is to grow big in the eyes of the street.

The imagination, as Bachelard (1969) states, strives to have a future. The images of gang war spread out like the ripples on a pond; the images form an interpretational matrix for action shared not solely amongst the kids on the street. The images, eventually, must find a concrete expression.

During the 1981 street disturbances Taylor was one of the first to know what was happening and where it was rumoured to happen next. He came into school excited. He was playing a central part in the impact of the riots on the school's fantasy life. He was called in to see a deputy head and questioned concerning the likelihood of coming riots. The school passed on whatever information it received from any source to the police. Taylor believed there would be a major riot, he believed eventually that soldiers would be needed to patrol the streets. The lads would be taking over, imposing a new social order. The streets would become 'no-go' areas for the police, only the army with tanks would be able to cope. The street boys would grow big in the eyes of the public.

Taylor drew upon the images of armed conflict currently available in our culture, taking the logic of playground fighting into the streets as a way of imposing a desired social order. And one night, there was the 'fight'. This was recounted by an adult, Harry.

Harry's father saw the barricades being put up by 'yobboes' in his road. He said. 'I'm not having this.' Harry, his brothers and his father began to dismantle the barricade. Some neighbours helped. 'The women were marvellous – they really belittled the yobboes. One of the yobboes yelled out as a reason for his actions, "I've got no fuckin' job." One woman replied, "If you 'ad a fuckin' job you'd faint."' The yobboes cleared off before the police came. Harry said, 'It's a law an' order thing here. People are very strong on it.'

On other nights in other areas the street disturbances were not so easily dampened. Darren Bailey was involved in one such incident although it did not develop into a large disturbance – at most there were about 250 involved. For him the disturbances were not isolated incidents but extensions of everyday gang or 'mob' activities. The images he used in his descriptions were reminiscent of the cinematic love of 'car chases' and dramatic confrontations:

> ... on the first night, right, I was up there, right, an' there was about 30 people there right, you know.... There was this bizzie car [police car] which come burnin' round right, an' some bizzie fella come out lookin' dead 'ard right an' he was sayin' 'Come, let's move, come on. Start movin'.'
>
> No one'd move, right. Everyone was just standin' there for a laugh 'cos he was by 'imself. So 'e got back into his car, right. Then everyone, you know, started shoutin' an' every-thin'. Then the car starts goin' back an' as the car was goin' back someone just 'ad, 'ad a petrol bomb an' thrown it, an' it landed in front of 'im right. An' about five minutes later, right, seen about ... about two meaties, you know, couple of others, you know, couple of other cars come burnin' round the corner. An' they all jumped out, started leggin' everyone, right, an' then that was it in the end, of the first night. An' everyone said 'Come on, we're gonna come back 'ere tomorrow. Everyone meet down 'ere.'

[On the second night there were] I'd say about 200 odd people there, 250 right, an' they were all there, right . . . the bizzies provoked everyone, that's all I can say. [If] the bizzies weren't there, there wouldn't have been no so called little riot at all. Everythin' would be just all passed on. But the bizzies come down there, right, decided to make somethin' of it, you know, the local police tried to make somethin' of it. When they couldn't 'andle it, well they called other officers in from all over the place. They come down. Then loads of people started gatherin'. They 'eard all about it. Then you got all little crews [gangs] from all over the place, down Edgeplace, all up Topside – an' all of them, all of them comin' over in crews to 'ave a go with the bizzies, to get their own back at them.

. . . The bizzies come down in the riot shields goin' 'Come on, come on', 'cos I 'eard them shoutin' see, 'Come on, get us', an' all this. They were not local bizzies. An' when I got dragged in I could tell from the accent. They didn't even know the way to the police station . . . there was just loads of fightin' an' everythin' goin' on, loads of stone throwin' – couple of bizzies gettin' caned like, couple of kids gettin' caned by bizzies. Oh . . . the bizzies were really givin' it to them, like they was givin' them plenty with all the sticks an' everythin' they 'ave.

Darren was charged by the police for his involvement in the riot. Darren's description is reminiscent of his earlier description of the first-year mobs fighting in the playground in order to determine the new leaders and new gangs (see chapter 5). In his interpretation of the riot he stated specifically that 'it wasn't a riot through hatin' bizzies.' He felt it was an act of police provocation which attracted the 'crews' who came to '"ave a go with the bizzies to get their own back at them.' Rather than hatred, there were scores to settle. For some, however, it was simply entertainment, a thrill, like watching TV. Some disappointed girls told me how dozens of primary school and first-year secondary school children sat waiting for a rumoured riot to happen. They would chase all over town hoping to see a riot.

The 1981 riots were over by the start of the autumn term. Perhaps little like them will happen again for several years. Or at least, the smaller more frequent disturbances will be overlooked. The 'riot' as a persistent structure of Slumptown street life is ignored. Thus we are perennially surprised when the big ones occur. However, we may note the structural similarities between Darren's description of a riot (large enough to merit attention from national newspapers) and fights between rival schools as described by these fourth-year girls:

> *Sally:* Only old Town Boys and Slumptown Comp. turned up.
>
> *Ann:* Was there um any of you there, Jilly Jones was there as well. An' there was loads of our first and second years waitin' by the gate too scared to go 'ome because there was a big gang of old Town Boys. We 'ad to take them 'ome.
>
> *Sally:* Rumours goin' round, there was rumours, a coupla months goin' round – all our girls were goin' to get raped by old Town Boys wasn't there?
>
> *Ann:* Yeah. That was supposed to be true 'cos I asked some of the lads at old Town Boys....
>
> *Julie:* Then there was supposed to be a battle over that wasn't there?
>
> *Ann:* Yeah.
>
> *Julie:* [acting ''ard'] Just knock them down, when yer 'ard with yer mates, don't yer?
> [laughter]
>
> *Julie:* Think yer 'ard with the gang.
> [laughter]
>
> *Ann:* They're all 'ard at old Town Boys though aren't they?
>
> *Julie:* Course they're all 'ard, they'd 'av to be tough, you know what I mean, an' you'd 'av to be tough in that school.
>
> *Ann:* I know.

The fights are exciting and eagerly awaited by these girls. I ask the reason for the fighting:

> *Ann:* They're just fightin', it's just fightin'.
>
> *Sally:* That's just it, it's good though isn't it, sometimes.
> [laughs]
>
> *J.F.S.:* No I mean....
>
> *Liz:* There's all police all the police round our school.
>
> *Julie:* There's all the police an' everythin'.
>
> *Liz:* Waitin' when they come....
>
> *J.F.S.:* Well, is it because you can't stand each other or....

Chorus: No.

Julie: No it's not that 'cos all the girls are mates....

Sally: Mates of old Town Boys.

Julie: Old Town Boys an' 'alf the lads 'ere are mates. But we just fight.

J.F.S.: What, just for fun?

Chorus: Yeah, fun.

Julie: But old Town Boys 'll start it. They'll say, 'Oh, we'll get Slumptown Comp. somehow....

Liz: I think It's 'cos they have no, 'cos there's not any girls, you know in the school.

Ann: That's why they're so jealous because we've got all the girls.

Sally: That's why they fight ours.

There is no particular feeling of hatred involved, the fights are exciting and when a fight is rumoured to occur people turn up. The police seem a natural accompaniment. Going to a fight is much like going to a dance. It is an ongoing drama with fun and occasional tragedy to add spice:

Ann: I was walkin' down an' then, the next minute, Oh there was seventeen New Town Boys lads that jumped us. One lad an' 'e's got a bad 'eart, an' e took an 'eart attack when they were batterin' 'im. An' the school didn't do nothin' about it.

J.F.S.: This school?

Ann: Yeah.

Sally: They didn't do nothin'.

Ann: They said they were gonna, 'cos I was there an' Jilly Jones was there, they said they was gonna take us into old Town's to identify them. An' they said. 'Well, then we're gonna need police patrol' to watch us, watch the school, 'cos we'd get done over. But eh, we'd get jumped an' that. We just lucky they didn't go any further with it.

Gang organization, and people held together by complicity in crime or criminal acts of violence, is, according to Freud (1979), at the foundation of our civilization. Along this line of reasoning there is 'fraternal organization' in rebellion against the 'father', that is, youth in rebellion and jostling for dominance against authority.

Brown (1966) develops the argument into the political sphere in the following way:

> The energy which builds fraternal organization is in rebellion against the family and the father; it is youthful energy. Ortega y Gasset can see that the primeval political association is the secret society, not the grey-bearded senate, because he is willing to acknowledge the youthful, or sportive, or playful origin of the state. 'It was not', he says, 'the worker, the intellectual, the priest, properly speaking, or the businessman who started the great political process, but youth, preoccupied with women and resolved to fight – the lover, the warrior, the athlete.' The ideology of utilitarianism which in the origin of the state and everywhere in life sees only obedience to necessity and the satisfaction of elementary vital needs, is senile, and in politics sees only senatorial activity. Youthful energy has that exuberance which overflows the confines of elementary necessity, and rises above labour into the higher, or is it lower, sphere of play.

The energy of youth when it is in rebellion, occasionally overflows the confines of adult social order, bringing to the street youthful concerns.

Classroom Violence

No clear assessment of the generality and frequency can be given. Teacher unions are beginning to collect information on reported incidents of assault or abuse against teachers. STOP brings to the public notice caning as a form of legalized assault. However, there is a variety of forms of unofficial assault and abuse against pupils, of the scale of which we have no knowledge. However, it is reasonable to say that underlying classroom control is a climate of threat which in some, perhaps most, classrooms results in expressions of violence or abuse, the frequency of which will depend upon the individuals concerned. Teacher assault and abuse, however, tend to be rationalized and concealed. For example, I entered the deputy head's office to find a boy, Duane, 'on the carpet'. Duane had insulted a teacher, Mr Wills, obscenely in front of the class. As I entered the deputy head was trying to convince Duane that it was in his interests to apologize. Duane refused. The deputy head modified the demand to Duane 'retracting' his statement rather than apologizing. Duane had frequently been in trouble and was currently in trouble with the law. Further trouble would mean he would lose any possibility of getting an apprenticeship. Duane refused to retract his statement. 'I don't want to suspend you', said the deputy. 'Do you understand the difference between an apology and retracting a statement?' 'Sir, no.' The deputy explained, using the example of politicians in the House of Commons, 'If one politicians uses hotly insulting language the Speaker would ask to have the statement withdrawn. There is no apology. You reserve the right to think it but acknowledge it wrong to state your thoughts aloud.' Duane said he now understood the difference but continued to refuse to retract his statement. The deputy then tried to get Duane to see that he was 'soon going to be a man, and a man can think things but also act in a way so as not to be rude. Would you like it if someone behaved to you in the way that you did to Mr Wills?' 'Sir, no.' 'Will you retract your statement?' 'Sir, no.' In frustration the deputy decided to postpone his decision to suspend Duane in order to give the boy time to think it over.

When the boy had left the room I asked the deputy why he had not suspended Duane. 'If I suspend him there will be a governors meeting and Wills will be called in front of the panel. It's well known that Wills strikes out at the kids and Duane will accuse him of doing just that. It could ruin his career.' The deputy did not approve of Wills' behaviour but thought Wills was a sufficiently good teacher not to harm him for a boy who was clearly bad. However, Duane had previously been told that if he got into further trouble he would definitely be suspended. The threat did not work. Duane was in a powerful position to hurt the career of a valuable, if not entirely respected, teacher.

The deputy had tried to give Duane a lesson in polite political duplicity: think one thing yet say another. He next tried to place the incident in the frame of reference of 'becoming a man'. He tried to use threats: suspension and losing a desired apprenticeship. The solution that 'worked' and satisfied both parties was this: 'You want to be suspended, don't you?' 'Sir, yes.' 'Well, then, in that case I won't do it. I'll give you work and detentions instead.'

The deputy thought the solution to be illogical yet satisfactory. Neither party lost face in the eyes of the other. It was a childish solution but one which befitted the childishness of the dispute. The daily drama between Wills and his pupils involved confrontations, threats and counter-threats. The relationship between Wills and Duane was one of open opposition, in short, they hated each other's guts. Duane could accept punishment because that was in the nature of the drama. He could not accept apologizing or 'retracting' his abusive statement because that did not serve in the construction of his own identity and his perception of the identity of Wills. It was not a part of the dramatic context of interpretation and thus could not make sense in his own eyes or the eyes of his mates. The dramatic context which Wills used to enforce discipline – while working with the great majority – set the conditions for rebellion and abusive behaviour by identifying roles in the drama, strategies and conflictual incidents.

In the classroom there is generally a climate of command which, if broken by pupils, will lead to a number of threats being carried out. Such threats may be experienced by many pupils as a violation of their desired freedoms of expression and action, and as a violation of their sense of security, their self-image and their sense of community with others. In short, certain kinds of teacher action may be experienced as abusive behaviour. For example, in my questionnaire, completed by approximately half the third year, only 6 per cent of boys and 8 per cent of girls said that teachers never shouted at them; and 60 per cent of boys and 43 per cent of girls considered teachers never called them names. About 58 per cent of girls and 44 per cent of boys said teachers at least sometimes frightened them. Shouting is a form of abuse. How may education – that is, critical reflection upon experience – take place in such a climate of fear?

The violent solution may seem irrational, dark, chaotic. But it may be the only rational solution left to an individual who feels abused. The violent solution is a course of action framed within a violent society, fuelled by violent images and violations of individuality. Indeed, there are many contexts for the interpretation, some official, some unofficial, of a particular act. School may be seen as an incubator for violent images and violations of individuality, and, indeed, of a healing sense of community. Such an effect may not be intentional, but organizational, impersonal demands step between the intention and the effect, acting as a distorting filter. In order to change the effect, the conditions of schooling require rational, reflective and critical reform. There is now at least a century of empirical evidence, of theory and of practice which supports the necessity for further reforms which will allow teachers and pupils to work together in a learning environment uninhibited by a climate of command and compulsion, impersonal authority, and violations of the dignity, sense of individuality and community of individuals who happen to play the roles of teachers and pupils.

[Through little things] you hope that you're doing something towards building the the uh the New Jerusalem. Y'
know, in very Romantic terms uh. And hopefully when we
get this, y' know, if we can get kids to believe a little bit in
themselves, to have some pride in themselves they might
start to take a pride in their home, in their street and maybe
eventually their town and we won't get the appalling conditions we've got round, around us at the moment, of vandalism and graffiti and so on. But the, the school is so limited
that that, in terms of what it can do about that on itself
because there are so many other uh pressures on these kids
that, that we have no control over um.... And I think the
biggest evil for them at the moment is uh um is the prospect
of unemployment and ... the work opportunities appear to
be shrinking. Um it's always been bad here. The last few
years it's got progressively worse and worse and worse.
(housemaster)

It is typically taken for granted that great reforms have occurred in
the education system: reforms in school organization, curriculum
and teacher-pupil relations. Perhaps simplistically, it has been
thought that in reforming school one might also reform society.
However, such reforms have not been clear-cut in their implementa-
tion, perhaps mismanaged, and frequently under-resourced despite
apparent massive injections of resources. Vaizey (1958) in 1955 found
that 70 per cent more was spent on grammar school pupils than
secondary modern pupils. However, from 1955 to 1965 the secondary school population rose by 50 per cent and real expenditure on
pupils more than doubled (Vaizey and Sheehan, 1968). However, as

187

Hough (1981:27) writes, the expenditure was unequally allocated 'due to the heavy weighting given to older pupils in the Rate Support Grant, the effect being that the most prosperous localities received the largest grants.' Areas traditionally poorly served continued to be poorly served. Hough's own research showed wide variations in the allocation of resources as between regions.

The New Jerusalem is still a dream. The old slums have frequently been replaced by vandalized new towns suffocating under the weight of unemployment and all the social evils which correlate so highly with poverty, such as crime, violence, ill health, children in care. Clearly, the anticipated results of reform have not been fulfilled. Indeed, there have been powerful pressures against reform which have subverted the potentiality for success. Plans for innovation which ignore the inherent conservativism of all institutions are almost certainly bound to fail.

This chapter, in focussing upon the theme of the reformation of maladjusted schooling, seeks to identify what may be learnt from some of the various attempts to reform schooling – as opposed to deschooling – over this century. Most major attempts at the reform of schooling have been aimed at adjusting individuals to the needs of society (say, producing more technocrats for the technological society) or reforming individuals in order to reform society (towards a captialist or a socialist ideal). The aim that is proposed in this chapter is that school be reformed to meet individual needs and problems as they arise in the context of everyday living. In a sense, the chapter is a *sketch* for facilitating the management of this innovation. There are three broad levels to consider in this programme: the classroom; the school; and schooling.

The Classroom

A class is typically a set of individuals reduced to some common denominator – age, sex, ability, exam group – and subjected to the control of a qualified expert who is charged with imparting portions of that expertise to the class. A classroom is any place where a class is subjected to the control of such an expert. Innovation takes place whenever a basic pattern is subjected to variation. The inherent threat of an innovation is that it may change the pattern beyond recognition and be interpreted as destruction resulting in chaos. In what ways may the basic patterns of the classroom be varied and with what results? The major task is to examine the possibilities for change in the teacher-pupil or adult-child relationship, one that allows a growing relationship taking into account how the child interprets the acts of the adult. If an innovation is to be brought about, this innovation must take into account the relationship between the participants.

Isaacs (1930:8–9) framed the problem of adult-child, teacher-pupil relationships within a Freudian context for interpretation as follows:

> It is not what we are to ourselves and in our own intention that matters; but what the children make of us. Our real behaviour to them, and the actual conditions we create, are always *for them* set in the matrix of their own phantasies. And what they do make of us in the years from two onwards is in large part a function of the already highly complex interplay of infantile love and hate impulses, and anxiety reactions towards these. The intensive study of instinct and phantasy in individual children by the technique of psycho-analysis has shown that, even at this early age, guilt anxiety and love invest any adult who has an active relation with the children with a prestige which he cannot escape. Whether he will or no, he is drawn into the ambit of the child's intra-psychical conflict. The child's world is a dramatic world, and the non-interference of the adult is interpreted in dramatic terms. The adult who does not interfere cannot be for the child himself a neutral observer – he is a passive *parent*. And if the parent is passive, one of two things happens; either the child believes that the grown up *endorses* what he is doing, or suffers internally from the tension of guilt which fails to find relief in his being told what he must *not* do, a tension which issues sooner or later in actions aimed at provoking anger and punishment.

Isaacs here justifies the adult as censor. Thus the traditional relationship between class and teacher is not under threat: that is, the power to judge, to enforce judgements and to limit behaviour. In her school, founded in Cambridge in 1924, this power relationship was however subjected to important criteria: 'there was no inhibition for inhibition's sake' and any commands 'were thoroughly scrutinised before hand' (p. 27). Limits to freedom were well defined and kept as few as possible.

The classroom ties pupil and teacher to one another in a series of reciprocal relationships and expectations. Disrupting such relationships brings the problem of how to handle such an experiment. Isaacs and her group solved the problem by having few but well defined limits to freedom. Furthermore, her pupils were well above average intelligence and from professional families. Such children, it could be argued, would be unlikely to prove difficult.

Neill at Summerhill 'got too many problem children, misfits that other schools did not want' (1973:122). Placed in a non-authoritarian context:

> I sometimes think that I have had more trouble with staff than I have had with pupils. I have had some odd bods in my time, the science man who let a boy of eight handle a bottle of cyanide and a girl of the same age pour fuming nitric acid into a tube so that she burned herself. So many reacted to freedom in the same way as unfree children do. There are no duties for our teachers barring being in their classrooms at teaching periods. Neurotic ones have taught their classes all morning and slept or read all the rest of the day. Good teachers have always used their free time mixing with the kids.

Clearly, if one tampers with classroom authority structures, one needs a strategy by which to introduce and maintain the innovation.

In the Humanities Curriculum Project (HCP), Stenhouse (1979) sought to bring about the notion of the neutral chairman. The authority of the teacher as the custodian of right and wrong answers was dismantled. However, the teacher:

> must learn to embody educational values in rules of procedure and in interventions from the chair which are neutral with respect to discussion issues but express commitment to educational values which, he is bound to assert by his actions are not controversial, at least within the context of the process founded on them. Such values may, for example, be: reasonableness (rationality tempered by a conception of its own limitations), aspiration towards truth, goodness and justice, respect for others, imaginativeness; and at a lower level willingness to listen, reflectiveness, recognition of the need for orderly procedures. These values are controversial

educational values of course. We are concerned with confining the teaching within an educational value position, which may also be debated, but which is clearly defined and adopted – subject to modification in the light of reason – and excluding from the teaching a range of substantive value stances with respect to socially controversial content.

It is a subtle course of action which disrupts the usual pattern of teacher control over knowledge. For this reason participants need to be prepared for the innovation. Ruddock (1980:3) quotes a pupil: 'All our life, we have been in schools. We been taught that what the teacher says is right. But when we're in this room, doing discussion, it's hard for us to disagree with him after all these years. We sort of come to conform with them.' Ruddock argues that as the innovation deskills and disorientates teachers it also deskills and disorientates pupils. Thus it is as necessary to help pupils come to grips with an innovation as to help teachers. Indeed, Hull (1982) elaborated the point as follows: 'a major agency of conservativism in the classroom is paradoxically the pupil group, through its learned incapacity to enter into dialogue with teachers about the management of class-room procedures and its consequent tendency to use group pressure to maintain the familiarities of the status quo.' Hull, in collaboration with Ruddock, wants to see the classroom as a place 'where teacher and pupils conduct the educative act as a collaborative enterprise the success of which is understood to be of benefit to all.' Their work uses the technique of video feedback as a 'route to a situation where teachers and pupils are able to discuss together the management and progress of the educative experience in which they are engaged so that "the hidden curriculum" of the classroom becomes one of co-operative collaboration rather than either cynical collusion or the stalemate of mutual suspicion and distrust.' The notion of the teacher as authority is here virtually replaced by a notion of collaboration through negotiation. The video playback of the group experience serves as evidence which the group explores in order to critique their own and others' behaviour, principles, values, expectancies and such like.

Potentially, at least, the discussion has arrived at a point where everything that happens in the classroom is under question by each member of the group who are *encouraged* to make their questions heard. Yet, there is not chaos. The group is bound by a common set of educative cultural values which have arisen during the common process of mutual critique. Thus 'the principles of procedure which constitute the value stance of the school may be characterized as 'a logic of inquiry' (Stenhouse, 1979). Classroom social order has been transformed from a 'logic of command' to 'a logic of inquiry'. Within such a position of inquiry-based-social order 'deviance' becomes a phenomenon for critical debate during a collaborative exploration of the 'deviant' position as but one controversial issue amongst others. It may be that the deviant position leads to creative change; or it may be that the deviant position is revealed to be hollow.

The 'logic of command' may further be broken through what Labbett at the Centre for Applied Research in Education (East Anglia) calls 'a sensitive neglect of pupils'. As coordinator of the current project, 'The Activity of Handling Information in the Class-room', Labbett shifts the focus of teacher attention from the pupil towards the teacher's own active engagement in his or her work as a 'craftsman'. The teacher is thus a genuine public model for the pupil of the craftsman at work – a testimony to the fact that such work can have intrinsic value and that the craftsman/teacher values such work. The emphasis is upon the creation of real products, that is, products which have intrinsic value (for both teacher and pupil) rather than extrinsic imposed value. The pupil learns through observation that work has a value.

From such a stance, it is open to the craftsman to share his or her skills with the pupils, but it is up to the pupil by showing interest to elect such a course. The move then is towards participation. Something of such an experience is recorded by Enright (in Nixon, 1981:50–1):

> The excitement I experienced as a participant helped me realise the importance of *planning* teacher participation in children's work, particularly when the experience is likely to be a new one for the teacher. Teachers are often unsure about their role in such sessions, but it is marvellous to see them getting excited with the work, to see them looking to the children when they get stuck, and to hear them afterwards describing how they managed to overcome insurmountable problems! Participation could also help teachers who can't resist 'helping' children – particularly in art and craftwork. If you've got your own model to make, your itchy fingers stay away from the children's work, and it's easier to help the children find their own solutions.

The classroom may become a society of craftsmen.

The classroom, however, is but a small unit within the school, and the freedom of the teacher to innovate even within the classroom is limited by organizational demands and pressure from colleagues or even parents. Reforming relationships within the classroom is thus not sufficient.

The School

The teacher who attempts to transform classroom patterns of relationships is detaching his or herself from the dominant professional norms and cultural expectations implicit in the ways teachers behave in the classroom. Kohl (1977) advised radical teachers to foster allies within the school if they embark upon classroom innovations. Another, and more important, source of strength may be in the developing relationship the teacher has with his or her pupils. If this relationship transcends the classroom, one may call it a 'school of thought' which has developed between teacher and pupils. It becomes imperative, therefore, to define what is meant by the term 'school' and hence appreciate anew the meaning of the terms 'class' and 'classroom'.

For the Greeks, school (*schola*) meant any place where leisure time was passed in disputation – a street corner, the market place, anywhere. This provides a fluid conception of school which might tentatively be formulated as 'a school is any place where two or more gather together for the purpose of disputation, or examining some point or object of common interest in detail.' The definition may cover such a range of activities as those involved in a 'school of cards players', 'a school of art', 'a school of crime'. Such schools exist and daily *attract* rather than *conscript* their members. Formally instituted schools do not compete with the records of 'success' of these, as it were, self-elected schools, nor can they boast of the level of commitment which such self-elected schools generate and maintain among their members.

With this revised notion of school the conscript state school may be analyzed as not one but as a complex interaction between the conscript and the many self-elected schools to be found among the members. Much research awaits to be done on the content of the curriculum (this is not to be confused with the hidden curriculum) of these self-elected schools, and the complex ways they interact with the official conscript-school curriculum (both overt and hidden curricula contents). In a recent paper (1983b), I wrote that individuals:

> choose those experiences of life which seem attractive and choose those 'teachers' who can provide them with the skills or knowledge by which to attain those experiences. Such experiences and teachers it would seem are not to be found in school.
>
> An image for the kind of curriculum such people wish to follow can perhaps be found in the Latin meaning of the word: 'racing chariot'. This conjures up an image of the individual who through skill and courage attempts to win whatever race he or she chooses to run. The school curriculum is indeed competitive and offers some prizes but none so attractive as those offered by everyday life.... Each individual in life elects his or her own curriculum, that course through life which they will drive with as much skill and daring as they can muster. A curriculum is not simply a syllabus of 'facts' or skills to be acquired, but an emotional obstacle course run in the hope of acquiring a number of desirable experiences. This kind of curriculum is self-elected. If the official school academic and pastoral curricula accord with the self-elected curriculum or is an integrated part of it, then there is likely to be little serious friction between the individual and the system of mass schooling.

Where there is a mismatch individuals will employ one of the many strategies for coping with or transforming the situation toward desired experiences, perhaps enlisting the aid of experienced 'teachers'. There is an implication for state schooling:

> If we accept such fluid definitions of teachers, teaching and schools then it becomes clear that professional teachers need to make themselves available to pupils in and out of time-tabled lessons. Time will be spent in conversation and disputation. The topics for discussion will arise from the self-elected life courses of the individuals concerned. Experiences and opinions can be shared and mutual interests developed. Through such sharing and disputation children can learn through being brought into contact with adults who can make available to them knowledge concerning

possible courses of action to attain experiences children desire. The curriculum of such a school is centred around the immediate concerns and practical solutions to the social, emotional and economic problems which confront children. Thus part of the teaching task becomes the identification of problems and the construction of courses of action to overcome those problems. In this way, children will take the reins of their own destiny in their hands knowing they have the help and concern of adults who have also negotiated such courses.

The concepts of the self-elected school and the self-elected curriculum bring practical problems to the professional teacher willing to take them seriously. It is conceivable that the humblest probationary teacher may be the leader or 'headmaster' of a self-elected school within the conscript-school, hence, potentially, undermining traditional power structures. The potential for conflict is enormous. The problem is how to manage the self-elected school within a conscript school. An insight may be provided by considering the position of the housemaster in a conscript school.

In Slumptown Comprehensive the formal structures of the pastoral care system may be interpreted in two distinct ways. A housemaster mediates between pupils and classroom teachers. Positionally, the housemaster may interpret his or her behaviour as either siding with pupils or with colleagues. It is difficult to be but a neutral chairman in pastoral issues but this, too, is a possible position to take. Such a housemaster is in a strong position to participate in some pupil-elected curriculum and hence influence a self-elected school of thought (or of action):

> [Some of my lads are] painting up some very badly graffitied toilets.... And they're loving it, believe you me John. And in that toilet, I'm amazed – I expected them to be in there smoking. I expected to go in and find it flooded, you know, them turning the taps on. But y' know, I've had none of that. The only thing was that they left a lot of paint on the floor. Yesterday I said, 'You know, I had to go in there and clean that up after you. I couldn't leave it like that.' Today they went in, after they'd finished, they got loads of mops and mopped it all up. Didn't need, you know, I didn't ask them. It's that ... I mean, that's kind of break-through stuff really. You're beginning to find out what these kids can do. I'm not

saying that's . . . they gotta, they've gotta learn other things but, you'd get more of that I think. There's loads, loads. It only needs some imagination, John. It doesn't need any brilliance. Teachers aren't bloody trained in the ways of getting kids to paint toilets. They're trained in test tubes, French books and English texts. Y' know, I'm sorry but to a great extent for a lot of our kids these are totally inappropriate skills. I could go down to the job centre here in Slumptown and find at least 20 men and women who would make a better job employed in schools here than 20 staff on this school. They would make a bigger and better contribution, more valuable and meaningful contribution. That's what I'm talking about. If, if schools like this would move pastorally in that direction, working in teams, and *teams* meaning just that. Your teacher and *you at fourteen and fifteen as a team.* Not that 'sir' and y' know, doffin' the cap business – deferential phrases y' know – [but] actually learning to grow up with an adult or other adults. (housemaster)

The teacher observes the content of the self-elected curriculum of some young people, participates in its construction as an adult team member rather than as boss. He has no higher ambition to transform this content nor to raise reflective awareness: 'If I can help a kid cope with now that's about the length of my ambition really.' Some teachers, however, do harbour ambitions to go beyond now and transform the life or the awareness of a pupil. Indeed, comprehensive reform attempted just that. Nevertheless, by behaving as simply an adult team member rather than as an authoritarian, the housemaster had succeeded in transforming his *relationship* with the young people. Many other teachers in the school found the housemaster's relationship with pupils threatening and were often scornful. To them, he seemed too lax.

Some radically inclined teachers may feel that the housemaster's reforms were too limited and too narrow in focus, that his ambitions were too modest. Many feel an impatience to right the world's wrongs; or at least, to make some firm change in the right direction. For example, a group of teachers decided to bring black culture to their pupils:

> *Lucy:* The teacher [a West Indian] brings in black culture, and uh, what [the white teacher] does, she brings in black and white and uh, . . . it 'urts me, you know, I'm black I'm

proud of it yeah, but the point still remains that it brings us
in a frame of mind of what, not *you*, but *whites* . . . 'as done
to us in time. And some boys really feel. . . .
Yvonne: It 'urts us and it 'urts them.

Carol, who is white, listening to this says of the black boys, 'They
take it out on us, right.' And Lucy says, 'It just causes contention.'
Lucy and Carol agree that, 'We've been the best of mates but when a
film [on black history] comes up, we're slaggin' each other down.'
They felt that the black history presented to them in films and talks
created more tension than they could handle, a tension that ripped
them apart. Such a sensitive issue requires skilful management if it is
not to violate the developing relationships of friendship and community between black and white youth.

A more successful approach was perhaps that of Kohl (1971),
who entered genuinely collaborative relationships with his pupils.
However, what success there was in his classroom was crushed in
later years by the following years of dull and painful schooling.
Working for lasting changes in the system is not easy. Kohl (1974)
attempted reforms from the outside; again there were painful
failures.

Nevertheless, many teachers have tried to reform their practice.
And this has led to a new phenomenon, the 'problem school', as
MacDonald and Walker (1976) called it. Such an example of 'teacher
defection from the role of the school as agent of cultural transmission
and conformist socialization' was the William Tyndale school affair
which brought a strong public reaction:

Although it was only a straw in the wind, the obvious
connections between Tyndale and the writings of Illich and
Friere, the 'de-schooling' movement of recent years, and the
popularity of the concept of 'pupil-power' are being made,
and are ringing alarm bells throughout the country. The
integrity of the school is in question, and the threat to the
erosion of public confidence is taken seriously, particularly
those who have most to gain by exploiting. The DES
memorandum, for instance, argues the case for closer supervision of teacher training on the grounds that teacher qualities of skill and personality have declined in recent years, a
subtle reference to the public dismay that was generated by
the Tyndale affair. (MacDonald and Walker, 1976:20)

The headmaster and several of his staff were sacked because of sufficient parental opposition to his teaching methods, dubbed 'progressive'. If a headmaster wishes to reform his or her school, strong allies must be sought. If none are forthcoming, it is likely the reform will fail. Any dramatic innovation requires detailed planning, with those who are most likely to endanger the innovation being brought into the decision-making process (see also the case of Risinghill, Berg, 1968). But failure may be the price of trying.

Sharpe and Green (1975) have shown how an apparently progressive school is constrained by wider socio-economic structures. Reform may often only be skin deep. Indeed, there is an inherent conservativism in schooling which individual schools find difficult if not impossible to overcome. Perhaps the only strategy left is to work at the fringes or outside the system in the formation of 'free schools' or 'alternative schools'.

White (1980:19) compares England with Denmark where there are:

> 120 after schools – residential provision that parallels the folk school provision. Of these a handful like Tvind cater predominantly for the working-class rejects of the ordinary state school.
>
> In addition there are about 40 small independent schools.... The Ny Lilleskole in Bagsvaerd, a suburb of Copenhagen, is an example of an informal school which operates an alternative curriculum approach to the state schools, and yet is supported by the local government school inspectors. The Danish law that says 'if a certain number of parents can start a school and run it on their own for a year, the government will from then on pay 85 per cent of the operating expenses' is the enabling legislation for the development of such Lille schools – as well as the after-school network of the Tvind kind.

No such provision exists in England. Instead, there are the variously titled Assessment Centres, Behavioural Units, Guidance Centres, and so on, where there is an interface between educational and social work concerns. The task of such places is to deal with children schools feel they cannot manage. The head of such a centre – it is residential – describes the work:

> We will accept a number of children who, because of behavioural problems, cannot be accepted in school outside.

So we're bound to get difficult children. We tell the staff, 'You will get difficult. . . . Don't expect to have an easy number, because if they're easy they shouldn't be here.' We help to resolve [many of the pupil's problems] by a lot of discussion and conversation, you see. We operate a three shift system . . . and everytime a shift changes over there's 30 to 45 minutes of a discussion between the two sets of staff: how the [unintelligible], how individual children are, what sort of problems there are, and how they dealt with it. So there is a consistent approach to it. Yesterday's staff meeting we discussed a boy who is having a difficult problem. And I had to point out to the staff saying, 'Now, wait a minute, we moved him from that group to that group because there was a problem and as we moved him I said I want you to concentrate on the relationships with his peers and we can build up confidence in adults. Now what is happening? You're allowing him to escape you around the building. He'll be isolated again.' They didn't see it happening.

The task is the systematic observation of behaviour and the critical reflection upon it. It is a paternalistic authority where, through systematic observation, interpretations are consistently applied to behaviour, and staff actions are concentrated upon small areas of pupil behaviour in order to bring adult desired changes in the behaviour of young people schools have ejected from their system. Pupils are torn from their social context, isolated in such centres and defined as problems. Torn from their social context, that context escapes attention. The schools themselves are not, therefore, under critical examination (or assessment) in order to bring a reform to meet the needs of the child. The head of this centre, however, was well aware that the problems of his pupils were primarily to be found in their school and their wider social contexts. He was also aware of the great power of the social worker to recommend children into twenty-four-hour care, with or without the blessings of parents or of the young people themselves. Everything is in the best interests of the child whether or not the child agrees. The task becomes to adjust the child to that which is in his or her social worker-defined best interests; ideally, to transform the way the child sees reality towards the way the social worker/teacher perceives reality. For the pupil to maintain or develop an alternative school of thought is not easy.

In 1969 the School of Barbiana wrote a 'letter to a Teacher', a message from a true school of thought to teachers around the world.

It was a best selling project authored by a group of pupils failed by the Italian schooling system. It began:

> Dear Miss
> You won't remember me or my name. You have failed so many of us.
>
> On the other hand I have often had thoughts about you, and the other teachers, and about the institution you call 'school' and the boys that you fail.
>
> You fail us right out into the fields and factories and there you forget us.

As a brief description of Barbiana:

> Barbiana, when I arrived, did not seem like a school. No teacher, no desk, no blackboard, no benches. Just big tables, around which we studied and also ate.
>
> There was just one copy of each book. The boys would pile up around it. It was hard to notice that one of them was a bit older and was teaching.
>
> The oldest of these teachers was sixteen. The youngest was twelve, and filled me with admiration. I made up my mind from the start that I, too, was going to teach.

And on children as teachers:

> The next year I was a teacher; that is, three half-days a week. I taught geography, mathematics and French to the first intermediate year.
>
> You don't need a degree to look through an atlas or explain fractions.
>
> If I made some mistakes, that wasn't so bad. It was a relief for the boys. We would work them out together. The hours would go by quietly, without fear. You don't know how to run a class the way I do.

Only recently is such 'pupil tutoring' receiving the research attention it deserves. For example, Bond (1982) took six persistent truants aged 15+ and made them 'pupil tutors' to six primary school pupils. Each of the participants benefited academically and emotionally and their attendance improved significantly. Such a system of teacher supervised 'pupil-tutoring' would not be hard to incorporate in any school with, say, fifth-form 'problem' pupils tutoring younger 'problem' pupils.

The members of the school of Barbiana created what may be called a real product as opposed to an exam-oriented curriculum. The work of the pupil teachers was *real* in the sense that the problems tackled were problems of mutual interest and concern; and the relationship between the members was not based upon feigned interests, concerns, and not based upon impersonal organizational authority but upon personal feelings of mutual respect. When young people are allowed to exhibit their creativity, and their care for others, the results can be spectacular:

> A third year class of mine performed in 1976 an improvised play which relied very heavily on Jamaican Creole speech forms. That play taught me a lot about Jamaican creole.... About two months after the play was performed, the girl who was the main character in it, the driving force, one of the most troublesome and talented children I've ever met, came into an English lesson at the head of the class, sat me down, and informed me that the class were about to teach each other to read, because, she said, 'There's some of us in this class who can't read very well, and there's only one of you and thirty of us.' For four weeks after that, until the girl was removed from the school as being too disruptive for the institution to handle, I had the astonishing sight for an hour and a half a week, of seeing fifteen pairs of heads, perfectly matched for social and academic compatibility, teaching each other to read. My relationship to the pupils was changed, so was theirs to me. Something which might be called research, th play which led to the work which I subsequently did on Jamaican Creole and the relationship between non-standard dialects and the school curriculum, came bouncing back to me before I had even written anything down, in the shape of a transformed attitude on the pupils' part to the possibility of something meaningful happening in their English lessons. The teaching and the research, the learners and the teachers, made a kind of inter-penetrating whole where things changed because things belonged to each other. (Richmond, 1982:33)

Instead of counterfeit relations between class members leading to counterfeit products, there were real relations leading to real products: the product of actually improving reading. It could be said that the pupil – the troublesome girl – became a self-elected school's headmistress. Richmond was its facilitator and pupil. Presumably the conscript-school's hierarchy learnt little.

It would require few, if any, resources to institute important reforms along the above lines. What can be learnt from the many and diverse successful programmes that have been instituted at school level? Most seem to have characteristics in common with those features of the White Lion Free School in London as reported by White (1980:33–4):

1 A lack of hierarchical authority characteristic of schools, where teachers are invested with status because of academic qualifications;

2 The number of pupils is small (fifty) and the ratio of adults to pupils is high (eight full-time workers and a whole host of voluntary helpers – especially parents);

3 Regular weekly meetings with all parents, teachers and children, and daily meetings involving all adult workers;

4 An emphasis on 'basic skill work' as a regular part of morning activity;

5 Tremendous local support and interest from teachers, colleges of education, institutes of education – but piecemeal support from the LEA (Inner London in their case);

6 Low rate of truancy, with 90 per cent attendance being the norm;

7 Discipline is enforced by a process of talking through confrontational situations (which some would describe as nagging!);

8 A multitude of rotas – for cooking, for cleaning, for washing up, answering mail, handling the petty cash, organizing the maintenance of the building;

9 Use of old premises that no one else really wants.

For us these points are open to critical debate. One may reflect upon the presupposed childrearing practices in 1, 3, 4, 7 and 8. The admission (in 7) that discipline is achieved via 'nagging' *suggests* that old-fashioned paternalistic authority is alive and well and buried just below the surface of more democratic procedures (as in 3). For comparison, the Educational Network of Norwich outlines its aims and principles as follows:

1 The network is open to anyone who wants to join it but is not available to children whose parents do not want them to

join it or to children who do not want to be there themselves.

2 All aims and structures of the network are to be explicit. All
meetings proceedings and records are open to the adults and
children concerned. Specifically, there are to be no discus-
sions which are unavailable to the persons discussed.

3 The physical well being and the security of the children are a
priority.

4 The network aims to give the children who attend it every
incentive to read, write, create and explore themselves and
their environment.

5 The network is open to appraisal by Education Authority
inspectors at their request, providing that notice of inspec-
tion is given a week in advance and that it is convenient to
the people concerned.

6 If and when any Education Authority decides to give money
for work done by teachers in the network, each teacher will
receive the same amount for the work done.

7 All decisions about the network will be made by the
children, the parents and the teachers at meetings with open
agendas.

8 No physical punishment of any kind is allowed. (unpublished paper by Rago, C/o 32 Argyle St, Norwich)

What is here seen to be necessary is to institute procedures by which
group members reflect critically upon their own and others' behaviour.

Collaborative reflection may be aided by evidence (video, tape,
diaries) produced with the agreement of those concerned. The object
of the exercise might be to identify behaviours which lead to a sense
of being violated and which lead to feelings of self-worth, individuality; or to aid the development of a school of thought engaged
in creating tangible products, workable solutions to immediate
problems, attaining skills or creating pleasurable environments; and
so on.

Assessment of the work produced in a school may be reconcep-
tualized. Instead of work being marked and assessed through impersonal means (public exam results) one may institute peer group
critique of each other's products so that assessment becomes a
collaborative work of appreciation. In such a way individuals may
retain control over judgement rather than surrender control to those

whose assessment procedures remain unchallenged, quasi-mystical, quasi-scientific and publicly unverifiable.

By retaining control over a social structure, one retains responsibility for it. In the self-elected school everyone is responsible and social order is creatively assessed and instituted through mutual responsibility. No conscript-school can claim such maturity.

In summary, professional teachers – scale one through to headteacher – may encourage reforms. The kind of reform, the scale of its operation and effect, and the degree to which it succeeds depend on the skill of the teacher in negotiating space for change. Daily, people take for granted the ways they and others behave. Through reflection and by inviting others to share experiences, the tacit is made explicit, habits may be revealed as hollow and the reified may crumble. Reflection and imagination set the rigid structures of everyday life into question which thus facilitates the emergence of new patterns. It is the wide sphere of schooling, entering as it does into local and national politics, which sets the most rigid limits and offers the greatest challenge to freedom of action for individuals who must take on the roles of teachers and pupils within institutions they did not design.

Schooling

Schooling defies precise definition. It involves an interaction of a complex of schools, where school is defined in its broadest, most fluid sense. It incorporates what is commonly known as the education system (constructed through an interaction of schools of political thought and action), which in turn services modern mass schooling to which children are conscripted as pupils. The term 'maladjusted schooling' refers primarily (although not necessarily exclusively) to modern mass schooling. Maladjusted schooling, like all institutions, can be transformed because such institutions are the product of man's mental life and, hence, a product of the manipulative webs by which people enchant, seduce and bully one another to get what they want.

At the level of schooling, reform tasks focus upon the *coordination* of the individual school efforts as a collaborative enterprise in the construction of community and the emergence of individuality among members; and focus, therefore, upon the *facilitation* of coordination and of individual school efforts. These facilitative efforts fall under four broad, somewhat overlapping, groups: organizational reform; curriculum reform; professionalization; and the development of support groups and pressure groups.

Organizational Reform

Organizational reform refers to changes in the ways decisions are made and enforced and the ways groups are formed, categorized and managed. Most school structures are hierarchical, with decisions and control retained at the top. A major reform involves shifting the balance of decision and control as between the top and bottom levels in the hierarchy. One such shift MacDonald and Walker (1976) call 'democratization'. Democratization describes 'a process which involves the dispersal of power and an increase of opportunities for citizens to have knowledge of and to participate in, decision-making which affects their lives.' Of course, democratization may lead in a conservative direction rather than a radical direction. Nevertheless, democratization is itself reformist; it is a move toward responsibility for the quality of one's life. It is likely that such a move may initially lead in a conservative direction simply because people will choose according to what they conceive as their practical interests; and such interests are largely framed by the political and economic structures of everyday life. For example, Goodson (1983) reminds us that secondary modern schools formed under the 1944 Education Act were initially free from external exams and hence in a position to experiment. However, more parents began to realise that certification led to better jobs, teachers found examinations a useful source of motivation and heads began to use examinations as a means of raising their schools' reputation and status.' Similarly, the new comprehensives had to justify themselves and chose examination success as the criterion (cf. Ball, 1981). Strangely, there persists a myth of the powerlessness of teachers to change such matters, condemned as they are by exam constraints to plough their furrows in the arid exam curricula! The myth is perpetrated everywhere:

> ... the examined curriculum is in need of some reform. Most of the teachers I know take a similar view; they feel a deep unease both about the academic curriculum and about the constraining power of public examinations. At the same time they feel entirely powerless to make any significant

changes – and so inevitably allow the issue to slide to the back of their minds – and in any event feel very unsure about the directions in which we might go. (Hargreaves, 1982:79)

In this chapter we have already reviewed enough examples of reforms to demonstrate the myth-like quality of this view. Furthermore, it is as much through the power of the teacher as any other cause that the reforming potential of the comprehensive school has been rendered impotent. Pupils have been categorized in comprehensive schools in much the same way as in grammar schools and secondary moderns – as bright or dull, as good or bad, as academic or non-academic (cf. Ford, 1969; Keddie, 1971; Ball, 1981). The pastoral system, by taking on discipline and control functions, has not seriously challenged the old authority structures and the over-valuation of so-called academic subjects (cf. Best *et al.*, 1980).

A potentially more radical reform in school than the comprehensive reform is that of the community school. Hargreaves sees 'four analytical dimensions to the concept of the community school. Any school may adopt one or two of these dimensions and ignore the others; and it may adopt a particular dimension in a 'strong' or 'weak' version (p. 123). Briefly, these dimensions are a community within the school; greater participation by members of the outside community; the school as a community centre; and the community-centred curriculum. Thus, within the school there is a greater democratization of control (even to the extent of including pupils). Parents and others are encouraged to act as governors and perhaps parents will be involved in classroom activities. The school itself is seen as the common property of the community. There is the possibility, therefore, of a greater rapprochement between the official school organization and those more fluid self-elected or community-elected schools described in the previous section. Hopefully, the barriers between the street, the home, the workplace and school become dissolved. However, the hope may not be realized for reasons similar to the comprehensive school (Hargreaves, 1982:125):

> The pressure on comprehensive schools to 'prove' themselves by examination results is exerted *a fortiori* on a community school. As long as this continues there can be no full development of a community-centred curriculum in the *secondary* school; it can achieve no more than a minor or peripheral position in relation to the grammar-school curriculum.

Curriculum Reform

There are many definitions of 'curriculum'. In practice, curriculum tends to be defined in terms of what a pupil should know at the end of a particular course of study. That is to say, a curriculum tends to divide into 'subjects' (say, maths, English, history) each having certain 'facts' or 'skills' to be learnt. Such a curriculum is imposed by an authority figure upon pupils who must be assessed according to their performance in following a prescribed course of study. Stenhouse (1975:4), in criticizing such a conception of the curriculum, does not erode the principle that curricula are typically constructed by authorities rather than pupils but does erode the concept of the teacher as one who transmits curriculum elements in a predigested form for pupil consumption. For Stenhouse (a working definition of) *'a curriculum is an attempt to communicate the essential principles and features of an educational proposal in such a form that it is open to critical scrutiny and capable of effective transmission into practice.'* However, the elements of the curriculum are selected, the mode of presentation planned and the means of pupil assessment constructed by authorities other than the pupils. In effect, the pupil is kept in a state of dependency upon the authority who constructs the curriculum.

Curriculum reform may focus upon two facets of the creation of a curriculum: first, the extent to which curriculum contents are open to critical scrutiny; secondly, the creator of the curriculum (that is, the authority, whether an exam board or one such as Stenhouse, or the pupil who elects and constructs his or her own curriculum). In any case, to be of use, the curriculum must be 'capable of effective translation into practice'; however, assessment differs according to who is to be the creator of the curriculum. Typically, assessment is in the hands of some authority rather than in pupils' hands. Curriculum reform then involves a progressive shift from teacher as authority toward teacher as, say, neutral, or as equal coproducer of the curriculum; and a shift from the pupil as dependent toward pupil as teacher-independent. A further reform focusses upon the nature of the curriculum product. Typically, the product stresses exam assessed knowledge or skill (what I have earlier called counterfeited knowledge) rather than stressing real products (books, chairs, music, artwork, interpersonal skills, the reflective analysis of a personal problem as a step towards its solution, and so on) which are of satisfaction to the producer rather than the examiner; thus the move again is from teacher to pupil.

Despite much apparent effort at curriculum reform, Goodson (1983:24) notes that there has been little real change in the curriculum in spite of radical *organizational* changes: 'It seems that it will be impossible to realise the ambitions of comprehensive educational reform unless we have a better understanding of the part played by the subjects of the curriculum in preserving a divided system in the face of organizational change.' Moreover, 'Within school subjects *there is a clear hierarchy of status which is based partly upon assumptions that certain subjects, the so-called 'academic' subjects, are suitable for the 'able' students whilst other subjects are not'* (p. 33)

Keddie (1971) has shown how teachers divide knowledge into 'expert' and 'non-expert', 'academic' and 'non-academic'. Teacher knowledge is expert, and academic forms of knowing, content and methods of presentation are reserved for 'able' pupils. In this way, many forms of knowing, content and forms of presenting knowledge are devalued and pupils categorized in terms of worth. Theoretical or abstract forms of knowing are set above concrete forms of knowing; exam success is placed above real products. Similarly, the community curriculum of the community schools, which may be examinable and include various schemes for community service, has the danger 'that these become options open to, or even compulsory for, the 'less able' or 'non-academic' pupils who are not working on courses leading to public examinations' (p. 117).

Again, therefore, the spectre of examination haunts maladjusted schooling, reproducing all the evils the various reforms have sought to attack. I believe the spectre of the exam has the quality of a myth simply because it is through the class control concerns of teachers that the breath of life is continually breathed into exams. Thus, rather than a community curriculum constructed by teachers, a real product curriculum brought into being by the needs, interests and concerns of pupils independent of, but in collaboration with teachers, is required as a means of overcoming the traditional divisions between 'subjects'.

Professionalization

Resort to the *Shorter Oxford English Dictionary* provides two broad sets of meaning to the word 'profession'. The first set focusses upon the act of professing, or publicly declaring, a belief, intention or practice as one does in taking a vow to join a religious order. The second set focusses upon 'the occuption which one professes to be skilled in and to follow,' or the way in which one earns one's money. By the profession of teaching, I refer to the act of making a public declaration of the beliefs, intentions and practices involved in being a teacher. Professionalization refers, therefore, to the act of bringing about a profession. Built into the notion of a profession is some form of public accountability through the profession of a code of intentions, beliefs and practices. This accords with my intention to see education as a collaborative act of critical reflection upon experience in the creation of schools of thought and action.

Sockett (1982), in arguing for a code of practice in the form of a 'codification of habits drawn from a variety of sources', sees such a codification as a major step toward winning public and political confidence in schools. Moreover:

> What is not unrealistic is that individual schools might develop and publish their particular codes of professional conduct.
>
> Such a code would be a major element in the quasi-contractual relations between schools and both parents and pupils as clients. The code could be made easily accessible to the constituents whom the school addresses. A school would need to devise its own procedures for constructing the code, for keeping it under review and for dealing with grievances, among which would be the matter of lay participation.

It is a move in the right direction. And some of the advantages of some form of code Sockett lists as:

> First a professional commitment of this kind would wrest the accountability initiative from those with myopic visions of its purpose. Second whatever the outcome of national deliberations on curriculum, it would give backing to the local concerns of schools and their relations with their particular communities. Third it would be a major step forward to gaining public and political confidence at large. Fourth it would provide a framework for the development of other critical aspects of the accountability of schools to their constituents. Fifth it could serve to bring pupils' judgements more seriously into account. Sixth it provides a way forward for a more detailed exploration of the appropriate extent of autonomy for teachers and schools without the rather general

arguments which are usually brought to bear on such matters. Last, but not least, it would provide a coherent empirical base of what teachers believe ought to be their obligations for the discussion of what improvements and developments should be examined.

Many may find such talk of professionalization ominous. Thus, I feel, many would agree with the headmaster of Stanground school, with whom Sockett opened a correspondence concerning his article. With permission, I quote the headmaster, Mr Barker:

> I'm tempted to see this article with its frequent references to rules, codes, law, and conduct as part of the dark 1984 rat-trap in which sensitive teachers are forced to live and note the closing hint (similar to that offered for other unattractive primitive-seeming schemes associated with the accountabi- lity movement e.g. self-evaluation, monitoring) that unless we adopt it something even nastier may happen. If we don't cane ourselves a policeman may come instead.... I would not give one ounce of energy to the creation of further elaborate lists of rules and regulations (or their more liberal- sounding equivalents – e.g. professional codes, aims and objectives, contracts) which start from 2 propositions (a) Schools are in some way failing parents/children (b) Teachers need prodding a bit converging in a 3rd, that this problem is significant enough for the expenditure of scarce psychic energy.

Certainly, one may feel that professionalization is simply another way of publicly harrassing teachers. However, the code is not to be a way of keeping teachers in line, by producing a way in which politicians or industrialists can keep the reins on teachers. It is a way in which schooling as a collaborative enterprise may be run in the interests of its members and not in the interests of some outsiders who would seek to exploit school to their own profit. Sockett thus replied:

> You find the implications of my paper dispiriting because you see it, quite largely, as not helping your management concerns: you see it as an invasion of your managerial privacy, as it were, and interpret it as directed solely at the inefficient. Perhaps I have not made enough of what I see as the need for the democratization of schools and the possibili-

ties of the code providing a focus for real debate and confidence in a school's purposes and activities.

Barker replied, setting the problem within 'leadership', 'management' and 'organization for 'teachers and pupils cannot achieve anything much on their own'. Thus:

> – I am MANAGING and have plans, tactics and strategies involving a fair degree of manipulation. I am working towards a far higher degree of participation and autonomy than my colleagues suspect; I have seen through the basic structural problems – now the next phase. So you are right to spot and detect in me a conservativism, an authority-consciousness, a sense that order and civilization are not inevitable, must in fact be won, planned, organised.

There is an implicit code and teachers and pupils become the objects of a benign plan, the objects of manipulative intents not of their making. Yet, it is a plan involving participation and autonomy. Hence, the listening leader may create a climate within which autonomy can develop. Or is it a climate of counterfeit autonomy? Nevertheless, there is here a real alternative to non-authoritarian collaborative organization, which many may prefer, which keeps open the potential for reform and the growth of autonomy in individuals.

In either case (leader-induced collaboration, or non-authoritarian collaboration), without effective translation into practice of either implicit or explicit codes of practice, confusion is the likely result. MacDonald (1978:187), for example, in an evaluation of a school participating in the Humanities Curriculum Project, reported on a situation where a headmaster of a mixed junior comprehensive Catholic day school held democratic ideals but did not have the full support of his staff. Thus, one of the HCP staff participants (Mr Parry) commented:

> In principle, I believe in the democratic "one man, one vote" structure, but it doesn't work. It's so hard to get 40-odd people to agree on anything, and in any case, there's no machinery for implementing decisions, and people feel that, well, if they don't really agree with the decisions anyway, why should they stick to it, and so nothing's done, and things go on as they were before. No, I never put anything up for discussion at a staff conference. I don't like the idea of

any young pup with three months' experience voting my
ideas out. So I never put anything on the agenda.

Perhaps people do not want to participate? Thus, there may be need
for clear leadership aimed at manipulating staff towards wanting to
participate? Clearly, where both leadership and community backing
are lacking, any innovation will fail. One cannot impose a code upon
a community which feels that code to be alien. The code must be
workable and hence either constructed by the community in its
initial stages or planned and managed by a capable leader until a
climate is manipulated into being which will accept the innovation.

In this particular case study, ironically, the HCP project
'appeared to have given rise to the establishment of a school-within-
a-school, an "authoritarian cell within a democratic structure", as
Mr Kelly was later to call it. Mr Parry saw it more as establishing an
area of co-operative order in a situation of permissive laisser faire'
(p. 233). Mr Parry was the 'headmaster' of his 'school within a
school'. It is perhaps true that we have not yet outgrown the
necessity for leaders; perhaps we never will. The birth of democracy
has yet to be accomplished; its structures are not yet fully established.
The creation of codes of practice by school members for school
members may prove to be a step in the right direction. It would at
least be a source of pressure which rose from the members themselves rather than from outsiders. Through collaboration there is
support. Many teachers, who do not have the power of a headmaster
and who cannot invoke the aims and principles of a code of practice,
may be isolated and feel helpless to realize desired reforms. In such a
case, the teacher must turn for support to support groups and
pressure groups.

Support Groups and Pressure Groups

A teacher alone is unlikely to accomplish much. Teachers must seek
allies if they wish to carry out reforms (cf. Kohl, 1977). A teacher's
allies constitute his or her power base. The first and most important
direction in which to seek allies is amongst one's pupils. Without the
active participation of one's pupils, nothing worth calling reform can
be accomplished. The task is to heal the splits, the tears, the
experiences of violation which have been the subject of this book.
The participation of the pupils is essential. Even where there is

apparent success, there is real failure if the pupils are left without a sense of determining their destiny, or following through their wants, plans, dreams, or realizing their autonomy in the world of others. Too easily reforms are subverted by habitual, traditional teacher methods and attitudes.

Returning to the MacDonald (1978) evaluation of the HCP school in which the project appeared to have largely failed, we see old teacher labelling processes in the following statement from a teacher: 'Only two things get these kids excited – football and pop music. Anything else leaves them cold. . . . The whole HCP set-up needs pupils who can respond to a gentle rein. It's too sophisticated and mature. The pupils find it boring and difficult' (p. 231). The attitude may seem superficially persuasive until we remember the accomplishments of the School of Barbiana, Kohl's children, Summerhill, Richmond's children and the many others who have over and over again demonstrated the truth that children – *all children* – can take the reins of their own destiny; the task is merely to help teachers to realize this. Thus the authoritarian teacher attitude and a curriculum which does not seek to collaborate but impose has had a predictable effect:

> We're always having to lay down the law. We're constantly switching roles. The kids are clear about when you're playing each role, but you have frequently to exercise authority in the chair, thus destroying the image. You know that whatever you do won't spring from the kid's need. These issues don't strike them as important. I'm literally sweating when I come out of these HCP lessons. Often I feel I have achieved nothing.

Switching roles, juggling masks – when will individuals make themselves known in the classroom? Together in our roles, behind our masks, we build counterfeit relations and make counterfeit products; action is recognized to spring from the kids' needs only whenever those needs conform to the role and are expressed through the mouth of the mask.

If teachers and pupils are not to be torn apart by the devouring masks, support must be found. After colleagues and pupils, support may also be found amongst parents. As in the Tyndale affair, parental disquiet may be made public and break a school. As in the case of free schools, parental support is vital. But parental support is not always enough. Kozol (1967), a reformist finally dismissed apparently for reading a poem by a negro to his class in a Boston public school, found gratifying support amongst the parents:

> I did not have any means of contacting them directly, but dozens of C.O.R.E. members went out into the neighbour-hood, knocked at doors, and told parents very simply that a teacher had been fired for reading their children a good poem by a Negro. A meeting was called by the chairman of the parent group, a woman of great poise and courage, and the parents asked me if I would come to that meeting and describe for them what had gone on. I arrived at it late and I was reluctant to go inside but, when I did go in, I found one of the most impressive parent groups I had ever seen gathered in one hall.

And afterwards:

> Looking back on it, I am sure that it was one of the most important and most valuable and most straightforward mo-ments of my life. A white woman who was present, and who had observed race relations in Roxbury for a long while, said to me after the meeting: 'I hope that you understand what happened tonight between you and those parents. Very few white people in all their lives are ever going to be given that kind of tribute. You can do anything in your life – and I don't know what plans you have. But you won't have a better reason to be proud.' (pp. 189–90)

The healing that was taking place was finally split; but we have here a potent image of what is ready to be achieved.

A further course of action is to form links with teachers in other schools and to link up with research departments in colleges and universities in order to monitor and analyze the course of the innovation as an aid to reflection in the guidance of action. Such 'action research' is becoming relatively widespread in a variety of forms (including teachers working for research degrees or being involved in university-based research projects – cf. May, 1981). Besides providing the teacher with support from a research com-munity, action research can provide a framework, a rationale and an opportunity for self-critical reflection. (Addresses for such networks supportive of action research can be found in the guide to action research edited by Nixon, 1981).

Support groups may also provide a base for the generation of pressure groups, although that is not their prime function. However, without organized pressure groups the reformation of maladjusted schooling will not be easy. Unfortunately, Hargreaves (1982:224, 225, 229, 230) considers that 'there are many reasons why it would be unrealistic to expect radical reform from headteachers'; and of teachers generally, 'their outlook and occupational culture is not conducive' to the various reforms he outlined earlier, nor are they conducive to the reforms I have outlined. He sees the various teacher unions as 'potentially capable of considerable leadership in educational reform, and some of their activities reflect that potential.' However, 'the active participation of teachers is at a rather low level'. However, he does see a glimmer of optimism, first in that teachers' jobs have become relatively more onerous due to various social changes whereas 'the work of many other groups has during the same period become easier and more satisfying.' Thus, presumably they will be prodded into some form of action through that oldest of wage-slave passions: the desire for comparability with others perceived to be on the same social rung. Of far greater importance, however, is the fact that many teachers have a genuine desire for reform because they have a genuine love of kids. However, if the New Jerusalem is to be built at all, it will be upon the solid rock of community commitment and not imposed upon a resentful conscripted pupil population. As always, the reforms rest in the hands of sensitive and committed teachers, headteachers and the pupils and the parents who have confidence in them. Thus the real optimism that changes, albeit gradually, will occur is based upon the kinds of experience daily faced by sensitive teachers which lead them to reflect and base their actions upon such reflections as these:

> sometimes y' see John, what [the pupils] are telling you is so flaming true and real that you don't want to hear it, because, it's, it's absolutely loaded, loaded with problems. What, what some kids are telling me in not so many words is tht they loathe and detest this system that we're forcing them through ... once you start lifting up stones like that ... y' know, you're into really serious sort of problems, aren't you, and the ramifications of it for all of us are very serious ... y' know, if, if you were to reflect on the messages that uh ... these kids ... uh, I think more and more [are] beginning to tell, then they're serious. Very serious indeed. They throw into doubt the whole purpose of what these schools are here for and what we're sending pupils here for in our present society anyway. (housemaster)

10 Last Words

I have created Slumptown Comprehensive as an image to remind us
of the pressures facing pupils and teachers in a multiracial, economically deprived community. Slumptown is a multilayered symbol. At
one level, it is a symbol of disadvantage, its historical causes, and the
pressures on people associated historically with such pressure. It is
also a symbol of reformist ideals and the subversion of ideals through
organizational structures maladjusted to the individual and the
individual's needs to innovate and to express inner needs, desires,
dreams. It is thus a symbol of control and of self-assertion through
rebellion. It is therefore a symbol of multiple stories and dramas
played out when self and other meet and conflict, or seduce each
other, manipulate each other, or reveal to each other the self behind
the masks. Teacher and pupil too often face each other as 'master and
slave', 'king and subject', 'boss and labourer', 'general and private',
'father and child' – never able to meet, to communicate across the
gulf created by patterns of dominance and subordination.

School as an institution is a foretaste for the young of what is to
come. Growing up in an institution maladjusted to the individual's
needs, one acquires a repertoire of necessary strategies to live an
alienated, apathetic, frustrated, or violently self-defeating life in a
maladjusted society of adults. One learns to live with the wardrobe
of masks one has to wear day by day. One learns to meet the masked
other, learns not to poke and pry – unless as a hired specialist in
poking and prying. Learning to keep one's nose clean, learning not
to rock the boat, learning to speak in code, learning to mind one's
own business, learning to keep a low profile, learning to be polite
and politic – these are the aims of too much schooling. After a decade
of such schooling the young person leaves with a fist full of
qualifications – a few CSEs, one or two GCE O-levels – as the mark

of his or her achievement, as the measure of his or her educational status. And then what? There is life-long distrust of education, of intellectuals, of 'pooffy' big words and literature. A grand achievement.

In the early 1980s there is yet another grand accolade to greet the school leaver – the Youth Opportunity schemes, Work Introductory courses, Work Experience on Employer's Premises courses (cf. Fiddy, 1983). Hundreds of thousands of young people must be introduced to work solely because at present work does not exist for them. The economy is maladjusted to the needs of young people to have real employment for the mutual benefit of all members of society. Everywhere young people are dominated by older people's ability or non-ability to provide work. Schooling has apparently raised a submissive, useless generation, which must now be paid to do nothing until 'the economic upturn', or until politicians start caring about people, or until fighting in the streets erupts.

Maladjusted schooling has grown out of the historical neglect of and violation of needs for individual expression, of needs for community, and the political control of the populace, or the mass. Qualification through mass assessment, not knowledge, has been the aim of schooling. Qualifications are awarded for recipe-recitation during annual speed-writing races. Knowledge, however, is a personal, individual achievement wrought through critical reflection upon first-hand experience – it has no place in maladjusted schooling.

Modern maladjusted mass schooling has the bureaucratic machinery and the philosophy of the totalitarian state. Popper (Vol. 1, 1966:136), in his analysis of totalitarianism stemming from Plato, has said of schooling:

> It has been said, only too truly, that Plato was the inventor of both our secondary school and our universities. I do not know of a better argument for an optimistic view of mankind, no better proof of their indestructible love for truth and decency, of their originality and stubbornness and health, than the fact that this devastating system of education has not utterly ruined them.

Eloquent words. But not the last. The debate will continue while there are teachers who work for reform:

> I would like to see the schools being community schools . . .

it's gotta mean finances and ... – you know, I don't accept there aren't finances available. I think it is society that is wrong – this is my political bias coming out – but I believe there should be finance available to pay professionals whether they be teachers or social workers or whatever to keep places like this open. I think it's a scandal that the place isn't kept open, it isn't used: that there are nights we can't use the place because caretakers can't be paid. I think it's a scandal. You, you ask teachers to give up their time and they're not paid for it. But I want to see the community more involved in the school, you know, my classes have been killed because of financial restraint. In an area like this where people are out of work with nothing to do except sit in front of the idiot box in the corner ... and, you know, I really do think it's a scandal ... what we're doing to people. The schools can play their part, I think ... organizing things – but it all costs money. (housemaster)

And there are the young people who will, rightly or wrongly, fight the system because they see through its masks:

Sometimes the teachers in this school are alright but that's only when they want you to do something. I hate the way they talk to us as if we were kids. I think teachers and pupils would get on much better if they were treated equally. This is what causes trouble. The way the teachers shout at us like we're a baby, this causes the pupils to retaliate and from there trouble is then caused because teachers don't like being shouted at. They think we can't shout at them because they're older, but if a teacher shouts at me I won't let [the teacher] walk all over me, I shout back. I agree we should be told off if we're in the wrong, but teachers pick on us for the least little thing.

Some of the teachers are O.K. I think Mr ... is great because he treats us equally. I like Mr ... and Mr ... because they're funny and I get on alright with them. The teacher I don't get on with is.... Every lesson we argue and pick faults with each other. I always get into trouble because of him. I've often had detentions because of when he's shouted at me and I've shouted back. I know my best mate feels the same way about teachers' attitude as I do. (fifth-form, high-set girl)

In the day-to-day pressure of the school, tempers flare, things are said and things done which should never have been. In the last word we must remember those who are swept under the organizational carpet. For example, a boy, with a very low IQ, had frequently been in trouble. In the first year at the secondary school, the father came into the school because of an incident concerning a teacher – the father had to be 'cooled down'. Previous trouble had led to psychiatric help for the boy. The father had been advised by the psychiatrist not to be as strict with the boy as previously. After being 'cooled down', the father requested help from the school, in order to avoid such trouble occurring again. It was agreed that all involved with the boy should know of his special problem and thus make allowances. Three years later nothing had been done. Now a teacher was accused – backed by some medical evidence – of assaulting the boy. The father claimed he had frequently been up to complain of the behaviour of teachers but had had no satisfaction. In the words of a senior teacher, the strategy with the outraged parent was to 'take as much as possible and to give as little as possible' in talking through the present conflict. He meant that, if pushed, he would be willing to admit *if* the teacher had hit the boy that this was wrong and the teacher should be reprimanded. But no more. The operative word was *if*. And the teacher in question admitted he *might* have 'rattled' the boy – and the boy was near a wall at the time, but certainly did not hit the boy. The senior teacher mused, 'I wonder what he meant by "rattled"?' He finally concluded privately that 'Slumptown Comprehensive has failed the father.' However, the father will lose his battle against the school because, as a senior teacher said, he is 'incoherent', 'inarticulate' – thus he will hardly know he has been beaten. But as one teacher put it, 'the boy, like his father, has that look in his eye which betrays the wildness pent up inside.' In this way such people are rendered helpless and must always bottle up their fury.

For such as these, school life, dealings with authorities, perhaps social life generally, becomes an ill-fitting mantle of explanations barely understood – not so much a social fabric as the rags of lonely, suspicious tramps, paupers, refugees in a world which slams shut the doors of comfort and help. Life becomes lived as accusation and denial. The demands and the needs of the organization prevent self and other from reaching out in mutual aid. Instead of collaboration, the battle is continued and a teacher, otherwise caring and responsible, shouts out in the heat of the moment when he or she might have listened had there been organizational resources available so that he or she could take the time and trouble. The relationship is torn when it might have been healed.

Teachers are not saints, nor are they superheroes; nor can we expect them to be. Their job is demanding and too much is expected from too few resources. Schools are failing not because of a lack of will nor a lack of caring on behalf of school staff but because they labour within an archaic, inefficient and inhospitable organizational structure and set of social demands. This intolerable situation will continue, as it has done for the greater part of this century, until individuals (teachers in collaboration with pupils and parents) wrest the initiative for school reform from the hands of their political masters.

Bibliography

ARNOLD, M. (1932) *Culture and Anarchy*, Cambridge University Press.

BACHELARD, G. (1969) *The Poetics of Reverie. Childhood, Language and the Cosmos*, trans. by D. RUSSELL, Boston, Beacon Press.

BAGLEY, C. (1975) 'The background of deviance in black children in London', in VERMA, G.K. and BAGLEY, C. (Eds), *Race and Education across Cultures*, London, Heinemann.

BAGOT, J.H. (1941) *Juvenile Delinquency*, Liverpool.

BALL, S.J. (1981) *Beachside Comprehensive: A Case Study of Secondary Schooling*, Cambridge and London, Cambridge University Press.

BANDURA, A., ROSS, D. and ROSS, S. (1963) 'Imitation of film-mediated aggressive models', in *Journal of Abnormal and Social Psychology*, 67, pp. 601–7.

BENN, C. and SIMON. B. (1970) *Half Way There: Report on the British Comprehensive School Reform*, London, McGraw-Hill.

BERG, L. (1968) *Risinghill: Death of a Comprehensive*, Harmondsworth, Penguin.

BERKOWITZ, L. (1972) 'Frustrations, comparisons, and other sources of emotion arousal as contributors to social unrest', in *Journal of Social Issues*, 28, 1, pp. 77–91.

BERNSTEIN, B. (1964) 'Elaborated and restricted codes: Their social origins and some consequences', in GUMPERZ, J.S. and HYMES, D. (Eds), *The Ethnography of Communication* , American Anthropologist, Special publication, Vol. 66(6), Part 2.

BERNSTEIN, B. (1971) 'Education cannot compensate for society', in *School and Society. A Sociological Reader*, London, Routledge and Kegan Paul, in association with Open University Press.

BEST, R., JARVIS, C. and RIBBINS, P. (1980) *Perspectives on Pastoral Care*, Heinemann.

BIRKSTED, I.K. (1976) 'School versus popculture? A case study of adolescent adaptation', in *Research in Education*, 16, pp. 13–23.

Black Papers (1969, 1970) COX, C.B. and DYSON, A.E. (Eds) (*Black Paper II, Black Paper III*), Critical Quarterly Society.

BOLT, C. (1971) *Victorian Attitudes to Race*, London, Routledge and Kegan Paul.

BOND, J. (1982) 'Pupil tutoring: The educational conjuring trick', in *Educational Review*, 34, 3, pp. 241–52.

BROGDEN, A. (1981) ''Sus' is dead: But what about 'Sas'?' in *New Community*, 9, 1.

BROWN, M. and MADGE, N. (1982) *Despite the Welfare State*, Heinemann.

BROWN, N.O. (1966) *Love's Body*, New York, Vintage Books.

BURRIDGE, K. (1979) *Someone, No One. An Essay on Individuality*, Princeton, N.J., Princeton University.

BURT, C. (1925) *The Young Delinquent*, London.

BYRNE, E. (1978) *Women and Education*, London, Tavistock.

CCCS (1981) *Unpopular Education. Schooling and Social Democracy in England since 1944*, London and Melbourne, Hutchinson in association with the Centre for Contemporary Cultural Studies, University of Birmingham.

CLARRICOATES, K. (1980) 'The Importance of Being Ernest ... Emma ... Tom ... Jane ...', in DEEM, R. (Ed.), *Schooling for Women's Work*, London and Boston, Routledge and Kegan Paul.

COARD, B. (1971) *How the West Indian Child is Made Educationally Subnormal in the British School System*, London, New Beacon Books.

COHEN, A.K. (1955) *Delinquent Boys, The Culture of the Gang*, New York, The Free Press; London, Collier-Macmillan.

COHEN, P.S. (1968) *Modern Social Theory*, London, Heinemann.

COLEMAN, J.S. (1961) *The Adolescent Society*, Glencoe, Free Press.

CSO (1983) *Social Trends 13*, London, Central Statistical Office, HMSO.

DE MAUSE, L. (Ed.) (1974) *The History of Childhood*, New York, The Psychohistory Press (a division of Atcom. Inc.).

DEUTSCH, R. and MAGOWAN, W. (1973) *Northern Ireland: A Charonology 1968–73*, Belfast, Blackstaff Press.

DOLLARD, J. et al. (1939) *Frustration and Aggression*, New Haven, Comm., Yale University Press.

EDGAR, D. and WARREN, R. (1969) 'Power and autonomy in teacher socialization', in *Sociology of Education*, 42.

FIDDY, R. (Ed.) (1983) *In Place of Work*, Lewes, Falmer Press.

FORD, J. (1969) *Social Class and the Comprehensive School*, London, Routledge and Kegan Paul.

FRAZIER, N. and SADKER, M. (1973) *Sexism in School and Society*, New York, Harper and Row.

FREUD, S. (1979) *Civilization and Its Discontents*, trans. by JOAN RIVIERE, revised and newly edited by JAMES STRACHEY, London, The Hogarth Press and the Institute of Psycho-Analysis.

FROMM, E. (1974) *The Anatomy of Human Destructiveness*, London, Cape.

GELLES, R.J., and STRAUS, M.A. (1979) 'Violence in the American family,' *Journal of Social Issues* 35, 2, pp. 15–39.

GOODSON, I.F. (1983) *School Subjects and Curriculum Change*, London and Canberra, Croom Helm.

GRINDER, R.E. (1973, 2nd ed.) *Adolescence*, New York and Santa Barbara, John Wiley and Sons.

HALL, G.S. (1904) *Adolescence: Its Psychology and Its Relation to Physiology,*

Anthropology, Sociology, Sex, Crime, Religion and Education, 2 vols, New York, D. Appleton and Co.

HALL, S. and JEFFERSON, T. (Eds) (1976) *Resistance through Rituals: Youth Subcultures in Post-war Britain*, Hutchinson University Library.

HAMILTON, D. (1980) 'Adam Smith and the moral economy of the classroom', mimeo, Department of Education, University of Glasgow.

HARGREAVES, D.H. (1981) 'Schooling for delinquency', in BARTON, L. and WALKER, S. (Eds) *Schools, Teachers and Teaching*, Lewes, Falmer Press.

HARGREAVES, D.H. (1982) *The Challenge for the Comprehensive School. Culture, Curriculum and Community*, London and Boston, Routledge and Kegan Paul.

HARGREAVES, D.H., HESTER S.K. and MELLOR, F.J. :(1975) *Deviance in Classrooms*, London and Boston, Routledge and Kegan Paul.

HARRIS, M. (1968) *The Rise of Anthropological Theory*, New York, Crowell.

HEER, F. (1974) *Challenge of Youth. Revolutions of Our Time*, London, Weidenfeld and Nicholson.

HENRY, J. (1971) *Essays on Education*, Harmondsworth, Penguin.

HIRSCHI, T. (1969) *Causes of Delinquency*, Berkeley, Calif., University of California Press.

HONDERICH, T. (1976) *Three Essays on Political Violence*, Oxford, Basil Blackwell.

HOSKIN, K. (1979) 'The examination, disciplinary powers and rational schooling', in *History of Education*, 8, 2, pp. 135–46.

HOUGH, J.R. (1981) *A Study of School Costs*, Windsor, NFER Nelson.

HOUSTON, S.H. (1969) 'A sociological consideration of the black English of children in north Florida', in *Language*, 45, 3, pp. 599–607.

HUGHES, T. (1976) 'Myth and education', in Fox, G. *et al.* (Eds), *Writers Critics and Children*, London, Heinemann.

HULL, C. (1982) 'Collaborative procedures in the classroom as a basis for co-operation in society', proposal submitted to Leverhulme Trust and funded for 1983–5.

HUSBAND, C. (Ed.) (1982) *'Race' in Britain*, Hutchinson.

IGLITZIN, L.B. (1970) 'Violence and American democracy', in *Journal of Social Issues*, 26, 1, pp. 165–86.

ISAACS, S. (1930) *Intellectual Growth in Young Children/with an Appendix on Children's "Why" Questions* by NATHAN ISAACS, London, Routledge and Kegan Paul.

JACOBS, J. (1971) *Adolescent Suicide*, New York, John Wiley.

JACOBY, R. (1975) *Social Amnesia. A Critique of Conformist Psychology from Adler to Laing*, Boston, Mass., Beacon Press.

JANOV, A. (1973) *The Primal Scream*, Abacus.

KAPO, R. (1981) *A Savage Culture. Racism – A Black British View*, London and Melbourne, Quarter Books.

KEDDIE, N. (1971) 'Classroom knowledge', in YOUNG, M.F.D. (Ed.), *Knowledge and Control*, London, Collier-Macmillan.

KETTLE, M. and HODGES, L. (1982) *Uprising! The Police, The People and the Riots in Britain's Cities*, London and Sydney, Pan Books.

KEY, W.B. (1973) *Subliminal Seduction. Ad Media's Manipulation of a Not So Innocent America*, New York, Signet and Mentor Books.

KOHL, H. (1971) *36 Children*, Harmondsworth, Penguin.

KOHL, H. (1974) *Half the House*, New York, Dutton.

KOHL, H. (1977) *On Teaching*, Methuen.

KOZOL, J. (1967) *Death at an Early Age*, New York, Houghton Mifflin.

KROPOTKIN, Prince P.A. (1904) *Mutual Aid: A Factor of Evolution*, London, Heinemann.

LABOV, W. (1977) *Language in the Inner City: Studies in the Black English Vernacular*, Blackwell.

LACEY, C (1970) *Hightown Grammar*, Manchester University Press.

LACEY, C. (1977) *The Socialization of Teachers*, Methuen.

LAING, R.D. (1965) *The Divided Self*, Harmondsworth, Pelican.

LAING, R.D. (1967) *The Politics of Experience*, Harmondsworth, Penguin.

LAING, R.D. (1969) *Self and Others*, Harmondsworth, Pelican.

LAING, R.D. and ESTERSON, A. (1970) *Sanity, Madness and the Family*, Harmondsworth, Pelican.

LEE, G. and WRENCH, J. (1981) 'A clash of cultures', in *Youth in Society*, November.

LEMERT, E.M. (1951) *Social Pathology*, McGraw-Hill.

LEMERT, E.M. (1967) *Human Deviance: Social Problems and Social Control*, Prentice-Hall.

LORENZ, K. (1966) *On Aggression*, New York, Harcourt Brace and World.

MACDONALD, B. (1978) *The Experience of Innovation*, Vol.2, Occasional Publication, CARE.

MACDONALD, B. and WALKER, R. (1976) 'The intransigent curriculum and the technocratic error. A British review of the curriculum reform movement', commissioned by Bettrift Erziehung, West Germany, mimeo, CARE.

MACKIE, L. (1982) 'My boyfriend threw my pills on the fire', in *Guardian*, 9 June.

MARCUSE, H. (1972) *Eros and Civilization*, New York, Vintage Books.

MAY, N. (1981) 'The teacher-as-researcher movement in Britain', paper presented to AERA, Los Angeles, mimeo, CARE.

MAYS, J.B. (1964) *Growing Up in the City. A Study of Juvenile Delinquency in an Urban Neighbourhood*, Liverpool University Press.

MEAD, G.H. (Ed.) (1962) *Mind, Self and Society*, University of Chicago Press.

MEHAN, H. and GRIFFIN, P. (1980) 'Socialization: The view from classroom interactions', in *Sociological Inquiry*, 50, 3, pp. 357–92.

MILGRAM, S. (1977) *The Individual in a Social World. Essays and Experiments*, London and Amsterdam, Addison-Wesley.

MILLER, J.B. (1958) 'Lower class culture as a generating milieu of gang delinquency', in *Journal of Social Issues*, 14, pp. 5–19.

MOHANTY, J.N. (1972) *The Concept of Intentionality*, Warren H. Green.

NEILL, A.S. (1973) *Neill 'Orange Peel': A Personal View of Ninety Years*, rev. ed., London, Weidenfeld and Nicholson.

NISBET, R. (1976) *The Social Philosophers*, Paladin.

NIXON, J. (Ed.) (1981) *A Teachers' Guide To Action Research, Evaluation, Enquiry and Development in the Classroom*, London, Grant McIntyre.

PARSONS, T. (1959) 'The School Class as a Social System: Some of Its Functions in American Society', in *Harvard Education Review*, 39, pp. 297–318.

PARTRIDGE, J. (1968) *Life in a Secondary Modern School*, rev. ed., Pelican.

PAYNE, G. and HUSTLER, D. (1980) 'Teaching the class: The practical management of a cohort', in *British Journal of Sociology of Education*, 1, pp. 50–66.

PEP (1976) 'The facts of racial disadvantage. A national survey', *Vol. XLII Broadsheet No. 560*, London, PEP.

PEROFF, K. and HEWITT, C. (1980) 'Rioting in Northern Ireland. The effects of different policies', in *Journal of Conflict Resolution*, 24, 4, pp. 593–612.

POPPER, K.R. (1966) *The Open Society and Its Enemies*, Vol, 1, London, Routledge and Kegan Paul.

RAGO (1982) *Preliminaries of Alternative Schooling*, The Education Network, C/o 32 Argyle Street, Norwich.

RAMPTON, A. (1981) *West Indian children in our schools. Interim Report of the Committee of Inquiry into the Education of Children from Ethnic Minority Groups*, Cmnd 8273, London, HMSO.

RICHMOND, J. (1982) 'Making it happen', in *The English Magazine*, 10, pp. 30–3.

RUDDOCK, J. (1980) 'Introducing innovation to pupils', paper given during series of SITE lectures Simon Frazer University, Vancouver.

RUTTER, M. (1979) 'Changing youth in a changing society. Patterns of Adolescent Development and Disorder'. *The Nuffield Provincial Hospitals Trust.*

SARGEANT, R. (1981) 'YOP washes whiter' *Youth in Society* November.

SARTRE, J.P. (1960; 1976 trans.) *Critique of Dialectical Reason* (translated A. SHERIDAN-SMITH), London, Verso.

SCARMAN, THE RT. HON. THE LORD (1981) 'The Brixton Disorders.' *Cmnd. 8427* HMSO.

SCHAFF, A. (1970) *Marxism and the Human Individual* (based on a translation by O. Wojtasiewicz) New York, London, McGraw-Hill.

SCHOOL OF BARBIANA (1969) *Letter to a Teacher*, Harmondsworth, Penguin.

SCHOSTAK, J.F. (1982a) 'Cries for help' *TES April 2.*

SCHOSTAK, J.F. (1982c) 'Revelation of the world of pupils' *Cambridge Journal of Education* Vol. 12, 3, 175–185.

SCHOSTAK, J.F. (1983a) 'Race, riots and unemployment' in FIDDY, R. (Ed.) *In Place of Work*, Lewes, Falmer Press.

SCHOSTAK, J.F. (1983b) 'Curriculum: the reins of destiny' *Curriculum* April.

SCHUTZ, A. (1964) *Don Quixote and the Problem of Reality* Collected Papers II: Studies in Social Theory 135–58 The Hague. Nijhoff.

SCHUTZ, A. (1976) *The Phenomenology of the Social World* trans by GEORGE WALSH and FREDERICK LEHNERT. London: Heinemann.

SCOTT, J.P. (1977) 'Agonistic behaviour: function and dysfunction in social conflict' *Journal of Social Issues,* Vol. 33, 1, 9–21.

SHARPE, R., and GREEN, A. (1975) *Education and Social Control. A study in Progressive Primary Education*, London, Routledge and Kegan Paul.

SIMON, B. (1974) *The Two Nations and the Educational Structure 1780–1870* London, Lawrence and Wishart.

SMITH, A.M.S. (1974) in HAIN, A. *Adolescent Suicide*, trans. by A.M.S. SMITH, Tavistock Publications.

SMITH, M. (1977) *The Underground and Education. A Guide to the Alternative Press*, Methuen.

SOCKETT, H. (1982) 'Towards a professional code in teaching', unpublished paper, School of Education, University of East Anglia.

SOREL, G. (1915) *Reflections on Violence*, authorized trans. by T.E. HULME, London, George Allen and Unwin.

SPENDER, D. (1982a) *Invisible Women. The Schooling Scandal*, London, Writers and Readers Cooperative Society Ltd.

SPENDER, D. (1982b) *Women of Ideas: And What Men Have Done to Them from Aphra Behn to Adrienne Rich*, Routledge and Kegan Paul.

STANWORTH, M. (1981) 'Gender and schooling. A study of sexual divisions in the classroom', *Explorations in Feminism*, 7, Women's Research and Resources Centre, London.

STENHOUSE, L. (1975) *An Introduction to Curriculum Research and Development*, London, Heinemann.

STENHOUSE, L. (1979) 'The teaching of controversial material and the rights of children', in VAN HERREWEGHE, M.L. (Ed.), *Educational Research in Relation to the Rights of the Child*, Ghent, World Association for Educational Research.

STEVENS, F. (1960) *The Living Tradition: The Social and Educational Assumptions of the Grammar School*, London, Hutchison.

STINTON, J. (1979) in Writers and Readers Publishing Cooperative (Ed.), *Racism and Sexism in Children's Books*, London.

SUGARMAN, B.N. (1966) 'Social class and values as related to achievement and conduct in school', in *Sociological Review*, 14, pp. 287–301.

TAYLOR, J.K. and DALE, I.R. (1971) *A Survey of Teachers in Their First Year of Service*, Bristol University Publication.

TAYLOR, M.J. (1981) *Caught Between. A Review of Research into the Education of Pupils of West Indian Origin*, Windsor, NFER Nelson.

THOMAS, W.I. (1928) *The Child in America*, New York, Alfred A. Knopf.

THOMPSON, E.P. (1980 ed.) *The Making of the English Working Class*, Harmondsworth, Penguin.

THRASHER, F.M. (1927) *The Gang. A Study of 1,313 Gangs in Chicago*, University of Chicago Press.

TOCH, H. (1972) *Violent Men. An Inquiry into the Psychology of Violence*, Harmondsworth, Penguin.

TUTT, N. (Ed.) (1976) *Violence. Social Work Development Group*, London, HMSO.

VAIZEY, J. (1958) *The Costs of Education*, London, Allen and Unwin.

VAIZEY, J. and SHEEHAN, J. (1968) *Resources for Education*, London, Allen and Unwin.

VERMA, G.K. and BAGLEY, C. (Eds) (1979) *Race, Education and Identity*,

London and Basingstoke, Macmillan Press.

WALLER, W. (1932) *The Sociology of Teaching*, New York, John Wiley and Sons; London, Chapman and Hall.

WARDLE, D. (1970) *English Popular Education 1780–1970*, Cambridge, Cambridge University Press.

WEDGE, P. and ESSEN, J. (1982) *Children in Adversity*, London and Sydney, Pan.

WERTHMAN, C. (1963) 'Delinquents in school: A test for the legitimacy of authority', in *Berkeley Journal of Sociology*, 8, pp. 39–60.

WHITE, R. (1980) *Absent with Cause. Lessons of Truancy*, Routledge and Kegan Paul.

WILD, JOHN D. (1963) *Existence and the World of Freedom*, Englewood Cliffs, N.J., Prentice-Hall.

WILENIUS, F. (1982) 'A focus of resentment', in *Youth in Society*, 63, February.

WILLIS, P. (1977) *Learning to Labour*, Farnborough, Saxon House.

WILSON, H. (1962) *Delinquency and Child Neglect*, Allen and Unwin, Sir Halley Stewart Trust Publications.

WOLFGANG, M.E. and FERRACUTI, F. (1967) *The Subculture of Violence. Towards an Integrated Theory of Criminology*, London and New York, Tavistock Publications.

WOODCOCK, G. (Ed.) (1977) *The Anarchist Reader*, Fontana/Collins.

WOODS, P. (1978) 'Negotiating the demands of schoolwork', in *Curriculum Studies*, 10, 4, pp. 309–27.

WOODS. P. (1979) *The Divided School*, Routledge and Kegan Paul.

WRONG, D.H. (1961) 'The oversocialized conception of man in modern sociology', in *American Sociological Review*, 26, 2, pp. 183–93.

Subject Index

aggression, 165–6, 168–9
  see also violence

Barbiana, School of, 199–201, 213

case studies, 12–15, 39–44, 45–67,
  71–2, 73–89, 92, 96–8, 98–103,
  103–11, 113, 115–16, 120–4,
  126–33, 139–63, 177–84, 195–7
classrooms
  control in, 115–25
  innovation in, 188–93
  reform in, 188–93
  violence in, 184–6
community, 6, 35–67
  see also community schools

community schools, 206, 208
comprehensive schools, 2, 5, 6, 38–67,
  94–111, 113–33, 175–7, 177–84,
  195–7, 205–6, 211–12, 217
corporal pubishment, 165
curriculum
  reform of, 207–8

death
  as symbol, 104–6
  see also suicide
delinquency, 38, 95, 100
  theories of, 18–23
'democratization', 205
Denmark
  schools in, 198
deviance, *passim*
  and racism, 69–89
  and school organization, 113–33
  and schools, 5–6

and sexism, 6, 91–111
and social control, 6
theories of, 9–34
'drama'
  in schools, 6, 54–67, 114
disadvantage, 35–67
discipline, 53, 59–60, 116–17

Educational Network (Norwich),
  202–3
Educationally Subnormal (ESN)
  schools, 79, 80
enfranchisement, 10
ethnic identity, 6, 82–9
  see also racism
examinations, 205–8

gangs, 101, 176–7, 183–4
growing up
  and school, 135–63

Humanities Curriculum Project, 190,
  211–12, 213

individuality, 6
  and control in schools, 113–33
  and deviance, 6, 9–34
  and racism, 71–2, 88
  and schooling, 5–6, 7, 9–34
  and sexual identity, 6, 91–111
  theories of, 5–6, 9–34
  and violence, 174
inequality
  in schools, 35–67
  in society, 170–2
innovation
  in classrooms, 188–93

231

Name Index